Getting Started in Business Law

Paul Bates

(G) **Goodfellow Publishers Ltd**

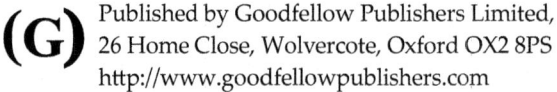 Published by Goodfellow Publishers Limited,
26 Home Close, Wolvercote, Oxford OX2 8PS
http://www.goodfellowpublishers.com

British Library Cataloguing in Publication Data: a catalogue record for this title is available from the British Library.

Library of Congress Catalog Card Number: on file.

ISBN: 978-1-911635-13-0

Copyright © Paul Bates, 2021

All rights reserved. The text of this publication, or any part thereof, may not be reproduced or transmitted in any form or by any means, electronic or mechanical, including photocopying, recording, storage in an information retrieval system, or otherwise, without prior permission of the publisher or under licence from the Copyright Licensing Agency Limited. Further details of such licences (for reprographic reproduction) may be obtained from the Copyright Licensing Agency Limited, of Saffron House, 6–10 Kirby Street, London EC1N 8TS.

All trademarks used herein are the property of their respective owners. The use of trademarks or brand names in this text does not imply any affiliation with or endorsement of this book by such owners.

 Design and typesetting by P.K. McBride, www.macbride.org.uk

Cover design by Cylinder

Printed by Printforce, Biggleswade

Distributed by UK Marston Book Services, www.marston.co.uk

> This book is dedicated to my two marvellous daughters,
> Steph and Chloe

Contents

1 What you need to know before you start — 1
Fundamental rules — 1
Terminology (Jargon) — 3

2 Sources of law: Where does law come from? — 13
Acts of Parliament – Legislation – Statute Law — 14
Delegated legislation — 21
Case law (judge made law) — 23
Some useful terminology — 28
The Law Reports — 31
Objective and subjective tests — 33
Common Law — 35
The Law of Equity — 36

3 The law of contract: Contractual 'ingredients' — 44
Background — 44
Offer — 47
Carlill v The Carbolic Smoke Ball Company (1893) — 63

4 The law of contract: Contracts in practice — 74
Terms — 74
The contents of contracts — 79
Duress and undue influence — 86
Privity of contract — 91
How contracts come to an end — 93
Electronic commerce and the law of contract — 96

5 The law of tort — 100
How the law of tort affects you and your business — 100
The basic principles — 101
The tort of negligence — 103
Economic loss and 'pure' economic loss — 114
An occupier's liability for premises — 120

6	**Types of business**	**130**
	Self-employment/sole traders	130
	Incorporation	134
	Partnerships	147
7	**Outline of the English and Welsh system of courts**	**154**
	Civil and criminal courts and the tribunal system	154
	The Supreme Court	156
	The Court of Appeal	157
	The High Court of Justice	158
	The Magistrates' Courts	159
	Overview of the tribunal system	163
8	**Employment law**	**167**
	Section 1: Contracts of employment	168
	Vicarious liability in workplace situations	179
	Section 2: The main rights of an employee	184
9	**Corporate governance**	**191**
	Failures of corporate governance	193
10	**Cases and Acts**	**206**
	List of cases used	206
	List of Acts of Parliament and Regulations	208
	Index	**211**

About the author

Paul was born in Coventry. This proved to be one of the biggest events of his short life. He grew up in Royal Leamington Spa which was, and still is, a very posh place indeed.

He attended the University of Exeter – staying there much longer than he had planned as he discovered the joy and lack of hard physical work in an academic environment very much to his taste.

In the following 20 years he founded and ran his own business after which he sold his business and decided to return to the academic world.

He now teaches law and economics courses at undergraduate and post graduate levels.

He lives in Dorset together with his wife and little black cat – 'Queenie'.

Acknowledgements

First, I would like to express my thanks to Sally North at Goodfellow Publishers for her help and encouragement at all times in the preparation of this book. My appreciation also goes to Mac, my editor at Goodfellow.

Enormous thanks must go to my wife Jacqui for her endless support and the most eagle-eyed proof-reader I have ever met.

Thanks must also be given to my stepson Tom and stepdaughter Sarah for their help with various IT issues which were completely beyond me. All responsibility for any errors or omissions must go to these individuals and not to me.

1 What you need to know before you start

In this chapter are the tools you will need to be familiar with in order to get a good running start with your study of business law. Please read the following and make sure that you understand reasonably well each of the principles (you can always come back to it). This will pay you huge dividends and put you ahead of the pack. I'll bet you that most of your colleagues who're heading for a First in this subject (you'll soon know well enough who they are) won't know a lot of the following. Also, they almost certainly won't be reading this book – it's not heavy enough.

> Please don't forget that the law you will be studying is English law and is the law relating to England and Wales only. I will be reminding you of this again. So, no statements about UK law or British law please! It upsets law lecturers a great deal if you do this as there is no such thing as UK or British law.

Fundamental rules

The following rules will help you to get the higher marks in business law. These are some of the rules I've developed and they're based on having been both a student and a lecturer in this subject and believe me they work.

General points

Attend everything you can. By this I mean all lectures, all seminars, all 'surgery' sessions, and this means any one-to-one meetings with your lecturers, and finally all social events where you can meet your lecturers. Remember that your lecturers, probably for the first time in your academic careers, are the people who will have written your exam papers. Cultivate them.

Forgive me please but I want to tell you a true story – when I was a law student, the law department of my university went on several outings – students and lecturers together. One particular event was a canal trip with a meal and a bar on board. On the outward trip we all had a meal and on the return trip the bar opened. One particular law lecturer started drinking when the bar opened (thinking about it they all did) and continued for the rest of the evening. As the evening progressed, most lecturers became mines of information about the exams we were shortly to take. The only trouble was, could we rely on what they were saying and indeed could we accurately interpret the indistinct method of speech they seemed to have adopted?

Very late in the evening one lecturer fell into the canal and we had to fish him out and dry him off.

My point is that you must do everything to become as friendly as possible with each lecturer in each of your subjects – when they'll let you. I very much doubt that any law lecturer has ever 'slipped' a law student a copy of a law exam paper but they'll almost always will give broad hints of what areas to concentrate on. It's in their interest to do so and in yours. They really don't want anyone to fail.

Be there

So, the best way to take advantage of any exam hints is to be present at every opportunity. You just don't know when some hint might come your way and also it gains you a good reputation. Remember, as alluded to above, that the university lecturers teaching you business law are the people who will be writing your exam questions. This is likely to be the first time this has ever happened to you. This is why it's really worth nurturing them. If you went the 'A' level route to university, there's no way that you'll ever have met the people setting the questions.

... And if you're not...

If you become ill, even for a day, you must contact the university administration people for your subject and let them know that you're unable to come in and why. This is also true if you have some family emergency or important event you have to attend. This is very important and I'll tell you why. I don't think I'm giving anything much away here because it's really just common sense. Someone, somewhere, in your university, is sooner or later going to notice that you're not present. There will be a record of your trail of non-attendance so you have to cover yourself. The reason why it is so important for you to do this is the following – at the end of each semester or exam period there will be a meeting of all your lecturers to finalise the total marks of every student. This is where it gets interesting. Particularly interesting if you are a student at the edge of a grade or even if you are at risk of failing the year.

Now no one wants to fail you and most lecturers want to do the best for you. In these meetings it is just possible that you may've missed a First or have failed the unit by a mark or two. The chairperson of the meeting will ask of everyone present something like "does anyone know anything about this student?"

This the moment for any lecturer or an admin person to speak up. It could be that an admin person may say "Well, this student had a long period of absence owing to a documented illness or family bereavement or something similar. It looks like this may have affected their final marks". A lecturer may say, "I know this student and they were very hard working and generally seemed to have applied themselves throughout the course". The general consensus often is, "can we find it in our hearts to find the fraction of a mark needed to edge this student from an upper second to a first?" It could also be that by finding just that tiny bit more could save you from having to retake the whole year.

You don't want to be a student with a bad reputation. You want to be known as a 'good' student. It doesn't take lecturers long to discover which student is engaged with the course and which student isn't.

If you are the sort of person who can 'sail through' everything by seemingly doing nothing and still pass all your exams, then fair play to you. To be honest I haven't met too many people like this. Unfortunately.

Terminology (Jargon)

Studying Business Law is honestly not as difficult as it may seem at first sight. One of the main problems you'll face if you haven't studied law before is the terminology. ('Terminology' is just another word for 'jargon'. Please don't write the word jargon down as lawyers really don't like to hear this word used about their subject).

> Remember that every subject has its own specific terminology and business law is no different. The only difference with law is that a good deal of the terminology tends to be in Latin. This situation is beginning to improve as in recent years there has been a movement in most areas of law to reduce the use of Latin in an attempt to make it easier to understand. So, why do you find still plenty of Latin words and phrases used in law today?

To explain this, let's use medicine as an example. As you will know if you've ever been to your doctor complaining of something, sooner or later (with luck) your doctor will diagnose what he or she thinks is wrong with you. Now you can bet your life (pun intended) that if you see your diagnosis written down, you won't have a clue what it means as it will be in Latin. Let's say that your doctor diagnoses you with "*febris petachiatis*". You might actually be secretly quite proud of having this – after all it sounds important. The doctor is likely to send you off with a prescription to the chemist for a mixture to be made up for you to apply '*femoribus internis*'. This in Latin to the doctor diagnosing you, means that you have spotted fever and asks the pharmacy to make you up a mixture to apply to your inner thighs. Nice!

The point I'm making here is that whatever it is that you've been diagnosed with it has to be described very precisely. This helps to reduce the chance that mistakes may occur later on. If accuracy isn't used, it could quite possibly happen that your pharmacist or some other medical specialist later on, may make a mistake as to what your initial diagnoses actually is. If ordinary English were to be used, a small mistake here could prove to be fatal.

Why Latin?

So, the use of Latin in medicine and law has a couple of advantages. First, the Latin language is not as ambiguous as English tends to be. Unlike the English language, most Latin words don't tend to have more than one meaning so they are far more precise than their English equivalent. Many words in English can have two or more meanings, and you can only work out which meaning the word has from the context of the sentence. As an example, think of the English word 'capital'. What does the word really mean? Well, it could mean the most important town of a country, it could mean the letter at the start of a sentence, it could mean the wealth owned by a person, it could even mean the ultimate punishment a serious offender might get in some countries. Ambiguity in the English language is vast, which is one reason why non-native speakers have so much trouble learning the language. With Latin you don't have the same problems.

Relating this back to the use of Latin in law, an ambiguity in the use of English means legal mistakes could easily occur. You could conceivably be sentenced to life imprisonment when all you should have received is a mere warning for whatever you've done.

This brings us to the second advantage of the use of Latin in law – it is a 'dead' language. This means that the meaning of words in Latin don't now change over time. The use of Latin in law then gives us a stable means of communication with less chance of mistakes occurring in understanding the meaning of the Latin terms used.

This 'exactness' is hugely important in law. Without it, you could be accused of some offence and a judge mistaking it for something else. There's quite a difference between being accused of creating a disturbance by rapping in the street or by creating a disturbance by raping in the street. The only difference in the English language is the single letter 'p', but what a difference it's going to make to the sentence you're likely to get. . .

So, how should you approach this use of Latin in your study of business law? You have a couple of approaches, but whichever you take does mean that unfortunately you will have to, at least once, to have made sure that you know what the expressions actually mean, i.e. what the terms translate to in ordinary English.

For example, you will often come across the term *'ultra vires'*. This simply translates as 'beyond the powers' of something or somebody. This could be that a government department is attempting to force you to do something that you don't want to do – maybe forcing you to sell your house to make room for a new road system, or a court sentencing you to a term of imprisonment that is beyond that which they are allowed to sentence. In these cases, the authorities have acted *ultra vires* – they have gone beyond the powers given them. Because they acted in this way you can question this and ask them to explain just where they think they have the authority to do so? On the other hand, *'intra vires'* simply means that someone or somebody is acting within the powers that have been assigned to them.

Assuming that you've made sure that you know what these Latin words or phrases mean, you now have a few options. The first of these is that you can sprinkle Latin phrases in your work, both in essays and in exams. The second is that you use the plain ordinary English words instead. There is nothing wrong with either of these approaches in theory. Some students feel that the use of Latin somehow improves the look of their work and will attract a higher mark by making it look as if it has more authority. Others students abandon the use of Latin completely and just use plain English. The choice is yours. Here I can only say that it is probably true that the use of the Latin phrases may well be more fruitful in the long run. Let me explain why this might be the case.

Often because of time limitations, your work may well be sometimes marked by lecturers whom you've never met, if this marker happens to be an 'old fashioned' type of lawyer, then they are probably going to like the use of Latin in the work they're marking. As you haven't met these individuals you can't ask them what they would like to see. Ask your law tutor which approach they think is better for your particular institution. To get over this you can use both plain English and put the Latin equivalent in brackets afterwards – or the other way around. This would cover you completely but would take more of your precious time in an exam. Largely it's a matter of the choice of the writing style that suits you. In theory you could write a whole exam answer in Latin, but I wouldn't advise it.

Jurisprudence

This is just a posh word for legal theory. You only need to be aware of the term as it's unlikely that in a business law context you'll ever have to explain it. It's handy to be aware of what it means because you may occasionally see it written, possibly within a case law judgement. It's one of these bits of knowledge that you'll be expected to know but probably never have to use – a bit like knowing how to properly address an archdeacon on the second Sunday after Pentecost.

The claimant and the defendant

Not too long ago, in the eyes of the law, as alluded to above, there was a campaign to make law a bit more accessible (or more correctly the use of the English language more accessible). One of the better outcomes of this was that the names used to distinguish between who was suing who in court were changed ('suing' a person just means taking a person or business to court).

Under the old system the person taking a court action i.e. the person suing the other person was called the 'plaintiff'. Nowadays we call this person the 'claimant'. This makes much more sense. The person being sued was kept unchanged and is still known as the 'defendant'. So, we now have Claimant v Defendant rather than Plaintiff v Defendant. In older cases you will still see the word plaintiff being used and this is why.

Criminal law and civil law

Criminal law deals with 'offences against the state', like murder, burglary or theft, and the laws here are made by Acts of Parliament, or are by-laws or regulations set by local authorities or other bodies with powers delegated to them by Parliament. In a criminal case it's the Crown (or rather the Crown Prosecution Service – the CPS) that takes the offender to court, and if the case is proved, the offender might be fined or sent to prison. We'll look at these properly in the next chapter, *Sources of Law*.

Civil law involves resolving disputes amongst ourselves, (civilians). Civil cases include such examples as, buying a car from someone and finding that the engine falls out after 5 miles down the road, or a business person buying a stockroom full of new items to resell and discovering that some of the stock is damaged. In these person to person, or person to business disputes, it is up to you or your business to find a way to sort it out, and that may mean taking them to court – to a civil court. If you win your case you would typically get some form of damages – money to recompense you for your time and trouble.

When the dispute comes in to the court, it becomes a 'case' which will generally be reported in the law reports. These law reports are available for you to read in the law library of your institution, and some of them do repay close reading!

Case law and precedent

Most civil law is *case law*, which has evolved over time, responding to the changes in the world, and is made by judges in courts. The judgement will be based on *precedent* – similar cases that have been heard in the past, and recorded in the law reports, under the names of the plaintiff and defendant, e.g. *Carlill v the Carbolic Smoke Ball Company*. If your case matches very closely to a previous case, then the judgement will be the same. If, however, your case breaks new ground, the judge will need to go beyond precedent to reach a judgement, and your case may become a new precedent for future reference.

> Some precedents are very important and are referred to regularly. These cases are often called 'leading' cases. Watch out for them, commit their names to memory and quote them – at the appropriate point – in your essays and exam papers. They are worth marks!

We'll go much further into case law in the next chapter.

Counsel

The word 'counsel', translated into ordinary language, just refers to a barrister or a team of barristers who have been appointed to represent you or your business in a legal dispute in a court case. The expression gets a bit tricky because different legal jurisdictions (i.e. different countries) use the term counsel in different ways.

Many TV programmes, particularly those concerned with criminal activities, frequently use the term 'counsel for the defence' or 'counsel for the prosecution'. I expect that you've heard this expression many times depending upon your viewing preferences. 'Counsel' though is not restricted to criminal cases. Many civil cases which you'll undoubtedly come across, will also use this term. Currently an ordinary solicitor, or team of solicitors, can't refer to themselves as 'counsel', which I bet annoys them greatly.

Separation of the Powers

Depending upon the design of the business course you're taking, you may come across this expression quite a lot or only once or twice. It is however, something that's worth knowing about as it can be included in so many contexts in work you may be asked to do.

The original idea for the concept of the Separation of the Powers stems from Charles de Secondat, Baron of Montesquieu in his publication *L' Esprit des Loix* in 1748. This title translates as 'the Spirit of the Law'. Montesquieu was a jurist. Jurist here doesn't mean that he sat on a jury (although he may have done for all I know) but it means that he was a political and legal thinker and writer. He wrote, "Everything would come to an end if the legislative, exjudicial powers of government were to be exercised by the same person or authority."

Powerful sounding stuff certainly, but what does it mean for English law? What the good old baron seems to mean is that the three main functions of any state should be entirely separate from each other. The three main functions (or organs) of the state are the **legislature** (Parliament, the makers of law), the **executive** (The cabinet and ministers of state in English law) and the **judiciary** (the judges). These functions should be entirely independent from each other so that there is no chance of one of these influencing any of the others. Imagine what might occur if there was a nice cosy relationship between the police and the judges or parliament and the judges? I really don't think any of us would be too pleased if the next time we're standing in front of a criminal court and we know that judge was the best mate of the policeman giving evidence against us. The idea is that if these different so called 'organs of the state' remain separate from each other, then it should be less easy for any individual to be influenced by any other one. So, Montesquieu's idea was that the more we can foster this separation of the powers, the less likely it should be that corruption will enter the system. Evidence shows that it'll do so anyway, but let's try to minimise the problem.

The amount by which politics and the English law achieves this separation is debateable and depends often on which source you're reading. It's certainly true to say that Baron Montesquieu's ideas have spread to many different legal jurisdictions. Well, they were bound to, with a person with such an imposing name as his, I guess.

Litigation

Litigation simple means taking court action (in civil cases), suing or being sued by someone or you suing someone else. A litigant is a person or business involved in some civil court action and being 'litigious' refers to a person (or company) who is always ready to start court action at the drop of a hat. The USA is often accused of having a very litigious society. Certainly, celebrities in the US seem to be forever suing their husbands or wives. The term 'prosecution' is reserved for use in criminal law, where you may be prosecuted by the state for some criminal offence. This would also be a form of litigation but for business law purposes the term 'prosecution' shouldn't bother us much further. Again, you must be aware of this term in case you happen to be asked (which is quite possible) to point out the main differences between civil and criminal law. We'll look at these differences in more detail when we look at the chapter on System of Courts.

The tests used by the courts to determine liability or guilt of a person

Civil cases

These are decided on the 'balance of probabilities'. This means that a person being tried in a civil court must bring sufficient evidence to the court to convince the court that he/she is the most likely to be believed and should therefore win the case. Remember that nowadays juries are not usually used for civil cases. The worst thing that can happen to you, in a civil case, if the judgement goes against you, is that damages (monetary compensation) will be awarded against you. If this is happens, this may damage your wallet a bit but you can't be put in prison for this type of offence.

The balance of probabilities test just means that if you can bring more evidence and more relevant precedents in a civil case to convince the court that you have the stronger case than your opponent can, then you're more likely to win your case.

Criminal cases

In a criminal case the position is much different. In a criminal case, sufficient evidence must be shown that the accused person is guilty beyond 'reasonable doubt'. This is decided by a jury and is a very much stricter test – for a good reason. Unlike a civil court, in a criminal court if you're found guilty, you can, at the time of writing, ultimately be put away for life. When these rules were originally put into place remember, it was entirely possible for a person that was found guilty by the court to be sentenced to be "hanged by the neck until you are dead". This is a pretty final sort of outcome and by then it's a bit too late to ask any more questions.

It's quite important then that the jury get it right. Unfortunately, history tells us that juries aren't always correct... So, a jury, which is mainly used in criminal cases, have to be pretty sure that you actually did what you are accused of. If the jury isn't convinced beyond reasonable doubt, then you walk free.

This thinking behind criminal case convictions seems to be based on centuries old legal maxim attributed to Sir William Blackstone in *Commentaries* where he stated that, "it is better that ten guilty persons escape than one innocent (person) suffer". This statement – known as the Blackstone Ratio – emerged around the 1760s, though isn't entirely original as variations can be traced back very much earlier than Blackstone statements.

Legal fiction

This is rather an odd concept which sometimes is a bit confusing to someone who comes across it for the first time. A legal fiction is sometimes just used as a handy way to ensure that the law gets the results it wants. It's certainly not a modern idea as it can be traced back to Roman times and arguably well before then.

We'll look at this in more detail in the chapter on types of business organisation. Here we'll see that once a company goes through the legal process of incorporation, the company becomes in law an 'artificial person' – sometimes referred to as having an artificial personality. This means, as we shall see, that for most purposes the incorporated company is treated in law as being a real person, just like you or me. This means that the company can sue or be sued in its own name and in almost in all other ways is legally equivalent to a real person. The fiction bit is that we all know that in reality we can't ask Asda, for example, out for a romantic meal. We could try of course, but I think we might be put away in a secure institution for our own protection.

Another example of a legal fiction is the quite often used expression that "we are all deemed to know the law". This of course means that all of us ordinary people are expected to be aware of all aspects of English law whether we are aware of it or not. The explanation for this is simple. If we are accused, let's say of murder, we can hardly turn to the judge in court and say, 'ooh! sorry your honour, I didn't know murder was illegal. I'll make sure that I won't do it again."

Now plainly none of us knows "all the law". No one does – not even lawyers. The legal assumption (fiction) behind the idea of all of us knowing all about all the law, is as that anyone is capable of finding out what the law is in a particular legal area, but in reality, of course we just haven't bothered to find out. So, given that the law is accessible to us all, then we can't hide behind a supposed lack of knowledge of any legal information at all.

These sorts of legal fictions seem to work pretty well. Another legal fiction which also works very well is the concept in company law which states that a company upon incorporation exists pretty nearly as much as a human being.

Queen's Counsel (Q.C.) and King's Counsel (K.C.)

QC stands for Queens Counsel whereas KC stands for King's Counsel. The individuals who are able to put these initials after their name are very experienced lawyers who stand at 'the top of the tree' in their profession. At the time of writing it costs a prospective QC over £2,000 just to apply. If you're lucky enough to get in at all, then it'll cost you another £3,000 each year just to stay a Queen's Counsel. It's a very exclusive legal 'club' to belong to. Top QCs nowadays can expect to earn several millions of pounds annually.

If you, or your business can afford it, in a legal dispute, by appointing a QC you expect to get the very best representation that there is. QCs are also called 'silks', referring to the robes they are allowed to wear in court. At one time this elevated status was reserved solely for barristers. More recently, experienced solicitors as well as barristers are now allowed to apply for these roles.

Vicarious liability

Vicarious liability occurs when someone is potentially liable in *tort* (a civil wrong where the rights of a person have been interfered with in some way) not done by you, but you become liable for the other persons' offence. At first sight this looks a bit unfair. Why should you become liable for the actions of someone else?

We will see this in more detail later when we come to employment law. As a little taster, ask yourself who should be responsible if the person or business you work for, (a building firm for example), asks you to demolish an old house and you knock down the wrong one because you got the address wrong?

Should it be you who should be liable, your employer or both you and your employer? Wait and see...

Sources of law:
Where does law come from?

> Please remember all through your course in Business Law that you are studying the law operating in England and Wales only. Please never say "British law" because there is no such thing as British law. Students unfortunately have often been known to use the expression, "under UK law", in their work. Please don't think, say or write this. If you do, the person marking your work will have a fit and will probably need medical assistance to recover from severe trauma. Occasionally, one or two of my students have made this elementary mistake in their final exams. Oh dear…

English law has a variety of origins. Most books refer to these as "sources of law". The main sources of English law are the following:

- ☐ Acts of Parliament – A major source. Also called legislation or Statute law.
- ☐ Delegated legislation – A major source. Sometimes called secondary legislation or secondary (subordinate) legislation.
- ☐ Case Law or judge made law – A major source. Also often called common law.
- ☐ Equity- also part of judge made law and an active source of law.
- ☐ ECHR (European Commission on Human Rights and The Human Rights Act 1998) – both major source of law (for the moment).
- ☐ Ecclesiastical law – a minor source for our purposes. Ecclesiastical law concerns religious regulations of the various churches and church members. It's very specialised and needn't concern us apart from being aware of its existence.
- ☐ Maritime Law – A minor source of law for our purposes. Maritime law (as the name might give away) concerns the courts of the admiralty - essentially, it's shipping law and collisions at sea etc.
- ☐ Local custom – a minor source of law and a bit of an annoyance for our purposes. Although certain old customs my still exist in some localities,

they really shouldn't concern us too much as you'll never be examined on them. Every student seems to have some story about how, for example, an old law still exists making it an offence for an MP to wear armour in the Houses of Parliament. A common story offered by students is that it is lawful to urinate in a policeman's helmet if you are pregnant – it isn't lawful in any circumstances – much as we might like it to be.

Please note that the last three sources of law above really are minor and in a business studies course you will not be asked directly about these. However, it is possible that you could be asked in a multiple-choice exam whether any of the three are a major source of English law. They are not.

We will take the major sources one by one and see how they fit into your business law course.

Acts of Parliament – Legislation – Statute Law

All three of the above terms mean the same thing and are completely interchangeable. Not only are they interchangeable, I suggest you practice using these terms interchangeably. Although you could use the term 'statute', for example, all the way through an essay or in an exam, I think it's better, to 'ring the changes' a little bit. That way you get a little less bored and so will the person who has to mark your work. Remember that the average business law lecturer may well have to mark hundreds of similar pieces of work. Believe me, this can get a little tedious after the first couple of hundred scripts. So, the more you can do to lighten up the life of the marker, the better we'll all feel. In the following paragraphs I am going to use all three of these terms to show you how it's done.

An Act of Parliament can be written with or without capital letters. Using capitals you can give an impression of your knowledge of how important they are. The choice of the use of capitals is yours. An Act of Parliament is a new law which has been passed by Parliament. Acts have to go through all the necessary processes of debate and amendment and be voted upon by members of Parliament.

When first introduced into Parliament, the document is called a *bill* and it can be introduced into either the House of Commons (sometimes called the 'lower tier') or the House of Lords (the 'higher tier') – though generally all finance bills and other high-importance bills start in the Commons. So a bill is able to be started in either House. After it has passed through several stages of debate in the first House, it is sent to the other. If the bill is amended in the second House, it is sent back to the originating House for approval. Assuming that this bill has gone through all the stages in both the higher and lower tiers and has successfully passed the debating and amendment processes, it is by tradition presented to the then ruling, Queen or King (currently the Queen) for her approval.

Nowadays this is not much more than a formality. The Queen, God bless her, would probably not understand much of the content of these pieces of legislation anyway as some of them can be very technical indeed. Of course, these days we cannot expect the ruling monarch to pay a great deal of detailed attention to these new pieces of legislation as they have enough on their hands already dealing with royal marriages (and divorces) and other intricate family matters must take up a lot of their time.

I hope that your business law tutor is not mean enough to expect you to remember in detail all the steps that a bill has to go through in order to achieve the stages of a new piece of legislation. If so, it's actually not that difficult as the stages the bill goes through in the House of Commons are simply repeated in the House of Lords. Just a quick note here, if as part of your exams, there is included a multiple-choice section of questions (MCQs) it is quite likely that these more detailed sorts of questions might appear. This is because it's really simple for your business law lecturer to ask something like "which of the following three stages are one of the stages which a bill goes through in its progress through Parliament in the process of becoming a statute?"

So, check if you're going to be taking multiple choice questions as part of your exam. If so, then concentrate for your main exam on the 'core' areas of your course for the written exam. These are highly likely to be contract law and the law of tort. Take a close look at your course specification which will be online or tucked away in your unit handbook or some such document with a similar title. Unfortunately for you, these MCQs are becoming more common in business studies courses as it is a very quick way for your tutors to check how much detailed knowledge of the subject you have. Here there is no substitute for repeatedly skimming through any up to date law book. Actually, there's no excuse for not doing this anyway.

So, by the above process we arrive at a new piece of legislation or a statute or Act of Parliament. These are said to be democratically arrived at as all members of Parliament have the chance to vote for or against the proposed new statute. This is why legislation produced by parliament is so important. Such a statute has overriding force throughout the land. In theory parliament has the right to pass any act on any subject that they want. An Act can overturn any law made by judges. Hence, it is said that Acts of Parliament are supreme. Historically this makes sense. Originally the monarch had ultimate power.

A King or Queen a few years ago (historically) could after all decide to cut your head off if they wanted to. Over the course of many hundreds of years for reasons I won't bore you with here, the power of the monarchy declined as the power of Parliament rose. Eventually Parliament became the supreme power so, it is argued, they can pass any piece of legislation that might take their fancy. It's often said that parliament can 'make or unmake' any law that they want.

If you want to know how many statutes are currently in force, I suggest you go to the Ministry of Justice website and start counting. Actually, I suggest you don't do this unless you're having a particularly sleepless night. Apparently, alcohol is a depressant. It may well be, but not as much as this website. There are literally thousands of acts. Some of these you will most likely be aware of, most of them you probably won't be aware of and have no need to be.

To give you a flavour of some of the acts that you will almost certainly need to be aware of, I will just take a handful and you can see if they affect you at all.

The Theft Act

This is the act which will kick into force if you decide to 'liberate' a tasty piece of brie from your local shop without paying and you get caught in the process. This of course is shoplifting which is to say, it's theft. You are likely to appear, probably the next morning, in front of the local magistrates' court (the lowest tier of the criminal court system). As you have not committed a really serious offence, although I don't personally recommend shoplifting, the magistrates will use their copy of the Theft Act. Under this act, and I quote directly from the act, "A person is guilty of theft if he dishonestly appropriates property belonging to another with the intention of permanently depriving the other of it: and thief and steal shall be construed accordingly."

It sounds a bit frightening when you hear the formal definition. Maybe now you wished you'd paid for the cheese. The Theft Act will be used in every criminal court in England and Wales assuming that someone is accused of taking something that doesn't belong to them. Each magistrates' court will apply the same definition to each case of theft. They will apply this to your case, to see if what you've done fits in with the definition given in the act. If what you've done is covered by the act and you have no defence, then you're guilty of theft. If it doesn't, then you walk free. But ask yourself, what defence could you possibly have to putting a couple of packets of cheese down your jacket pocket and walking out? Answers on a postcard please.

In a recent visit to Bristol, I picked up a copy of the local paper. Glancing idly through it, my attention was caught by a report about a student who had been caught walking out of a shop with a bottle of vodka in her bag. Naturally, she hadn't paid for it. When she duly appeared before the Bristol Magistrates Court, she pleaded 'necessity' as a defence. Now, this wasn't a small bottle of Vodka. This was a bottle as big as you can get (I think), at least I've not been able to find a bigger one). "Necessity", shouted the presiding magistrate! "Yes", she replied. "I can't afford to pay for food as well as vodka on my student loan." Needless to say, the Theft Act applied very fittingly to her. Worth a try I suppose.

The Theft Act, rather interestingly, also covers robbery, burglary, blackmail, taking a motor vehicle without authority and rather curiously, taking or destroying fish. It seems that you can't remove anything these days without the full weight of the law coming down on your head.

The Road Traffic Acts

There have been many of these Acts governing motor vehicles and road use. Even more numerous are the amendments to them since it began to be recognised that motor vehicles have to be regarded as quite dangerous objects. One of the first major pieces of legislation relating to cars dates back as far as the Motor Car Act in 1903. This statute allowed motor vehicles to legally travel at a mind blowing 14mph! Although an official driving license was required (I now am beginning to think I should apply for one of these) amazingly you did not have to have taken or passed a driving test. Another milestone was the Road Traffic Act of 1930 which abolished the upper speed limit for all cars.

This in itself is not too surprising as very few cars at this time could achieve a speed likely to unsettle driver, passenger or pedestrian. This, of course, has now changed.

Needless to say, the legislation governing motor cars has been expanded greatly over the years to cover such matters as careless and inconsiderate driving, driving while under the influence of drink or drugs (what's the difference?) and now covers offences relating to riding your bicycle down the road in a dangerous fashion.

At the time of writing, the Road Traffic (Amendment) Act 2018 is the latest Act in force, and amongst other things it makes it an offence to allow another person to drive your car on a public road if they don't hold a licence or learner's permit for the correct category of vehicle; or if they have a learner's permit and are not accompanied by and under the supervision of a qualified person.

Acts protecting the consumer

This is a really important act to all of us as consumers. It is also crucial to businesses as the act lays down the rights of ordinary buyers of goods in any retail outlet if something goes wrong with what is bought. Most of us have grown up knowing that under English law if we buy something from a shop and it doesn't work or is broken in some way, then we have an automatic right to take the product back and either get our money back or accept a replacement.

Most of the time the ordinary person doesn't think too much about this and assumes that the shop will put it right for us should something go wrong with it. However, this has not always been automatically the case. In a sense we have always had the right to dispute the purchase of a faulty item from a shop. But unfortunately, prior to this act and a trail of similar acts coming before 2015, we may well have had to take a very expensive route and threaten to take a court case against the shop. If you had purchased a fairly cheap item from a shop and it was faulty, the cost of taking an action against the shop was mostly just not worth it. This left us as consumers in a pretty bad situation.

Parliament began to be aware of this imbalance of power between retailers and consumers quite early on. One of the first acts of parliament which was aimed at trying to put this right was the Sale of Goods Act way back in 1893. This Act went some way to give us ordinary consumers, a degree of rights against unscrupulous sellers of well, frankly, dodgy goods. It was a good start. Over the years this original act has been replaced by more updated pieces of legislation. These later acts extend the rights we as consumers now have as we go about our day to day shopping knowing that we have a degree of protection.

We had the introduction of the Sale of Goods Act in 1979 and the Supply of Goods and Services Act 1982... Notice 'Services' here? Parliament, in its wisdom, extended consumer rights to the situation where they may not have actually bought just a physical item, but also as part of the service, had this item fitted. If this item is badly fitted you now have extra rights. An example of the fitting of a new boiler in your house springs to mind here. You have arranged to have your expensive new gas boiler delivered to your house and paid to have it fitted. Let's suppose that the first time you turn it on it sets your kitchen on fire. You would not be a happy person. Alternatively, you may have bought a new set of tyres for your car and as you drive down the road the tyres pop one by one leaving you and your car in the hedge. Not good. This piece of legislation is designed to protect you here.

It's true to say that Parliament only began to get really interested in our rights as consumers when large supermarkets began to invade our high streets, this was in the late 1950s and 1960s. The retail model of supermarkets is an idea borrowed from America where these types of shops first emerged. The concept was quite quickly adopted by English retailers. They were, and still are, a much more efficient way of selling goods to people. The retailer no longer had to employ large numbers of staff to deal personally with each customer. Just give them a basket and let them choose their own goods. Perfect! The trouble was that the old days of shopping, where the shopkeeper was likely to know each customer by their first name, had now gone.

The incentive for the local butcher, greengrocer or fishmonger to keep each customer happy was also gone. It was going because independent shops were slowly going one by one. They still are.

So, shops were more than happy to adopt the new self-service model and can we blame them? Tesco, Sainsbury, Boots and many other still existing stores had a gleam of £ signs in their eyes. The slogan, "pile it high and sell it cheap" was adopted by Jack Cohen the founder of Tesco and ex market trader – he did pretty well out of it.

It was argued by such retailers that this new method of selling would cut costs which could then be passed onto us as consumers. This may well be right, but the personal touch in buying goods was being lost. Large retailers became to be called 'faceless corporations' by many. Now if you had some grievance against one of these giant organisations what could you do? Well we've already seen that if you could afford it you could take a court action against them. But would you? Who would want to sue Tesco, Sainsbury or The Boots Pharmaceutical Society as it was then known? Who would want to do it now?

Parliament it is argued, decided to try to equalise the power of these large shops and that of the ordinary consumer. They did this by the series of Acts of Parliament we have seen above. At the time of writing this series of Acts has culminated in the Consumer Rights Act 2015. This Act is an excellent example of Parliament being paternalistic. It's Parliament looking after us as ordinary consumers giving us automatic rights when going about our ordinary shopping in the high street or elsewhere. I for one don't mind this one little bit. If you buy anything from a shop and go up to the till to pay, somewhere behind the till you will see a notice giving the policy of the store regarding the return of goods in the event of you being less than satisfied.

Please take a look the next time you buy something from say, Primark. The notice will say something like, "This notice does not affect your statutory rights". Which statutory rights do you think this refers to? Well it's the Consumer Rights Act 2015. Translating this notice, it means that store may have such and such a returns policy but they cannot mess with legislation. No store can. In fact, no retail outlet can. Before leaving this act, let's just give you an idea of the rights conferred on you under the act.

It says that in every purchase you make, the goods must be "of satisfactory quality". In addition, all items purchased by a consumer, "must be suitable for their particular purpose". They "must match their description", and if you do not see all of the goods you buy, then all of the unseen goods must "correspond to the sample".

Also, what is worth knowing is that under this act if the goods you have bought do not "conform to contract" – that means that you are unhappy with them for any of the reasons given above – you have the right to reject the goods within 30 days ("the short term right"). You can insist upon a quick and effective repair of the goods and have a final right to reject the goods if a repair is not done properly and within a reasonable time. Strong stuff indeed.

It's difficult to think of any area of human existence or anything we may wish to do, where somewhere in the background there doesn't lurk some statute telling us what we can and cannot do. I'm not saying that this is in any way a bad thing at all – we all need to agree to some sort of regulation in order to live amicably with one another.

Imagine what would happen if for some reason or other a proportion of car drivers decided to drive on the wrong side of the road just for a laugh one day. If all drivers decided to do the same thing on this particular day things would not be too bad. But imagine if only half of car drivers decided to have an unusual and exciting days' driving and the other half didn't? Apart from sheer common sense and the human instinct for self-preservation, what stops us are the various Road Traffic Acts. Acts of Parliament, you see, are really very important.

Apart from laying down regulations about our day to day living, legislation is important to you in your study of business law. There are Acts of Parliament which govern the setting up and running of the various forms of business organisations that exist, as well as statutory rules governing the rights and duties of the directors of companies, the rights that shareholders have in certain businesses and what can happen if any of these rights and duties are not properly conformed with. As said before, luckily for you, there are not too many of these pieces of legislation you need to be aware of on an undergraduate business law course. However, there are a few, and we will return to these in the sections on employment law.

Also, it is not normally required for you to remember a huge amount of detail about statute law. Usually just an outline knowledge is quite good enough, depending on your particular course. For example, the main act governing the operation of limited liability companies, a type of business which you may well have covered elsewhere in your studies, is the Companies Act 2006. Normally you only need to be aware of the existence of this act but you do not need knowledge of the act section by section. We will see some more of this act later in the chapter on types of business organisation.

Delegated legislation

Parliament likes to think of itself as the supreme maker of laws for England and Wales. At one time the then reigning monarch (King or Queen) was indeed the supreme power and thus the chief lawmaker in the land. Over the centuries, the power of the monarchy declined and was gradually replaced by Parliament. So, the power as the ultimate law maker nowadays rests with Parliament. The theory is that as Parliament is democratically elected, then the ultimate power to make or unmake laws rests with Parliament.

Assuming that we can now ignore the effect of the EU on English law, then it is true to say that Parliament can do virtually anything they may want to. Of course, Parliament is in practice limited in what they can and cannot do to by us the voters. If it turns out that Parliament introduces some law which is extremely unpopular within society, then just occasionally they may have to change their minds and 'undo' these laws. This has been evidenced in fairly recent times with the very unpopular 'Poll tax' introduced by the Margaret Thatcher government. It's fairly well accepted that the attempt to introduce this unpopular law was the start of the decline of Mrs Thatcher and her government.

Given that, within the constraints as described above, Parliament can make any law that it wants to, then it can not only make its own law via statutes, but it can also give the power to make law to other bodies or institutions. This is exactly what delegated legislation is. This process is used where Parliament decides that, owing to such matters as lack of parliamentary time, it will grant the power to make certain regulations, rules, and orders to other bodies.

Parliament passes what is called a 'Parent Act' giving the power say to a local authority, to make its own laws within that local area. These Parent Acts are also called 'Enabling Acts'.

There are three main types of delegated legislation. These are orders in council, statutory instruments and by-laws. The easiest to understand, and therefore to remember, are by-laws. By-laws are the local laws given to local councils, governing for example, where you can park your car, where you can use your skateboard, how you must control your dog in a park, where you can ride your horse, and even where you are allowed to bury someone (not in your garden unless you have special permission). Interestingly and unexpectedly, some of these local laws also can regulate hairdressers and barbers to ensure that their premises, tools and personnel are clean and sanitary.

Some people argue that the passing of the ability to make laws to others, mainly local authorities, which enables them to make their own laws affecting local areas, is not democratic. Parliament essentially would argue, well, we're the one with ultimate power so we can do exactly what we want, and we will. In practice delegated legislation (alternatively called subordinate legislation), is very practical in effect. After all, Parliament has limited time – or so they tell us – I often wonder do they really need a summer break of 6 weeks, a 2-week break at Christmas, a further 1-week break at the end of May? This is ignoring a further 2-week break for conferences? By my reckoning that makes 11 weeks of doing well...what?

In reality though delegated legislation seems like a good idea. After all this type of legislation is aimed at local areas and who knows the most about local areas than local authorities? The alternative would seem to be to hire a series of coaches to bus the current 650 members of Parliament around to each local area equipped with clipboards in order to see whether skateboarding should be allowed in your local park, whether you've buried you granny in the garden without obtaining the proper permission, whether the local park closes its gates on time or more importantly, whether your hairdresser has a dirty sink.

I like to see the positive side in all things. I often think that had these pieces of delegated legislation been in power at the time, they'd have caught Sweeny Todd the Demon Barber of Fleet Street, a whole lot more quickly.

Case law (judge made law)

When we have a dispute with someone, perhaps with one of our neighbours or we find something that we've bought from a shop is broken, we obviously need to have some system to resolve these situations. Here we're in the area of what is called 'civil law' cases as opposed to 'criminal law' cases. The term civil law is used as it involves resolving disputes amongst ourselves, (civilians). Here we are not dealing with criminal offences or 'offences against the state', like murder, burglary or theft (more about criminal offences and courts later). Civil cases include such examples as, buying a car from someone and finding that the engine falls out after 5 miles down the road, buying a house only to discover that the foundations are crumbling, buying an expensive stereo system and finding that no sound comes out of the speakers, or as a business person you might buy a stockroom full of new items to resell and then discover that some of the stock is damaged in some way. Obviously, you need to be able to do something about this.

In the above cases and millions of similar situations, we naturally expect some method of putting things right. We can't expect to involve the police for these types of offences because in themselves the above are not criminal situations. Imagine what would happen if you called the police because your next-door neighbour's cat had taken a pee on the roses in your garden? Annoying certainly, but hardly a criminal offence. If the police did come out at all they'd have a good giggle at your expense. I doubt if they'd try to arrest the cat. I know they wouldn't catch mine...

So, in the sort of person to person, or person to business disputes that may occur, it is up to you or your business to find a way to sort it out.

In civil law you may have to resort to taking the other party in the dispute to court. You would sue (take a legal action against the other party). This would be heard in a civil court and obviously you would be hoping to win your case. If you do win your case you wouldn't really expect the other party to go to prison. You would, however, expect them to pay you money in recompense for your time and trouble.

The object of winning a civil case then is normally for you to receive the appropriate monetary reward in order to put you back to where you were before you started. This sum of money is simply called 'damages'. When you win your case, the judge will award you damages of the appropriate amount. The purpose of damages is to compensate you for your losses.

Similarly, if you have your own business and have a dispute with another business or an individual, whereby your business has lost money, you might well decide to sue the other party to recover that money. This becomes a court 'case' which will generally be reported in the law reports. These law reports are available for you to read in the law library of your institution. Also, they're available online, but try to avoid paying for this service. There are plenty of free websites, which means that you can get free access to most case law. I've always found that it's important to keep costs down wherever you can.

Precedent

This brings us to the concept of 'precedent' as used by the courts. The concept is really quite simple to understand. It just means that if a case comes to court, the court will look to see if sometime in the past, a case similar to the current dispute has been decided. If there has been a case with very similar facts to your own which has produced a ruling, then the court will use the same principles as used in the earlier case to decide your case. This is called following precedent. So, a line of precedent is set when the facts of a later case are sufficiently similar (or the same as) an earlier case, then the court saves time by simply following the earlier decision.

The word 'precedent' is not specifically a legal term at all. It's in fairly common use in ordinary English usage. To give you a non-legal example, a while ago a kitten arrived in our household. For reasons that I can't now remember, I took it upon myself to feed this little ball of fur called Bobbie first thing in the morning. As I bet you're able to guess, the job became mine for life. The cat now tries to wake me up at some unholy hour and won't let anyone else feed her. I had set a precedent as far as the cat is concerned. I wish I hadn't.

The principle is the same in law. So, once a dispute comes to court that has been already decided in a previous case, if the facts of the present case are sufficiently similar to the earlier case, then the court will follow the already decided precedent. In the many centuries that English law has developed there are thousands, if not hundreds of thousands, of already decided cases. Of course, owing to the enormous changes in society over the years, new situations arise that simply haven't happened before. If this happens, then the court has no older cases to look at to guide it in the new circumstances. When this happens, the court has to decide these cases on their own merits in the light of current day knowledge. This is called creating a new precedent. The principle(s) of law upon which a court reaches its decision is called the *ratio decidendi* of that case (see below).

The system of precedent, arguably, has great advantages. It's said that the system brings a great deal of certainty to the law as we can look at any dispute that we may currently have and see if anything like this has ever happened before. If you can find one (or hopefully more than one) case where the situation is the same or very similar to your case, then you can see how the older cases were decided. You can then make a reasoned decision whether to go ahead with your case or not. Obviously, if other similar cases to your own didn't succeed then you'll probably decide not to go ahead with your case. If older cases similar to yours did succeed, then obviously you'll be far more likely to take your own case to court. This can save you or your business a great deal of time, money in lawyers and court fees.

A strong argument against the system of precedent is that it's too rigid or too inflexible. Imagine, we have a whole structure of thousands and thousands of decided cases which form precedents in each area of law. This makes it a very complicated system to use. How can any one individual be expected to know each and every one of these cases? Well, of course, no one does know all of these. This is why there are specialists in law, just as there are specialists in medicine. An analogy to medicine is that a solicitor knows a great deal about a wide range of legal problems but is not a specialist. If a solicitor finds that the problem facing them is outside of his/her experience, then they'll refer you to a barrister. A barrister will have a much more in-depth knowledge about a smaller range of law. In medicine when the same thing occurs, a GP will be likely refer you to a consultant. A GP knows a substantial amount about a wide range of illnesses but a hospital consultant has a much deeper knowledge about a smaller range of ailments.

Modern technology is nowadays a huge help in searching for previously decided cases and precedents. Any of these precedents remain good law unless they are overruled by a later case in a court higher within the system or by an Act of Parliament.

One of the earliest cases and its associated precedent you're likely to come across in business law is that of *Lampleigh v Braithwaite*. This case took place in 1615. It's concerned within the area of contract law and is still good law today. As one of my students pointed out about the system of precedent, "ah if it ain't broke, don't fix it". My sentiments exactly.

All of the disadvantages you'll see about precedent are exactly countered by their opposite advantages. So, someone can argue that the precedent system is too rigid while someone else can argue that it's too flexible. Another person can say that the system is too complex having to trawl through thousands of cases while this can be countered by saying that it saves time as the courts don't have to redecide cases. Ah well as the old saying goes, "you pays your money you takes your choice". Law being law, you can argue whichever way you want and you won't be wrong as long as you can bring enough law.

Unfortunately, you will have to learn some of this case law to make and argue legal points in your work. You'll have to support your legal arguments by using the appropriate case law as it's from these cases that the precedents come. You might be asked a question on contract law: for example, whether it's possible to make an offer for the sale of something not to a specific individual, but whether such an offer can be quite generally addressed to anyone at all? This could occur say in a newspaper advertisement. (Don't worry about the specifics here as we will look at this in more detail in the section on contract law).

So, the question may say something like:

> *'A' puts an advertisement in a newspaper stating that you can buy some item from him – say a second hand car. 'A' doesn't know who has read the advert. By the time someone comes to buy this item it's already been sold. The prospective buyer insists that 'A' has broken the law by advertising for sale an item which they now do not possess. There is, 'A' maintains, no contract between himself and the disappointed customer. State, using legal arguments and decided cases, whether 'A' may have committed some offence?*

Now your job as a student is to be aware of the decided cases in this area and be able to state that it is indeed possible to make an offer to someone that you haven't met. Actually, in the present case, the advert actually isn't an offer for sale as we'll see later. But you'll be expected to know this from the decided case of *Carlill v Carbolic Smoke Ball Company* in 1893 and/or similar. This is your **legal authority** backing up your argument. You can't just guess at the answer unless you want zero marks.

If you don't back up your arguments with some kind of legal authority you will simply fail. I've marked exam papers where the student has not attempted to supply any legal authority at all – oh dear, what a pity.

So, you'll be expected to know some case law and use it in the appropriate places. A frequently asked question by new law students is, how much case law do we have to know? The answer is unfortunately, the more the merrier. You can't know too much case law. Realistically you should aim to know at the very least one piece of case law for each legal point. Better two, better again three. I'm tempted to say that the more (relevant to the point) case law a student knows the better she/he will do in their exams. This is why the students who I see standing outside exam rooms with crumpled lists of case law testing each other before they go in, are the students most likely to walk out with an excellent result. The more effort, the better the result. Simple.

One of my students truly once wrote in one of my exams, "Ah, I know the answer to this. Something similar happened to my Uncle George and he went to the Citizens Advice Bureau and they told him. . ." I expect this student is now gainfully employed stacking shelves in his local supermarket.

Leading cases

In each area of law there are some cases which are of great importance because of their influence and continuing legal significance in modern law. These are often referred to as 'leading cases'. For example, a case which we will be using often in the area of contract law is *Carlill v the Carbolic Smoke Ball Company*. This is one of the leading cases in this area of law. Please feel free to call such cases 'leading cases'. In fact, I encourage you to do this.

Hierarchy of the courts: Their ranking in order of importance

In the English legal system some courts are more important than others. As we will see in more detail in the chapter on the court system, each court has its own position within the system. Some courts are called higher courts and some are called lower courts.

The reason that I'm talking about this here is just to explain a bit more how the system of precedent actually works. The lower courts are usually called 'inferior courts' (bet they don't like this) and the higher courts are called 'superior courts (bet they love this). For the sake of political correctness, I'm sure, some writers are now referring to the court system as being split into 'senior courts' and 'subordinate courts'. Whatever the words used, the system is the same.

In general, the lower courts have to follow the judgements made by higher courts. That is, precedents set by the higher courts must be followed by courts lower down in the system.

Points of law

Points of law are questions of law which need to be clarified. This means that a court when hearing a case may need clarification on what the exact law is on a particular issue. Remember that these are purely issues of law (and not questions of fact, i.e. what actually happened in each case), which need explanation. These opinions are given by a higher court at the request of a lower court.

Case stated

An appeal by way of *case stated* is an appeal from a magistrate or a tribunal which goes directly to the High Court (Queen's Bench Division). This can occur where you think that a magistrate (or a tribunal) have acted over and above their powers or jurisdiction in hearing your case. There are very few of these types of appeals.

Some useful terminology

Prima facie

This is a bit of Latin which is very useful and is used throughout the law as it is in ordinary English usage. It simply translates as 'at first sight' or 'at first appearance'. An example of its use in law would be, "*prima facie* this problem looks like a case involving reckless driving".

What you mean here is that your first impression is that the case involves reckless driving but you've covered yourself by the use of the phrase by suggesting that if greater investigation is made into the case it may turn out to be some other offence. It's also a very handy way of covering yourself if you're asked an awkward question in a seminar.

Stare decisis – Let the decision stand

This Latin expression is the basis of the operation of the above system of precedent. It is one of the Latin *maxims* (sayings) which simply means that once a case has been decided and a precedent set, later courts must follow the same reasoning and apply this precedent to cases with similar facts to the earlier one. It translates simply as, 'let the decision stand'. This is every easy bit of Latin to learn, remember and use.

Ratio decidendi – Reason for the decision

What the courts are actually doing when following precedents is looking at the reason why a decision has been made in earlier cases. They then look to see if these earlier decisions apply to the current case. If the earlier facts do fit the current case, then the court will apply the earlier *ratio* to the case now in front of them and decide accordingly. An expression you may see is that a case 'stands on all fours' with an earlier case. This just means that the facts of an earlier case on the same legal point, are the same (or virtually the same) as the present case; therefore, the precedent set earlier will be followed. The *ratio* of each case is the bit you need to know as it gives the legal principle that comes from the case. More strictly, the *ratio* includes the principle(s) by which a court arrives at its decision and it includes all the relevant facts of each case. Some case gives us more than one *ratio*. Any or all of these *ratios* become legally binding upon courts in the future – particularly binding to courts which are lower down the in 'pecking order' of the court system. By now you will know that the full expression is *ratio decidendi* but you can just use *ratio* in all of your work. Everyone will know what you mean.

Obiter dicta – Things said 'in passing' by a judge

When a judge (or judges) are in the process of hearing a case, they can say whatever they want in their own court. They can talk about the case at hand. They can use examples from the case currently being heard or from any earlier case or cases. They can if they want digress into any hypothetical instances that they may think relevant to the present case. Please remember that a judge does not have to do any of this if they don't want to – it's up to the judge individually. Judges, should they want to, may just stick rigidly to the facts of the case that they're currently hearing. Some judges are keener than others on speculation about different case scenarios. Lord Denning, one of the more famous and influential English judges, was well known for his theorising around possible different case scenarios.

Now, this type of judicial discussion doesn't form a part of the precedent coming out of the case at all. It cannot be relied upon as part of the *ratio* which must be followed in later cases. This speculation is called *obiter dicta* – or just plain *obiter*, it could be described as mere musings by a judge – a sort of 'what if . . .' or a contemplative sort of activity. The importance of this is that although this speculation does not form precedent, it may later be very important in some later case.

So how could this speculative type of judicial talk possibly be important to a later case?

To explain this, I'll use a made-up criminal law example. Let's suggest that Fred has entered a school with a shotgun. The court is told only that Fred pointed the gun and fired it. As a result, the court is told, a child has been shot and killed. Now on these facts Fred is being tried for murder. The court has to decide whether Fred is guilty of murder or is guilty of the lesser offence of manslaughter. The judge, as we know, can speculate on this matter as much as he wants. He or she may say, "Given the facts of the present case, I do not doubt in my mind that Fred must be found guilty of murder". But the judge may go on, "had the facts had been different, for example if a person had been a school caretaker and had been told that the school was infested with rats, and the caretaker then went into the school with his shotgun in the middle of the night and fired his gun up at the ceiling towards where he thought rats were hiding then my decision might well have been different. The caretaker would have no reason to suspect that any child would be hiding in the attic of a school at that time of night. If these facts were to occur, I would conclude that the accused person would be likely to be tried on the lesser charge of manslaughter."

Now, as we know, all this speculation by the judge doesn't create any kind of precedent but is just something said by the way (or said in passing). It's 'mere' *obiter dicta*. But nevertheless, it's now on record what the judge said he would decide should this hypothetical situation ever come about.

Lets' go onwards in time and imagine a different scenario. Let's now suggest that Charlie, a school caretaker in a different school, has been told to watch out for rats during the night. He does the same thing as Fred and shoots his gun at night seemingly at rats but by accident shoots and kills a school child not knowing the child is there. Charlie is accused of murder. Charlie, or his defence counsel (his defence lawyers), do not have a definite precedent to rely upon but they do have the statement of the judge in Fred's case.

The statement by the first judge does not form a precedent but Charlie and his legal team may bring this earlier judicial statement to the present court. It can be pointed out that the judge in the earlier case said that if the facts were to occur which have actually now happened to Charlie, then the judge would have found there to be no offence of murder. This may not get Charlie off completely but would be heavily suggestive that the court should look strongly in his favour.

This is the importance of *obiter dicta*. There may not be a full precedent for a later court to follow but any *obiter* can be strongly influential in later decisions. If there doesn't seem to be much previous precedent to follow in a later case then the more *obiter dicta* you can bring the stronger your position. Of course, we must remember that the lawyers on the other side of the case are also looking for precedents and *obiter dicta* which suit their own line of argument – the prosecution want Charlie found guilty of murder. *Obiter dicta* therefore have what is called 'persuasive' authority. Very handy though if you've run out of ideas. *Obiter* is particularly important in English law if it comes from one of the superior courts – the courts that rank higher in the system of courts.

Obiter or persuasive authority, can come from a variety of sources – as above, from within the English legal system, from certain overseas jurisdictions, notably from Commonwealth countries, and 'dissenting judgements' from superior courts.

The Law Reports

Given the operation of *stare decisis* and precedent above, it follows that there should be a careful record kept of legal cases which have taken place previously. This is because lawyers, judges, business law students or anyone with an interest should be able to look back at previously decided cases and read the facts of the case and be able to see what precedents, if any, were set in the earlier cases.

Perhaps unfortunately, the written record of legal cases is a relatively modern thing. It was only in 1865 that the records of cases began to become more formal and standardised. This was when the Council of Law Reporting was established. The All England Law Reports series is the main source of law reports which are commonly used. There are plenty of other law reports, but I doubt as a business law student it's very likely that you'll be asked to look at too many of these. Of course, you can take a look if you want to.

Usually, as a business law student, as previously said, it would be rare for you to be asked to read these original law reports. Your course notes and handbook will give you the main cases and these are usually in sufficient detail for essay and exam purposes. You may want, however, to look up some of the original case law from time to time either out of interest or for some deeper insight for essays, project work or exams – or because you want a first.

To look up these cases you'll need to be able to follow what are called the case citations. These are the mysterious letters and numbers you will see written after each case.

Case citations

Let's take the case of *Carlill v The Carbolic Smoke Ball Company* again as an example of how to find an original case in the law reports. This is the case mentioned above which we'll take a closer look at in the later chapter on contract law. Wherever this case is written down you should see after the case name, the following: '*(1893) 1 QBD 256*'. This indicates where you will find the case. This is known as the case citation. Go along to your university law library. If you don't know where this is don't worry because the librarians usually do.

Having reached the law library, you will see a lot of law books. This is not a bad thing, so don't be put off. Now, what you're looking for is a whole series of books with QBD imprinted on the side. This stands for the Queen's Bench Division (of The High Court). Once you've found the right shelf, look along at the dates printed on the side of each volume. Pick out the book dated 1893. You want volume 1. Turn to page 256 and you'll find the original of Carlill's case right in front of you. Enjoy.

As a final note on looking up cases, sometimes students get a bit confused, and rightly so, about the dates of cases as seen in a law book. Occasionally a law tutor will write down a case and give the date of the case. Unfortunately, the date given to you will not always agree with the dates given elsewhere. Students have often come running to me asking why more than one date appears for the same case and which one is correct. The answer is quite simple. Usually the earlier date of the case refers to the date when the original case was first heard in court. The later date (usually about a year or two later than the original case) refers to the fact that this case has gone to a higher court on appeal. If this worries you it's probably better to use the later date as this is likely to be the decision of a superior court. The different date of the cases (sometimes two or more years apart) also reflects how slowly English law sometimes works.

There are lots of online resources where you can access legal case reports so it's always worthwhile having a look there. Quite often you can find online 'case summaries' which are often enough for most purposes. There are plenty of websites that offer case reports for you to read, but often they want you to pay – never a good thing. You'll be able to access cases using your university law website so have a trawl around there and see what you can find – at least it'll be free.

Usually just entering the name and date of the case you want to find in Google brings up most cases and case summaries and once more this'll cost you nothing. With a little bit of time you can almost always get free access to the original case law reports on the internet. As mentioned, case summaries can save you a lot of time. You may want to access the original case reports for insights into cases which you're may want to use in really important work: like anything which is going to count towards your end of year grades.

Objective and subjective tests

The courts need some method of understanding what a persons' intent was when they performed some act, whether it's the causing the death of another person in criminal law or whether a person intended to enter into a contract with another party in civil law.

Unfortunately (or not) given the current state of technology, it's impossible to look into the mind of a person and discover what their exact thoughts were at the time an act was performed. The marketing boys have a great interest in being able to discover the reasons why a person tends to be attracted to some product – and you can guess why. The last time I looked the marketing people haven't yet been able to get into someone's head. Frighteningly, according to a scientific study I was reading a couple of years ago, they're getting dangerously close.

It doesn't help much if you ask someone what they were thinking after the act is over, as they'll probably just lie. "Did you actually intend to rob that bank or was it just one of life's little mistakes?" "It happened entirely by accident officer". Well, these things do happen, I suppose – at least on other planets. Because people don't always tell the truth (and they forget), some sort of test is needed for the court to apply in order to discover whether a person 'intended' to do whatever it is she or he has allegedly done. A truly subjective test would have to get into the mind of an accused person and read it like a book. Then it would be easy for a court to pronounce whether a person is guilty or innocent of some particular crime. Thankfully, with business law, we are dealing virtually exclusively with civil law and we apply an objective test, i.e. what would an ordinary person think that the person being sued in court must have been intending when they did what they are being sued for, given knowledge of all the facts of this particular case? You may want to read that sentence a few more times.

Anyway, we can leave the fancy subjective side of things (what was the person actually thinking) to the criminal lawyers and I personally wish them all very best of luck with that.

Enter 'the man on the Clapham omnibus'

The expression above was first used by Sir Charles Bowen in a court case in 1871 (or it appeared in a later case in 1903 depending on your sources). Whatever the origin of the phrase actually is doesn't really matter too much for our purposes as it's the meaning of the statement that's important. It's just that I'm trying to reintroduce the expression. The "man on the Clapham omnibus" refers to you and to me and to the man or woman in the street. He (or she) is the plain ordinary person whom you might ask an opinion of. To be clear here, Clapham is an area of London: an omnibus is just the old-fashioned name for a bus. So, the expression refers to the ordinary person sitting on a bus in London. He or she is just the average citizen only interested their own concerns and being asked what they might think about particular situations as put to them. This person also doesn't have to be sitting on a bus.

This fictional person is someone going about their business in an ordinary way without fuss. This person isn't fabulously intelligent, doesn't possess super powers and could well be quite boring. He is what English people refer to as 'Joe Blogs' and the Americans usually call 'John Doe' (or 'Jane Doe', as I recently learnt from an episode of *Homeland*, which I was watching when I should've been working). This is the man or woman you might see on any average street.

Remember that in civil law cases, which is virtually all you will be dealing with in business law, the test is overwhelmingly always objective. It's what the objective person (the man on the Clapham omnibus) would think that the person entering into a contract for example, must have been thinking at the time, i.e. taking account of any evidence they may've left behind them to prove their possible intent. So, for example, are there any letters going from one party to another? Any there any records of conversations? Has any money passed between the parties? Has the person shown by their actions that they intended to contract perhaps by putting money in a bank in readiness to transfer funds? Has this money been stopped just before the date it was due to be transferred to the other person? All these things might give evidence of the person's intent to enter a contract as shown by their actions – or evidence that they quite obviously had no such intent to contract. How do we know what their intent was? Well because the ordinary person says so when informed of all the facts of the case.

The court will look at all the evidence and ask the question, "what would an objective person infer from all the evidence about the conduct of the person under review?" If the answer is that the ordinary person, given the available evidence, would certainly take the view that this person intended to enter into the contract, then as far as the court is concerned, he did intend to contract. If, on the other hand, the objective person would say that of course there was no evidence of any intent to contract, then no contract came into being.

Obviously, the court doesn't just grab some ordinary person passing by the court in the street to ask them this. They just pose the hypothetical, question would the ordinary person have concluded whether there is sufficient evidence for the court to decide either way in each case?

The man on the Clapham omnibus is nowadays seen as a very old-fashioned way of looking at the objective test and has fallen out of favour. But I like it and as I said above, I'm trying to reintroduce it with my students. This tends to annoy my fellow lecturers which I think is all the more reason for me doing it.

Common law

Please note that the origin of common law really just refers to law common to the people. It's very easy to think that common law is based on Roman law because as most of us are aware, Britain was invaded by the Romans – actually three times. The final and successful invasion was in 43 A.D. The truth of the matter is that the Romans didn't really try to force their systems of law upon the ordinary people living in the land at this time. They were quite happy to accept the law that they found already existing here. This mistake I think is often made as there is so much use of the Latin language in law. For the reason why this is the case see Chapter 1, '*What you need to know*'.

Unfortunately, the expression 'common law' can have more than one meaning. This doesn't really matter very much as long as you're aware that different writers sometimes are referring to different definitions of what they mean by common law.

☐ It's used at times to refer to law which was historically made in the early court system after 1066 following the Norman Conquest, as opposed to 'equity' which was developed later in an attempt to improve the older system. Equity it has been often said, is "a gloss on the common law". More on this below.

☐ Sometimes the expression is used for law made by judges in order to distinguish judge-made law from law made by Parliament (Legislation)

The Law of Equity

Equity is just another word meaning fairness.

The common law, and here I am using the term to mean to the law made by judges which eventually became common throughout the land, was to be truthful, pretty basic and 'rough and ready'. Actually, it still is. Most people centuries ago didn't have access to the law at all unless they happened to be very rich (what's changed?).

Originally if you wanted to obtain a remedy for some legal wrong which you'd suffered, then you had to obtain an official document (called a *writ* simply because it was a piece of paper where your complaint was written). A writ was very difficult and very expensive to obtain. If the legal complaint you wanted to take action upon was not covered by an existing writ, then you had no remedy available to you.

You had to choose between existing writs to see if you could slot your particular claim into one or other of these. You may come across the statement, "where there's no writ there's no remedy". Unless you had plenty of money and/or had access to the King, it was far easier to just give up. Most people did just that.

Compressing centuries into a few paragraphs, some of the more important legal difficulties came to the attention of the reigning King. The King's attention was drawn to the inadequacy of the law at that time. Specifically, that the old remedy of damages (money) did not properly cover all eventualities. The then law of contract was not developed enough to be able to deal with the growing needs of the business community: some individuals were just so powerful and rich that they could think themselves above the law and were effectively untouchable.

In an attempt to deal with some of these problems, the King would look at specific claims himself and try to deal with each one according to what his conscience told him was fair in each case (hence 'equity'). Then by all accounts, he got too busy to deal with all these legal claims himself so he started to pass them to his Lord Chancellor to resolve. The Chancellor eventually took over all this work and became known as the 'Keeper of the King's Conscience'. I really like this idea – let someone else decide what he thinks the King would decide.

Anyway, this was the start of the branch of law called equity. The Chancellor began to feel that he was superior to the old-fashioned and rather crude common-law system and common law judges. The Court of Chancery was established and this Court did not consider itself ruled by common law. Thus, the Court of Chancery could decide cases in a new and fair way, when they thought this approach was required.

So now there were two separate systems of courts and two systems of judges. There was the older common law system and the newer courts of equity. This was simply asking for trouble and trouble there was. Decisions made by the common law courts and the new courts of equity often disagreed with each other. Each court at times tried to overturn the decisions of the other court. The quarrelling between the separate systems of courts continued and got worse and worse until it came to a climax. This happened in the Earl of Oxford's case in 1616. The then King, James 1st, was a bit unsure what to do. He asked his Attorney General, Sir Francis Bacon for advice. Famously, Sir Francis stated, *"where common law and equity conflicted, equity should prevail"*.

This was probably one of the last pieces of good advice that he gave. Famously Sir Francis died two years later attempting to see if stuffing a dead chicken with snow would preserve the meat for later consumption (it did).

So, there we have it. The law of equity should have the final say in any case law legal dispute. Eventually the two court systems were united by the passing of the Judicature Acts of 1873 to 1875. Now common law and equitable remedies are available in all civil courts. (upon request)

> Equity has often been called a "gloss on the common law" because it fills in some of the cracks in the common law system, much like using car body filler on the dents and rust spots on your car before trying to sell it.

Let's take a quick look at how equity or equitable remedies may affect you in your studies of business law.

Specific performance

This is a remedy which you can ask the court for when you feel that the common law remedy of damages is not good enough. Let's say that you are very rich and a collector of fine artwork. You attend an auction where there is a Rembrandt painting to be sold. This is the final painting that will complete your collection so you are very eager to buy the painting. You bid £30 million and the painting is yours... you think. You pay the auctioneer and take the Rembrandt home and put it on the wall next to your other paintings.

A week later the auctioneer gives you a call saying sorry but the painting shouldn't have been included in the sale. It was in the sale by his mistake and he wants it back.

You don't want your money back because you're rich. What you want to do is to keep hold of that painting. In a contractual dispute like this the only common law remedy is damages (money). So, you could in common law ask for your £30 million back.

In this situation you can ask the court to apply the equitable remedy of specific performance. You want the contract to be performed specifically as you had arranged between you and the auctioneer. This remedy is available at the discretion of the court and you have to ask for it. If you don't ask for it you won't get it. This is why it's worth knowing about.

Other equitable remedies you may apply for are the following: I've chosen these for their suitability to business law in particular.

Injunctions

An injunction in general terms is an order issued by a court to order a person or a business to not do some act which in contract law would be likely to breach the contract.

Rectification

This is where the court may 'dig into' a contract and make changes (corrections) to the contract where they are certain that the intent of the parties to the contract have not been correctly expressed within it. Possibly some mistake has been made in the drawing up of the contract and only noticed afterwards. This most commonly can occur in business contracts but even here it's not something you see every day. As we said elsewhere, the courts won't rewrite a contract that's been drawn up in a sloppy way.

Rescission

Here a court order may be issued in contract law to put contracting parties back to the point they were at before they entered into a contract in the first place, i.e. back to the pre-contractual situation.

European Law (EU Law)

At the time of writing this the UK has finally left the European Union. Whether this is for the better or worse is of course a matter of opinion. Just over half of the voting population thought it a good idea to leave the union and just under half disagreed. So, what's done is done. For business law students, the leavers have done you a real favour. Let me tell you why. All the years I've spent teaching business law, I have to admit that I used to not look forward to coming to the section on EU law. I can't remember a single student saying "oh goody we've started EU law". I can't remember ever thinking this myself either.

Of course, EU law was a very important source of law and had to be covered as part of the law specification. It probably will remain as an important influence in the shaping of English law even today. Thankfully you should no longer have to learn much about the various institutions of the EU and their functions. Rest in peace.

Now, what you will have to learn about is the influence of the European Convention on Human Rights and the Human Rights Act 1998. That's fine because it's far more interesting than EU law ever was.

The European Convention on Human Rights and the Human Rights Act (HRA 1998)

First, I have to warn you that this area of law has absolutely nothing whatever to do with EU law (above). I know it looks as though it should do, but it doesn't. This is another reason why dropping the study of EU law has got to be a good thing for you. It was very easy to get the two confused with each other and this used to happen a lot with many students. I can understand this – after all the two subject headings both have the word 'European' in them.

The European Convention on Human Rights (ECHR)

The origin of the ECHR can be traced back to the years immediately after the Second World War, around 1945. During this war, as I'm sure we all know, many monstrous acts took place in Europe and many violations of human rights occurred. After the war ended, Sir Winston Churchill in particular became a leading figure arguing for some kind of European movement to be established in the hope that such horrific acts should never be again repeated.

It was a sort of Friends Reunited or Facebook idea, but of course this couldn't be used as it hadn't yet been invented. Instead Churchill became a leading advocate of the United Europe Movement which eventually became the Human Convention on Human Rights. This became operative in the UK in 1953. Currently there are 47 member countries.

Originally, a person having a complaint under the Convention had to take their case to the European Court of Human Rights which is based in Strasbourg (north east France). This process was notoriously slow – some cases taking 5 years or more to be heard in the court. The Human Rights Act (1998) passed into law in the UK in 2000 and this significantly improved matters for UK residents. What this act meant was that any cases involving the rights laid down by the Convention could now be heard by courts in the UK.

Some of the human rights which signatories to the ECHR are able to include: the right to life and freedom from torture, the right to liberty, the right to a fair trial, the right to respect for private and family life, and the right of freedom of expression.

These are just a few examples of the fundamental rights which we are entitled to under the ECHR. Section 6 of the Convention states, it is unlawful for "a public body to act in a way which is incompatible with a Convention right". 'Public body' here refers to any institution such the government itself, local government, the courts and police force or indeed hospitals. It's clear though that, as the Convention mentions, natural or legal persons (remember the concept of incorporation – page 10), that the provisions extend to companies as well. An incorporated company is a 'legal person' so that's why the convention affects businesses and therefore affects any course in business law.

The ECRH and the HRA have had effects upon English law which are argued by some as not all that favourable. You see, a court action involving a case which allegedly involves some infringement of a human right, must inevitably make the ECHR law relevant to the case. English courts, of course, decide cases which are not remotely concerned with human rights at all, but they must now decide domestic cases in a way that is compatible with the ECRH. It's often argued that this stipulation of compatibility must affect the reasoning of the court even with domestic cases. Courts also have to take into account the European Court of Justice previous rulings. Some writers argue that this has had the effect of undermining the well-established system of precedent in English law. Also, looking at statute law passed by Parliament, the minister responsible for introducing a new bill (legislation) must now state how compatible this new bill actually is with the ECHR.

In short both some politicians and some (but not all) of the judiciary, frankly seem to be a bit fed up with the whole system. Some parties seem to think that the ECHR is trying to 'muscle in' on our own recently regained parliamentary supremacy – trying to push us around and tell us what to do.

Let me give you a few examples of comments made about this. David Cameron, ex-prime minister (Conservative) suggested that the ECHJ has become "a small claims court" and was "dealing with enormous amounts of trivial claims". Theresa May, again Conservative ex-prime minister, in her early election manifesto promised to scrap the Human Rights Bill. This didn't happen. To be fair, some of the top judiciary are on record as defending the ECHR.

There has been much talk in recent years in the UK of getting rid of the HRA and pulling out from the Convention. There seems to be a fair bit of support for separating the UK from the existing European system and introducing our own Human Rights Act. Time will tell…

Answers to questions on the sources English law must include some discussion of the effects of the ECHR, unless this has been specifically excluded in the question. There have been several cases in the area of unfair dismissal which have involved alleged infringements of human rights. Other cases involving the ECHR have involved possible conflicts between an individual's right to privacy and the right to freedom of expression: particularly the right to freedom of expression in the media. These sorts of cases often involve famous people, strangely enough often footballers, who get up to naughty things in nightclubs but don't want the media to report what they've been up to. The media (newspapers etc) argue that reporting dodgy behaviour is in the public interest but the famous people argue that they have a right to privacy. It's all a bit of a dilemma don't you think?

An important aspect to remember here is that English law must to some extent be affected by the ECHR and the Human Rights Act as both the courts and ministers introducing new legislation into parliament, must evidence compatibility with the Convention. This is now the case with any proposed new piece of legislation.

Summary

We started this chapter by introducing the main sources of law which you'll be expected to know and looked at some more minor sources of law which you'll be expected to be aware of, but not know in any great detail.

The details were given of how Acts of Parliament are introduced through both the lower and upper tiers of parliament and finally become law. We followed this with some examples of actual acts of parliament and how they may affect you and your business.

Next, we turned to delegated legislation (secondary legislation) where parliament delegates the power to make laws to other bodies, notably local authorities, and saw some of the effects of this secondary legislation.

Then we looked at case law (judge made law) and the importance of the use of precedent in the court system under the heading of *stare decisis* (let the decision stand). This was followed by introducing the concepts of *ratio decidendi* and *obiter dicta* and how they both work in case law.

The importance of law reports was explained, and we saw how you can look up an original case should you ever be asked to do this (unlikely for business law students). Case citations were looked at (the letters and numbers you see after each case) and how they work to enable you to find any case you may have to in the law library.

The tests the courts use to come to their decisions was then given. We stated the importance of the objective test used in civil law (the only type of law you'll need to know about on your course). The idea of "The man on the Clapham omnibus" test was emphasised and the fact that, to annoy other law lecturers, I am trying to re-introduce this expression.

The point was made that in your business law course you'll only be asked about how the courts use an objective test so we can leave the subjective test to the criminal lawyers. We thanked the heavens above for this.

The concept of common law was introduced and the fact that different writers use different meanings of this expression and to be careful to make sure which meaning a writer might be using.

After this we looked at the law of equity (fairness) and how it forms a 'gloss' on the common law which even now, left to its own devices, can produce some pretty rough and ready decisions. A quick history of the development of equity was given and its importance in law today. Some of the more important equitable remedies were given.

Finally, we looked at the importance of the European Convention on Human Rights and the Human Rights Act and pointed out their influence on English and Welsh law today.

Revision questions

1. Give the main sources of English law and write a sentence about each one.
2. Describe the importance of the use of precedent in case law.
3. What is 'obiter dicta' and which are the main sources of obiter?
4. Why is the use of 'equity' still so important in English law?
5. How does the European Convention on Human Rights influence the development of English Law?

3 The law of contract: Contractual 'ingredients'

Background

I'll bet that by the time you are reading this, you'll have already made a large number of contracts this week. Every time you go into a shop or supermarket to buy something you are making a fully legally binding contract with the shop or supermarket to buy whatever the article purchased may be: crisps, a bar of chocolate of a bottle of water or wine.

Contracts of this type are called 'simple verbal' contracts. By their nature these contracts do not have to be made in writing. Some contracts of course do have to be made in writing and these are referred to by lawyers as 'speciality' contracts. The reason that these speciality contracts have to be made in writing is historical more than anything else and these types of contacts shouldn't bother you in your study of business law. You are unlikely to come up against too many of these, but please be just aware of them. You are very unlikely to be expected to analyse these on a first-year undergraduate business course.

However, there are good reasons why some contracts should be made in writing. If, for example, you are buying or selling a house, English law requires that you will need the contractual document to be in writing. This is also true when buying or selling shares in a public limited company. By and large I think it's safe to leave these types of contracts to the lawyers. For yourself, of course, it is quite handy to have a written document stating that you actually own the house you've just bought. As far as your study of business law goes, the chances are that you'll only be asked to analyse certain internal aspects of contracts and you can largely ignore whether they were written or verbal contracts.

To get an idea of just how many simple verbal contracts there are, think of a supermarket that you regularly use; now try to think how many people use this shop each day. Then multiply this number by 364 for the number of days in the year. We'll allow them Christmas day off. The number you come up with will certainly be in the hundreds of thousand or even millions. This is just taking one supermarket and ignores all the others. It also ignores all the other retail outlets throughout the land.

So, if anyone tells you that all contracts have to be made in writing, ignore them and tell them to clear off. Only a minority of contracts must be made in writing. To emphasise the point, the vast number of fully legally binding contracts being formed each day are simple verbal contracts. All of these are just as 'legal' and enforceable as any written contract would be. I've had students, even towards the end of some of my law courses, telling me that all contracts must be made in writing. This sort of thing worries me.

Just out of interest and to put matters in context, over 540 million tins of baked beans are sold in the UK every year. I'll bet that not a single tin changed hands using a written contract

Having fully legally binding verbal contracts is a very practical arrangement. It would be silly if each time you used a shop, you had to sign a written agreement before you could buy anything. The queues would be so long that it would take you hours to do your shopping. I bet you'd think twice before buying frozen beef burgers (or frozen Linda McCartney sausages for the veggies amongst us).

For verbal contracts, the term 'simple' is used not because these contracts are simple in themselves, but to distinguish them from the above mentioned 'speciality' contracts.

In business, naturally most transactions form written contracts, but as said above you will not be asked to analyse the written aspect of these contracts in any detail. It is much more likely that you will be asked to consider the underlying principles of contract law itself. These principles are pretty much common to all contracts whether written or verbal. It's these we'll look at shortly.

Before we do this, let's take a little aside and consider the value of contract law to businesses. Businesses can't trade with other businesses, and indeed customers, for very long without some underlying system of trust. Would you do business with another business that you know won't pay you? I doubt it very much. It's the framework of contract law which reinforces this trust.

All parties to business contracts have the underlying concept in their heads that if, for example, a company to which you've supplied with goods ends up refusing to pay you, well you'll simply sue them for the money. That doesn't mean that you won't meet people and businesses which are slow to pay you. You will – that's business.

To continue, contracts form an agreement between two or more parties which are intended to be legally binding – we will look at the legally binding part shortly. These can be agreements between one person and another person, one business and another business or between a business and a person – or any combination of the above.

☐ *One person and another person* – You agree to buy a car belonging to a friend.

☐ *Business to business* – Tesco buys milk from a farm to sell in its stores.

☐ *Business and a person* – You buy a packet of mints from a shop.

For all of these contracts to be legally binding, English law requires that there must be certain basic elements present to ensure that the contract is enforceable. If one or more of these ingredients are not present then there is no contract. The most important of these contractual requirements are the following:

Contractual 'ingredients'

A. It must be established that there has been a proper (formal) offer and a proper (formal) acceptance.

B. There has to be an intent to enter into a legally binding agreement (sometimes this is written as legal intent or an intent to create legal relations – they all mean the same thing).

C. It has to be established that there must be 'consideration' flowing from each party to the other party, i.e. something of value (to each contracting party) flowing in each direction from one party to the other party. *Consideration*, please be clear, is not a difficult concept. It's simply the benefit you get from entering into any contract. It's also the benefit the other person gets from entering into a contract with you. If both parties aren't going to each benefit in some way by contracting, then they wouldn't contract in the first place!

D. The contracting parties must have the capacity to contract (this normally is concerned with the ability of children to make contacts or people who've had one Carlsberg too many and can't remember what they may have agreed to).

E. There must be a clarity of the terms in a contract. The terms agreed within each contract must be sufficiently clear so that a later dispute in a court enables the court to establish what each party meant when they were contracting.

F. There must be established that there is *consensus ad idem* – this just means a 'meeting of the minds' or agreement between the minds of the contracting parties. As this aspect of contract formation is rarely mentioned in the main textbooks, it's wise for you to be aware of it, as it's worth extra marks.

Offer

Normally the 'offer' side of the offer and acceptance situation doesn't create too much of a problem in business law. Of course, all contracts have to start with an offer and this must be made known (communicated) to the other person or business to which you want to make the offer. The offer can be made in several different ways, orally, in writing or indeed by your conduct. It might seem strange that your conduct may actually become an offer.

Consider this – you drive your car to a car park and walk up to the ticket machine ready to put your coins in the slot. Is it you who is making an offer to park your car to the parking machine or is the parking machine making an offer to you? This was decided in court nearly 50 years ago by one of the most respected judges in English law, Lord Denning, who was mentioned previously. The answer is that it is the machine (or the owner of the machine) who is making the offer and it's you who is making the acceptance by inserting your coins to get your ticket. So, by your conduct, you have accepted the offer made by the machine.

Is there an offer or not? Could it be an invitation to treat?

At first sight it would seem to be obvious whether someone's made an offer to someone else or not. The trouble is that law is law and things are not always as obvious as you might think. An 'invitation to treat' is not an offer for sale. An invitation to treat is also not an invitation to a party. Pay attention to this because it's important. Put that shot down.

When you walk into a shop and pick up a tin of beans and you take it to the checkout person in order to pay, it's you that is making the offer to buy and the checkout person that is accepting your offer (or rejecting your offer if they think that you're under age and shouldn't be trying to buy a six pack of Guinness).

At first sight this seems the wrong way around but believe me it really isn't. It's actually a very good thing for retailers. Let me tell you why. Imagine that a store is running a sale. It makes it clear to potential customers that it's selling new smartphones at half price. You eagerly go along expecting to get a real bargain. The trouble is that the store has run out of the smartphones. You might well get a bit annoyed and say so. But when you realise that the store is not actually offering these phones for sale but it's you that's making an offer to buy, this begins to makes more sense.

What the situation legally is, is that the store has issued an 'invitation to treat'. This means that it's an invitation for you to go in and make an offer to the store for the phone. Looking at it this way the store can decide to accept your offer or reject it. This is the legal position for goods on open display in shops and for most advertisements, wherever you might see these.

When you start to think about this on a personal level it makes even more sense. Imagine that you decide to sell your car and you put an advertisement in your local newspaper saying something like "Ford Fiesta, 2004 model, low mileage, £1,500". Now, it is just possible that the first person that comes to see your car buys it straight away. Unfortunately, you have no idea how many other people have seen your advertisement.

In theory 100,000 people may have seen the ad and are interested in buying your car. If this is the case you could have another 99,999 people knocking on your door complaining that you have advertised the car for sale when you no longer own it. Surely, they will say, it must be a breach of some law or other to advertise for sale something that you actually haven't got? But we now know you were not advertising the car for sale, but merely announcing an invitation to treat – that is, you are issuing an invitation for prospective buyers to come along and negotiate with you regarding the sale of the car – effectively to haggle with you. Crucially it is the prospective buyers who are making an offer to buy and it's up to you to accept it or reject these offers. So, you have broken no law. The trouble is that most people don't know the law.

This concept (or *ratio*) of an invitation to treat comes from very many cases which you will come across during your course, but we only need to look at one of these to illustrate the principle. Ideally you should be aware of two or three of these cases. This will add authority to your work.

Fisher v Bell (1960)

In this case a retailer in Bristol had a shop with articles in the window for passers-by to view. Amongst these articles was a knife with a ticket attached to it saying "retractor knife" and the price was written on the ticket. There is an element of criminal law involved here as there was (and still is) a law banning the sale of this type of knife. So, the police became involved and took out a prosecution against the shop owner for offering to sell a knife which is more commonly known as a "flick knife". The court had to decide if the shop owner had broken the criminal law by "offering for sale" such a knife. The court decided that this was not an offer for sale but just an invitation to treat. This was a situation where any prospective buyer could look through the window, come into the shop and make the shop owner an offer for the knife. As this was simply an invitation to treat and not an offer for sale, there was no offence committed.

This principle has been tested in a large number of other cases and holds true today in the civil law of contract. The result of this precedent is that most, but not all advertisements (see Carlill's case later) are not offers to sell you something but an invitation for you to make the advertiser an offer. So, when you see say, an advertisement in a magazine for that Ferrari which you have always wanted, it is only an invitation for you to go into your nearest Ferrari garage and make them an offer for the car. They can accept your offer or refuse it. Normally if you offer £100,000 for a Ferrari priced at £200,000, they'll refuse it. Still, worth a try.

Lecturers, particularly near the start of your law course, are fond of making up simple questions to test your understanding of this. I am no different.

The sort of question I may make up is the following:

Charlie is driving past a garage which has second hand cars on the forecourt. Charlie has spotted that one car, say a Merc, has a price placed on the inside of the windscreen using the sort of plastic stickers that garages put inside cars. The car should have been priced at £25,000 but unfortunately unknown to the garage owner, one of these plastic stickers has slipped off the windscreen and the price now reads £5,000.

Charlie, not knowing any law, approaches the garage owner and insists that the owner is obliged in law to sell the car to him for £5,000 as the owner has advertised it for sale for at this price. Using decided case law, advise Charlie as to his legal position.

This is dead easy. You simply say that the garage owner is not obliged to sell the car to Charlie as the price placed on the car is not an offer to sell the car at this price, but merely an invitation to treat. The authority for this is given in many cases but particularly is *Fisher v Bell (1960)*. You could go on to say that as it is Charlie who has made to offer to buy the Merc at £5000, the garage owner could, if he wanted, accept Charlie's offer. Somehow, I don't think Charlie's offer will be accepted. What do you think?

This brings us neatly to ...

Counter offers

This is really no problem as it simply means that if someone makes an offer to sell something to you and you want to accept it, then you have to agree to all the terms that the person (or business) have specified in their offer. This idea is often described to be that your acceptance of the offer must be a 'mirror image' of the offer. If it is not a mirror image then what you have done legally is to end (terminate) the offer made to you, and you may have not only ended the offer but replaced it with another offer coming from yourself.

Another one of my examples is the following;

> *Fred says to Graham, "I am selling my car. I want £2,000 for it, are you interested Graham?"*
>
> *Graham says, "wow, £2,000, that's a bit expensive. I'll tell you what I'll do, I'll give you £1,500 for it". This statement has terminated Fred's original offer and replaced it with an offer coming from Graham to Fred. Fred then says," There's no way I can accept £1,500, but I would accept £1,750 for it". If Graham then says, "that's great you've got yourself a deal", then there is a good contract between Fred and Graham.*

Of course, this is a simple example of haggling, which goes on every day. For our purposes we must appreciate that in this process of haggling, a refusal to take the first price offered by Fred is a refusal to accept the original contract offered (it is not then a mirror image because there has been an attempt to change the terms of the contract). The legal effect is to destroy the first offer and replace it with another offer coming the other way. This process of offer and counter offer may continue until both parties come to some agreement that they are both happy with. So, it's a process of offer/counter offer/new offer/new counter offer... until both parties are finally happy with the agreed terms of the contract

As usual there are a huge number of cases which show this principle. A leading case on this to take on board is *Hyde v Wrench (1840)*.

Hyde v Wrench (1840)

Wrench offered to sell his farm to Hyde for a sum of £1,000. Hyde said no, the farm's not worth it but he would pay £950 for it. Wrench refused this lower offer. Then Hyde came back and said OK then I'll give you the £1,000 you wanted in the first place. Wrench, presumably a bit exasperated by Hyde said, no he wouldn't now accept this. Hyde sued Wrench saying that they had a contract.

The court said that there was no contact between them as the offer of the lower sum of money was a counter offer and this destroyed the original offer.

This case is very well known and you are welcome to use it in any work on contact law (in the right place of course). You can just say, ah, this is a Hyde v Wrench counter offer situation. You don't need to remember the facts necessarily as it's the principle that matters (the *ratio*).

I like to remember it myself by saying, Hyde couldn't wrench Wrench's farm away from Wrench. I think this is funny… not everyone agrees.

Acceptance

This is a little more complicated but the general rule is that once an acceptance is made to an offer, then the contract becomes legally binding on both parties. You cannot revoke (take back) the offer once it has been accepted. A concept known as 'privity' of contract means that only the person or business to which an offer has been made can accept the offer. For example, if Samantha, Julie and Pete are having a coffee in a café. Samantha turns to Julie and says, "I need to get hold of some money quickly so I'm selling my stereo system for £250; do you want to buy it?" Pete says, "sure I'll buy it at that price". Pete cannot buy Samantha's stereo because the offer was not made to him. Legally speaking, Pete was not 'privy' to the contract, i.e. he was not part of the proposed contract as the offer was not made to him. Privity is just a posh way of saying privacy. Pete actually was trying to push himself in where he wasn't wanted. We'll return to the concept of privity in more detail in the next chapter as this is an area where law lecturers often sneak in an exam question, particularly in the written part of your exam rather than in any MCQs you might face.

Returning to acceptance above, remember that acceptance must be a 'mirror image' of the offer. As we will see in more detail below, any attempt to change the terms of the offer has the legal effect of terminating that offer. It must be an acceptance which agrees to all the terms of the offer without any attempt to vary the terms at all.

In general, the rule is that acceptance must be relayed (communicated) back to the person making the offer. One exception to this rule is where acceptance may be made by conduct. See the Carlills case on this below. Generally, also, if the offer specifies the method by which the acceptance must be made, then this is the only method you can use, otherwise it's not a mirror image.

This position is reversed in what are usually called 'social and domestic' arrangements. So, the courts make the assumption that when you agree with your best mate to meet outside the cinema to see a film at 7.30 p.m. and your friend doesn't turn up, you cannot sue them for breach of contract. Both of these assumptions (or as the law calls them presumptions) are overturnable if you can bring some evidence that to show that there was an intent to contract in a social/domestic agreement then you may well have a legally binding contract. Similarly, if there is what appears to be a business agreement but you are able to show strong evidence that there was no intent to be legally bound under the agreement, then there is no contract. If something can be overturned, in law it is usually called 'rebuttable'.

The postal rule of acceptance

This is a bit of an old fashioned but still existing rule of acceptance which you'll have to know about even though it's a bit quirky. Being a bit of an odd and peculiar rule, it's something which is often examined both in seminar work and in exams. Some of you, I know, won't like this at all, but there's not much we can do about it ourselves whether we like it or not.

The general rule of acceptance by post is the following. Where using the postal service in accepting a contract is a suitable method of acceptance, as long as the acceptance is also sent back by post, then the moment that the letter of acceptance is put in the post box correctly, it becomes a full acceptance. By 'correctly', here I mean that the letter sent back has the correct name, address, postcode and a stamp fixed on it. Now, even if the letter never gets to the person it's sent back to, then this doesn't matter. It becomes a fully, legally binding acceptance upon posting.

This seems odd to most of us because what it can mean is that, if for example, you send a letter to someone with an offer to sell them something and they respond to you with their acceptance by letter, once they've correctly posted the letter, even if you never receive it, you're now in a legally binding contract. The quirky bit is that you're now in a fully legally binding contact without knowing it, but as you never received the acceptance, you don't know that you're legally bound. The expression 'where it is suitable' to accept by a contract by letter, normally means that the person sending the offer has used the post office to get the offer to the other person. If the offer is sent by post, then it's perfectly reasonable for the person who wants to accept to also use the postal service to get it back to you. It's often said that as the person sending the offer has chosen the post office as his/her agent to get the offer to the other person, then the person accepting the letter is quite within their rights to also use the same method to accept the offer.

Let's use an example where you can unknowingly be in breach of contract under this rule. So, you decide that you want to sell your original Gibson SG 1969 electric guitar to you best friend because you know he's always wanted one. You write him a letter offering to sell the guitar to him for £2,500. He receives your postal offer and immediately sends back his letter of acceptance. The post office loses his letter so you never get it. Assuming the return letter has the correct address etc. when posted, you're now in a contact with your mate. As you never got the acceptance you assume that your friend just isn't interested. Accordingly, you sell the guitar to another friend. Now you could be in trouble. As you are legally bound to sell the guitar to the first friend you offered it to, you are now in breach of contract to him. Depending on how your friend looks at this (how understanding he might be) he might just sue you for breach of contract. If he did so, under these circumstances, he'd win.

Weird or what, say many of my students! They also make other unprintable comments. This is sometimes said to be a legal anomaly which should've been got rid of years ago. Actually, it does make some legal sense although I admit that it doesn't seem to. There are about three methods you can use to explain this. I use what I think is the best example – I think it's the best because I made it up.

So here goes. What we have to do is to get you to imagine yourself on the receiving end of some offer which you've received by post. You are a businesswoman living in London called Judy. You have a business acquaintance living in Coventry called Fred.

> *One day Fred decides that he wants to make you an offer to buy a piece of land in Coventry which he knows you've expressed an interest in some years ago. Now, Fred doesn't trust the postal service (probably from previous experience) so he thinks that he'll use a motorcycle courier person called Michael to get the offer to you personally. He gives Michael a letter containing the details and the price of the land he thinks you'll be interested in. He says, take this letter to Judy in London, wait for her written response which I've asked her to put back in the letter and bring it straight back to me.*
>
> *Michael gets the letter to Judy in London which she immediately accepts. Michael gets back on his motorbike with the letter of acceptance and starts the journey back to London to deliver the letter. Michael gets a bit thirsty on his return journey and pulls in to a pub he knows well. He gets a bit carried away and seemingly without thinking drinks 6 pints of Guinness. As a result, two miles down the road, Michael and his motorbike spins off the road and smashes into a tree. The motorbike and Michael disappear in the resulting explosion – neither to be seen in this world again. Fred, in Coventry, expecting Michael back in a few hours, gets fed up and thinks, oh well, I gave Judy her chance, so he sells the land to someone else.*

I expect you've worked this out by now. OK, I know Michael isn't part of the postal service so the formal postal rule wouldn't apply but the principle is much the same. We have to ask ourselves who's really at fault here? Well quite obviously Michael is, but he's not here to answer any questions. Is it the fault of Judy? Hardly. She didn't choose to use Michael as an agent. Fred did. So, we must put the blame on Fred as it was his choice of transmission mechanism. So, by analogy and by a stretch of the imagination when we apply this back to the postal rule, it's Fred that stands to lose. Similarly, under the postal rule above, the seller of the Gibson SG stands to lose out as much as unfair as this may seem.

Please bear in mind that the postal rule of acceptance only applies to the postal service and not really to Michael. Also, it does not apply to offer only acceptance. If you post a letter making an offer to someone which never arrives then naturally there is no offer so there can be no acceptance. Students sometimes get this the wrong way round or think the rule applies both to offer and acceptance. It does not. It's quite specific to acceptance only and only then when the post is used. That's why it's called the postal rule.

The leading case to use here is *Adams v Lindsell (1818)*. I did say it's an old rule. See the much later case of *Holwell Securities v Hughes (1974)* for a far more modern interpretation of the old rule. It's really worth looking at the earlier rule as it's so easy for your lecturers to make up exam questions on this. If you see a question on contract law with dates (particularly a date of sending a letter mentioned in them) then you can be pretty sure that you're into the postal rule and Adams v Lindsell. Once you understand the concept, no matter how silly it might seem, you'll have no problem in answering.

Consideration

This is the third ingredient of a contract: there must be 'consideration' flowing from each party to the other party, i.e. something of value (in the eyes of the contracting parties) must be exchanged from each person to the other. The concept of consideration is the one which frequently confuses students. This is probably the fault of the English language as the word consideration has more than one meaning.

Consideration can mean being kind to someone, it can also mean giving some problem deep thought. In contract law it describes nothing like these two meanings at all. What it means in law is that consideration is the things (or items) which are being exchanged between the contracting parties. "I will sell you my car if you give me £2,500".

This means that one party is losing his car (his consideration) in exchange for £2,500 which is the consideration given to him by the other contracting party. Normally for most of us, consideration is money being exchanged between you and the person or business that you are dealing with. The thing that you're buying comes your way and money goes from your pocket to the other party – often grudgingly as far as I am concerned.

Although consideration is usually money, it doesn't have to be. As long as there is no fraudulent activity going on, consideration can be almost anything which both parties agree to exchange with each other, but it must be something which is said to be legally 'adequate'. It usually has some economic value, however small. I could agree if I wanted, to sell my house to another person if they gave me used chocolate bar wrappers. See *Chapple v Nestlé (1959)* on this. Also, keep your eye on the sports news. Whole football clubs often change hands for £1.

Consideration can also be the alleviation (putting right) of a disbenefit (getting rid of something disadvantageous) to the other party. You make a contract to buy a phone from a friend for an agreed price of £500. Now, unknown you, your friend owes £500 to another person who we'll call Tom. Your friend says that he is quite happy to buy your phone for £500 but could you pay the money into Tom's bank account? You would, I expect, be quite happy to do this as it doesn't matter to you where the money goes. What has happened here is that your consideration has removed the debt your friend had to Tom. This is called 'valuable' or good consideration. Please see more on this below.

> **Consideration** – A promise to do something for someone in exchange for the other party promising to do something for you.

Below are the main rules on consideration which you will have to know for an exam on contract law. I've included a couple more rules here because they're interesting – and true.

It must be shown that both parties want to exchange something for something else. This is the 'consideration' and as mentioned it usually take the form of money. In most contracts you exchange money for whatever you want to buy in a shop or you expect money from the other party for something that you're selling. But the consideration doesn't have to be money. It can just be a promise to do something for someone else in exchange for the other person promising to do something for you. So, "I will mow your lawn if you let me borrow your car", is good consideration. Or, "I will mow your lawn this weekend if you promise to wash my car" would also be good consideration.

However, if there is just a promise to do something for somebody else with nothing coming back your way, this does not form a contract because there is nothing flowing both ways. An example would be a promise to clean someone's car for nothing in return. Here there is no consideration as nothing is coming back to you, so there would be no contract in the legal sense – this promise could not be enforced.

So, the essence of a contract is based on an exchange of something for something else. The assumption is that that if you and someone else have decided to enter into a contract for the exchange of whatever the article or service is, then you must both be happy with the arrangement.

You could agree for example, particularly if you are mad, to sell your house in exchange (for consideration) of a plastic carrier bag. Why not if it suits both parties? The court then allows us the freedom to make our own 'bargains'. 'Bargain' here do not mean a cheap pair of earrings you found in the sale in Primark. It means the agreement we have come to with the other contracting party. Consideration, going either way, does not have to be of equal value from an outsider's point of view. As long as each contracting party is happy with the exchange then everyone is content and no one is able to interfere with the agreement.

Generally, if no deception is involved by either party to a contract, the courts are simply not interested in what the terms of exchange are (what the consideration is) but only in discovering whether there has been some valuable consideration recognised by the courts.

Of course, if some threat has been used to get you to enter into a contract then the law says that there is no contract. This is called being induced to enter a contract by duress or undue influence and there are, of course, plenty of case law examples of this. This thankfully is generally outside the scope of a business law course in your first year. Just to give you a flavour of this, think of an example of someone holding a large heavy weight over your head and saying to you, if you don't sign this contract, I'll smash this down on your head. Well clearly you have been forced into the contract. On a number of grounds, the law will say that here there can be no contract.

There are some 'rules' of consideration which you will be expected to know. Some writers call these 'maxims of consideration'. Don't worry because these two means exactly the same thing. However, using the term 'maxim' makes it sound like you know what you're talking about. A 'contract' where there is no consideration is called a *'nudem pactum'*.

An example would be where someone makes a promise to do something for you but you promise nothing in return. This would be a *nudem pactum* – a bare promise, and no contract is formed. Add this to your list of Latin phrases.

The following rules have been developed by the courts over the decades and form the main precedents that the courts will apply to any new case coming before them. You will be expected to know the main cases on this.

Consideration must be sufficient, of some value, but does not have to be a 'fair' bargain

This seems a bit odd at first sight but as long as there's been no dishonest activity involved here, what's to stop you selling anything you own for anything you like? If you feel like it you could sell your house in return for a banana, I'm sure you wouldn't do this, but if both parties agree to this exchange then there's nothing to stop you from doing it. This reinforces the fact that the courts are not there to question your ability to make your own decisions regarding your own possessions – however mad they might seem to other people. The court, should it ever come to it, will just enquire did the consideration here (the banana) have some economic value however small. Well, of course, it does.

Consideration must not be in the past

Consideration is a time related concept as it must not be in the past. This means that the formation of the agreement must not be over and done with when the consideration is offered or later discussed. For example:

I stand up in a seminar group and ask whether any student with a car can give me a lift to town when the seminar finishes?

A student puts up his hand and says that he would be happy to give me a lift. When the seminar finishes I get my lift to town and just as I get out of the car, as it's driving off I shout through the drivers open window "thanks very much, I'll give you a £10 note the next time I see you for your petrol money". I never pay the student (which is incidentally very possible).

Now, the question is, can the student sue me in court for his £10? Well the most likely possibility is that I can't be sued because the promise of £10 (the consideration for my lift) came *after* the agreement was made in the seminar room. In short, there may well have been an agreement but there was certainly no legally binding contract because the consideration was offered too late.

OK, let's consider a similar situation in the seminar room. I stand up this time and ask if any student will give me lift to town. A student says that she would be happy to give me a lift. I now say thanks very much, "I'll give you £10 when we get to town."

We get to town and I then refuse to pay. Can the student now sue me for the money? Well it's likely that the student would win her case because this time the consideration was offered before, *not after* the agreement was made. Unfortunately, most of my students have now got used to this little ploy.

This rule is shown in many cases of course. I suggest you take a look at *Re McArdle (1951)* on this. It's an easy case to understand and concerns promises made to a lady to pay for house improvements by her children – after she had finished the improvements. Also, a very interesting case which is an exception to this rule you may want to look at is *Lampleigh v Braithwaite (1615)*. This is worth a look because it's such an old case, but it's even more interesting as it involves murder and a potential hanging and is still good law today. You can use it in any essay work or exams.

Consideration must not be illegal

You make an agreement with a friend to rob a bank. Your friend promises to steal a fast getaway car and you promise to get the shooters. On the day of the robbery he turns up outside the bank in a stolen Porche and you bring two water pistols. He gets angry and threatens to sue you for breach of contract. I think I can leave this point there…

Consideration must be more than an existing duty

If you're under an existing contractual or legal duty to do something anyway, then you can't use this as good consideration. One of the very many cases you can use here is *Collins v Godefroy (1831)*.

Collins v Godefroy (1831)

Here, a lawyer made a private promise for a sum of money to appear in court to give evidence as a witness. As he is already under a legal duty to appear in court, this private agreement was held to have no consideration. Legally he had to appear anyway. This is an area which you really must explore further as there are quite a few case law variations on this theme.

What about where you have an existing contractual duty to do something?

Suppose that you are working as a receptionist at a doctor's surgery and a patient says to you that he will give you £20 if you ensure that he gets the next available appointment if there's been a cancellation. This is not valuable consideration because as a receptionist you are contractually bound to do this anyway. It is not contractually binding as no 'extra' has been supplied. A receptionist at a doctor's surgery is contractually bound to ensure that all patients are given the best possible service. This automatically includes offering an appointment when there's been a cancellation.

Consideration must move from the promisee

First, we need a little more terminology the *offeror* and the *promisee*.

- The *offeror* is just the person making the offer. This is also the *promisor*.
- The *promisee* is the person accepting the offer. This is also the *offeree*.

This can get confusing at first so it needs a little practice and it is useful to draw yourself a few diagrams with arrows pointing each way just to make the position clear.

An offer from someone must go to someone else. If A makes an offer to B then it is up to B to accept the offer or reject it. If B wants to accept the offer then it is up to B to ensure that the consideration he has been asked for by A, is supplied to A. It is possible that A can ask B to supply the consideration to another party, C, if A wants this.

So, Terry is making an offer to John to sell his car to him for £2,500. John wants to accept this offer so it's up to John to make the necessary arrangements to get this sum of money moved to Terry. Hence, consideration must move from John, as John here is the promisee – so consideration must move from the promisee.

Note that although the consideration must move from John, it doesn't necessarily have to move to Terry. If Terry said to John, "would you mind paying the £2,500 into someone else's bank account please," I don't think John would mind too much as long as he's sure that the car has been fully paid for. It could well be that, unknown to John, Terry owes some other person a certain sum of money and Terry is discharging this sum (or some of it). This is an example of privity of contract again.

Other rules of consideration

The above are the main rules of consideration which you will be expected to know along with some key cases.

I have included the following rules just for fun, but they are quite real and you are very welcome to use them if you want to impress (or annoy) your law lecturers.

Consideration cannot be impossible (at the time of the offer, at least)

So, Pete makes an offer to Sarah saying that if Sarah gives him £10,000, he'll arrange for her to be transported back in time to meet Napoleon. He says he's a good mate of Dr Who.

Consideration cannot be too unclear or vague

In *White v Bluet (1853)*, a father made a promise to forget a loan made to his son if the son stopped complaining about how his father would distribute his money to the family after the death of the father.

The court decided that this was not good consideration as it was in effect just a promise "not to bore his father" and was too vague. Anyway, "the son had no right to complain" to his father. Let this be a warning to all business law students.

The terms of the agreement must be sufficiently clear to each party

This is because if a court is later asked to determine whether a contract is valid or not, it must be clear to the court that the terms were transparent (intelligible) to each party involved. For example, if a person is trying to make out that there is a contract for the sale of his car to a friend and the court has evidence that when the offer to sell the car was made it was met by the answer, "oh I'll give it some thought", then the terms are not clear enough and there will be no contract.

If the person to whom the offer for sale of the car keeps completely silent, making no reply at all, then this is not a good acceptance. The courts have, over the years, asked anyone who is making a contract to please make sure that all the terms within a contract are as clear as possible. Of course, this hasn't happened with many contracts so it's still up to the courts to unravel an unclear contract. Oh well... this is their job after all.

Let's have quick look at the main methods by which an offer can end:

☐ When a counter offer is made. As we have seen this acts as a rejection of the offer and terminates it.

☐ When the contract has been 'breached' (broken down in some way) – see the following section on this.

☐ Where a time limit has been stated by the person making the offer, and it has not been accepted within this time.

☐ When an offer has been taken back, before it's been accepted. You can't take an offer back after someone has accepted it. This is called 'revocation of an offer'. So, you cannot revoke an offer after it's been accepted.

☐ When the offer lapses within a 'reasonable' time. What is meant by reasonable here depends on the circumstance of the case and often what is involved in the offer. For example, shares in a company trading on the Stock Exchange might be offered at a particular price. Twenty years later you cannot realistically attempt to 'accept' these shares, as no doubt the share price will have changed even if the company still exists. The question of what is reasonable depends, as always, on what the court tells us is reasonable in each case. If you make an offer to sell a bunch of grapes, the time it may be reasonable to keep the offer open is likely quite different from an offer to sell your house.

Legal intent/intent to create legal relations (the two mean the same)

There must be "an intention to create a legal relationship" with the other party involved. This means that the law assumes that both parties are aware that they are entering into a legal arrangement. In most cases in the real world of course, most of us don't even think about this (until things go wrong). But for a legally binding contract to exit the law (i.e. the courts) make an assumption that all parties to a contract have this 'awareness' that they are intending to be contractually bound by the agreement.

It must be shown that the parties attempting to form the contract intended for the contract to come into existence. This is the basis of legal intent. Arguably, this is the most important of the all the ingredients in a contract. This why an agreement between you and your best mate to meet up to go to the cinema, for example, is not a legally binding contract, so if your mate doesn't turn up, you cannot sue them for breach of contract. The court would say that this would just be a social or domestic agreement between two friends. Crucially, the court would say that neither you nor your friend had any intent to go to get involved in law if one of you didn't turn up.

Look at one or more of the cases on this. Specifically see *Carlill v the Carbolic Smoke Ball Company (1893)* (below) case and *Balfour v Balfour (1919)*. This case will lead to the concept of contrasting cases. There are plenty of other cases showing the difference between the courts presuming that there is legal intent to contract and the court presuming that you hadn't, as in the above example. It is wise when looking at contract law construction, to be able to state when it is likely that the courts will find that there is a legal intent (mainly in business contracts or when you buy something in a shop) and where there is not likely to be legal intent (mainly just agreements between you and a friend or your family). Of course, law being law there are exceptions to the above rules. So, if you intend to enter into a binding contract with, your brother, for example, to sell him your car, then you really should make this clear to him and perhaps keep some kind of record that you both intend to be bound by the agreement. This should help you if your brother ends up not paying you for your car.

What you have done here is going to be a good way to prove at a later time (in court) that this, on the surface, mere domestic "agreement" was in fact intended to be a legally binding contract. Mind you, you've probably lost a friend in your brother.

☐ It must be shown that there is an offer from one person to the other and an acceptance coming back from that person to the person making the offer.

☐ The party making the offer must be in a position to make the offer. Children, for example, are more limited in their capacity to make or receive offers and acceptances. This is normally called "the capacity to contract" which must be shown to exist for a legally binding contract to come into existence.

Let's take a look at one of the most famous of cases in contract law and see how some of the above precedents can be teased out of it.

Carlill v the Carbolic Smoke Ball Company (1893)

We will be looking at this case in some detail because, well, it's interesting and it is one of what are called leading cases in the law of contract. It is a case which is so fundamental that it changed the law of contract at the time and is still used by the courts today. It established a number of new precedents in this area of law and we will use it to explain how these precedents can be used to resolve some modern-day contractual disputes. Perhaps not surprisingly, virtually every person who has any knowledge of the law at all knows about Carlill's case. I've even seen questions come up about this case on TV quiz shows.

The case

So, what are the facts of this case? Well, it's really quite simple on the surface.

The Carbolic Smoke Ball Company placed an advertisement in *The Illustrated London News* on January 21st 1892 attempting to sell their Smoke Ball product. The advertisement claimed that if anyone bought their Smoke Ball and used it as the Smoke Ball Company directed (written instructions were included with the Smoke Ball) then they would be cured from an absolutely staggering number of ailments. These included: "Coughs – cured in 1 week, Snoring – cured in 1 week, Cold on the chest – cured in 12 hours, Asthma – relieved in I week and Throat Deafness – cured in 1 to 3 months" (what on earth is throat deafness?) The list goes on, but more importantly for our purposes, the list included influenza. Influenza is what we would now call 'flu. The smoke ball was very much like an ordinary candle with a wick. The candle itself had carbolic material imbedded in the wax which is a powerful astringent, i.e. it kills germs.

The advert went on to say that the Smoke Ball Company was so sure that their product worked, that they had deposited £1,000 in a London Bank on Regent Street in case anyone buying a Smoke Ball contracted any of the above ailments. If any buyer contracted any of these afflictions after using their product, they would pay £100 to that person as a reward. They actually did deposit this amount in the Alliance Bank.

Importantly, the advertisement stated that anyone buying their Smoke Ball and using it three times a day for two weeks would not catch 'flu. Now, a lady called Louisa Carlill saw the advertisement in her copy of the newspaper, and bought and used the Smoke Ball exactly as she was instructed and caught 'flu. Oh dear. When Mrs Carlill was sufficiently recovered from her bout of 'flu she tried to claim her £100 reward. Naturally, the company was reluctant to pay her what she considered to be her rightful reward. It's worth pointing out here that although £100 might not seem a huge amount of money today, if you scale it up to its present value, it amounts to a sum most of us would not turn down.

I used the Bank of England Inflation Calculator online and plugged in £100, chose 1883 and pressed the button. It came as a bit of a surprise that at the time of writing, £100 would be equivalent to £11,944.09 today. That would be worth having! It would more than pay for a year's university fees with a fair bit left over for Wetherspoon's (other eating places are available). No wonder Mrs Carlill wanted her money. Who could blame her?

The legal arguments

Then the fun began. A huge legal row started. The Smoke Ball Company were adamant that they wouldn't pay out a penny to Mrs Carlill and they used the then existing contract law to try to show that there was no contract between themselves and Mrs Carlill. The case ultimately went to the Court of Appeal to decide who was right.

The company brought to the court quite a few legal arguments in an attempt to show that they shouldn't be contractually bound. We'll look at just some of these arguments to show how this case changed the law of contract quite fundamentally and developed the basics contract law to what it is today.

Initially, the company insisted that the advertisement was a mere "advertisers' puff". Nowadays we would call this advertisers' hype. This means that they were saying that it was just a marketing gimmick. You see this sort of thing every day. Here are just a few examples of some modern advertising puffs: "Persil washes whiter than white" – how can you get whiter than white? (Interestingly, I never believed that Unilever, the makers of Persil, would ever have used such a silly advert. The nice archiving department at Unilever went to a lot of trouble for me and after extensive searches back to the 1950s, told me that they've never ever used this slogan. They've used, "Persil washes whiter" and other variations. This just shows that the writers of the marketing books, which often quote this example wrongly, haven't ever bothered to properly check that it is true.

"*Heineken reaches parts of the body which other beers cannot reach.*" Really? "*Clairol – does she, or doesn't she?*" Does she or doesn't she what? "*Red Bull gives you wiiings.*" I wondered why I couldn't get my jacket back on. Of course, we mainly understand nowadays that this sort of thing isn't actually meant to be taken too seriously. At least I hope so. Anyway, the court rejected this type of argument immediately by saying that the deposit of £1,000 in the event of the smoke ball not working properly, showed the intent of the company to be legally bound or, putting it another way, showed that the company had the intent to create legal relations. So, no, this wasn't a mere advertisers' puff.

The company then said that an advertisement was not an offer for sale, merely an invitation to treat. Now as far as the law went at that time, they might well have been right about this. Contract law up to this time generally considered most advertisements not to be offers for sale but to be invitations to treat, i.e. an advertisement was looked at generally as allowing you, the individual who saw the advertisement, to be in a position to make an offer to the company placing the advertisement, thus an invitation to treat. This is still the position today with most advertisements. Here the Court of Appeal made a distinction between the Smoke Ball advertisement and other ordinary advertisements in newspapers and magazines. The Smoke Ball advertisement was not like an ordinary advertisement.

With an ordinary advertisement all you do is look at whatever is advertised and it's up to you whether you go to the shop and buy the item. But with this advertisement you had not to go buy the product, but crucially having bought it, you had to agree to use the product exactly as the manufacturer specified (to use it three times a day for two weeks) and in addition in Mrs Carlill's case, you had to catch 'flu.

This level of detail, and the number of steps you had to go through to respond to this advertisement, turned it into, according to the Court of Appeal, from what may arguably have been a mere invitation to treat, into an actual offer for sale. Strike one to Mrs Carlill. The Company didn't stop there however and tried another tactic (it still didn't want to pay out the money).

They came back with what they must have thought would be a clincher. They said ah ha! OK, if the court says we made an offer then so be it. But, how could we make an offer to someone we didn't even know existed? We had no idea that there was a 'Mrs Carlill' and that she'd read our newspaper and had seen our advertisement. In short, how could we have made an offer to someone out there with the person reading it being quite unknown to us? After all, most contracts require one party to make an offer and another party to accept it. The Court of Appeal deliberated over this point and decided that yes, it should be entirely possible to make an offer to the world at large. As soon as the court were clear that this was an actual offer then it makes sense to say, well, it's now up to the individual reading the offer to accept the offer or not as they chose. Mrs Carlill had accepted the company's offer by buying the Smoke Ball and using it as instructed and contracting the 'flu. Strike two to Mrs Carlill.

The company were by no means finished (they really didn't want to pay out the money). They argued that, OK, we accept that we've made an offer, and that Mrs Carlill bought and used our product but – using the contract law of the time – Mrs Carlill didn't make us aware that she'd bought and used our product so how can we be part of any contract with her? The normal rule in contract law states that there should be a formal offer made and a formal acceptance should be given back to the party making the offer. But the company argued Mrs Carlill had not *communicated* her acceptance of the offer back to the company. Therefore, there could be no contract. I suspect that the company were getting a bit worried by now. The Court of Appeal then rejected this argument also stating that, in this case, Mrs Carlill had accepted the offer by her conduct. By buying the product and going through all the steps required of her in using the product she had fulfilled all that was required of her, she had in effect accepted the contract by her conduct in acting as the advertisement asked. Strike three to Mrs Carlill.

The Carbolic Smoke Ball Company were still not finished yet. They then argued that for a contract to be legally binding in English law there has to be consideration from both parties. The company said that in this case not enough consideration had been supplied to make this a legally binding contract.

This was firmly rejected by the court. One of the judges, Lord Justice Smith stated, "It was said that there was no consideration, and that it was a *nudem pactum*" (bare promise). "There are two considerations here. One is the consideration of the inconvenience of having to use this carbolic Smoke Ball for two weeks, three times a day; and the other more important consideration is the money gain that was likely to accrue to the defendants by the enhanced sale of the Smoke Balls. . ." Strike four to Mrs Carlill – and out! Actually, I think I've wrongly stated the number of strikes needed in baseball to be out, so apologies to our American friends.

So, Mrs Carlill won her case and got her money. I often wonder what she spent it on.

The precedents

Let's now take a look at some of the more important precedents and new precedents that emerged from the case:

- It is possible to make an offer to the world at large – an offer to someone you don't know and didn't even know existed.
- It is possible to accept an offer by your conduct.
- Depending on the detail or number of steps the advert wants you to go through, an advertisement can be an actual offer and not just an invitation to treat.
- Intent to create legal relations for the contract was shown by the action of the company in depositing the £1,000 in the bank. That is, intention to create a legally binding contract can be done by conduct.

Bilateral contracts

It's time to clear up a confusion that occurs frequently in this area of the law. Many authors will talk about *bilateral* and *unilateral* contracts. The 'bi' bit in bilateral contracts simply means two parties to a contract (of course theoretically there can be any number of parties to a contract) but the more common number is two – the buyer and the seller. One party offers to sell or do something for the other party and other party accepts the offer by promising something in return – usually, money.

Unilateral contracts

This can be where a little bit of trouble can enter. As usual this is mostly caused by the English language. An example of a unilateral 'contract' is Carlill's case as above. This is where one party to the contract makes an offer saying that they will do something in exchange for some action by someone else. If you buy a Smoke Ball from me and use it as I say and get the 'flu, I promise to give you £100 as a reward. At this stage there is no real contract as such yet, only an offer. No one has to accept my offer, so a fully formed contract only starts when someone takes me up on my offer. It is sometimes said that the offer then 'crystallises' at this point into a contract. Probably it would be better for all authors to stick to the terms, 'bilateral contracts' and 'unilateral offers'. I don't expect this will happen very soon. There are some philosophical arguments about this so, it would be best for all writers to stick to the same terms but also make clear that in the unilateral case, a full contract has not yet been formed.

Consensus ad idem – a meeting of the minds

Often this aspect of contract formation is forgotten completely, which is good for you as not everyone will know about it. The idea seems very obvious in that it must be shown that if there are two contracting parties (we usually assume this to make life easier) then both parties must be thinking about the same thing, that they are trying to buy and sell to each other.

Several writers who do cover this aspect of contract law, have used the possibility of contracting parties confusing the word 'crane'. One possibility of course is that a 'crane' is a bird. But a 'crane' it's also a great big tall metal thing used in building construction. If one party is thinking of one of these meanings and the other party is thinking of the other, then obviously there is no real meeting of the minds and no contract.

Let me give you two examples where this is also possible – well just about.

A lady walks into a mobile phone shop and says, "I want a battery for a Nokia 3310". The person behind the counter says, "that sounds like a good swap, thanks".

A man walks into a car parts shop and says, "I'd like seat covers for my Bugatti Veyron". The sales assistant says, "Lovely, I'll take that".

Quite obviously in these two examples there is no real meeting of the minds so again there would be no contract.

Misrepresentation

OK, so we now have all the main 'ingredients' of a legally binding contract, as seen above. But what about the situation where someone has told you something about whatever it is which you're seriously considering buying, and this information, which you may well be relying upon, is just not true? If you rely upon something said to you as a contract 'clincher' and as a result you go ahead and make a contract, you are going to be seriously annoyed when you find out later that you've been told a complete set of lies. If this occurs then it's said that there have been one or more types of contractual *misrepresentation*. Misrepresentations, as we shall see, have their own remedies. There are three main types of misrepresentation, each with its own remedy.

I just have to point out here that this part of contract law can be really quite confusing. It has been called, "an incredibly complex area." And so, it can be, however, in your first year you should be fine with making yourself aware of the three different types of misrepresentation and their general remedies. Check with your law tutor if he/she wants you to look further into the subject. If so, it will probably just mean that you will have to study the various exceptions to the rules we are about to look at. If this is the case you will have to add a few more cases to your memory bank.

The following example is one I use regularly with my students as it seems to cover most possibilities.

> *Imagine that you're thinking of buying a second hand car. There you are on a garage forecourt looking at perhaps 50 cars and wondering how far your money can stretch. All of a sudden, the car salesman appears beside you (if it's a man, no doubt he'll be wearing a three-piece suit with a watch on a gold chain dangling from his waistcoat). As he's working on commission, he's very likely to tell you anything he thinks you want to hear to induce you to buy one of the cars on display. He'll be very friendly and give you an award-winning smile which will gleam, as if he's in a toothpaste advertisement. Invariably, his suit will be at least one size too small for him. He'll be your long-lost friend. The conversation may go something like this:*
>
> *"Good morning sir, lovely morning, am I correct in thinking that you're looking for a car?"*
>
> *"Ah yes, well, that's why I'm standing on your garage forecourt. . . Of course, I am just looking today".*
>
> *"Well, this is your lucky day, sir as I have some special offers this week. May I direct your attention to this model, sir? It's in a lovely shade of pink which would suit your hair, if you don't mind me saying so, sir."*
>
> *"Well thank you, I was looking at that one actually. Is the mileage it states on the clock correct?"*
>
> *The salesman, not bothering to check the vehicle history or documents says, "Oh yes sir. I'm sure it is. All our cars have the correct mileage. You can tell that from their fantastic condition."*
>
> *You then say, "OK, what about the car's MOT?"*
>
> *The salesman, knowing very well that the car only has three months' MOT, says, "It's got a full 12 months MOT, sir, as have all of our cars; I wouldn't sell a car with any less."*

> *He goes on to say, "also, you may be interested to hear that we put a brand-new engine in the car last week". He actually believes this as the garage manager told him about it the day before.*
>
> *You then say, "has the car been serviced recently?"*
>
> *The salesman doesn't answer this because he hasn't heard you or has just pretended not to hear you.*
>
> *As a result of this conversation you go ahead and buy the car. You've entered into a legally binding contract. You pay for the car and drive it home, for the moment quite content – until you later check the vehicle documents.*
>
> *You check the car's paperwork and find out that its mileage is twice what is says on the milometer.*
>
> *You find that it only has three months' MOT and not 12 as you were told.*
>
> *You find out that there is no history of the car ever having had a service and it hasn't got a new engine.*
>
> *Your wife doesn't agree that the pink colour suits your hair.*
>
> *Oh dear. You've been had.*

Some of the salesman's statements have induced (persuaded) you to enter into a legally binding contract. But this surely is unfair? If you hadn't listened to the salesman, you might well have just walked away from the whole situation. If he hadn't flashed his gleaming smile at you and complemented you on your hair, then you may well have instead bought a good second hand Volkswagen Golf from a reputable dealer and also got some kind of guarantee. We live and learn...

The statements made by the salesman are called 'pre-contractual statements' or 'representations' (the two are the same and you can use either of these expressions interchangeably). The 'pre-contractual' part gives it away. These statements do not normally form part of the contract. So, they can't be treated as contractual terms which actually are contained within a contract. We will look at the different types of term within a contract in the next chapter.

For a misrepresentation to be actionable, it must be a statement of fact not opinion. So, when the salesman said that the car was a lovely colour which suited my hair, this is a mere statement of opinion. Actually, being a second hand car salesman, I doubt if it was a real opinion anyway. I have no course of action here. But I may well have a course of action for the other statements the salesman made.

There are three different types of misrepresentation. These are:

- **Negligent** – this is where a person makes a statement relating to whatever it is that you're interested in buying, but that statement has been made in a careless way. The statement has been made believing that it is true but not bothering to check if it really is true.
- **Fraudulent** – where a person makes a statement which they know isn't true. It is a deliberate lie – see *Derry v Peek (1889)* on this for a full definition.
- **Innocent** – This is where a person makes a statement honestly and has good (reasonable) grounds for believing that the statement is true.

Let's see how we can apply the three types of misrepresentation to our second hand car salesman. We already know that his 'opinion' about the colour of my hair has no legal significance. When I asked about how many miles the car had done the salesman, without checking any records of the history of the car, simply said that that the reading was correct. This is likely to be *negligent* misrepresentation. He could've checked but he didn't. When he stated that the car had a full 12 months' MOT knowing full well that it only had three months, this is likely to be a *fraudulent* misrepresentation. However, when he informed me that the car had been recently fitted with a new engine this is likely to be an *innocent* misrepresentation as he had been told of this by the garage manager, and presumably believed him.

So, what can we do about these misrepresentations? The case law on this was a little confusing and as a result the Misrepresentation Act 1967 was introduced. Some people argue that this Act, far from simplifying things, has actually made matters worse.

The remedies for these misrepresentations are generally damages and/or *'rescission'* (This is an equitable remedy which is only available at the court's discretion). Rescission involves putting back the clock to return both parties to the position they would have been if they had never started negotiating in the first place. If damages are to be awarded, the amount will as usual be decided by the court.

In the next chapter we will dig more deeply into the actual contract (the terms of the contract) itself and see what happens when these terms have been breached by either of the parties to the contract. This will be fun.

Summary

In this chapter we introduced the idea of 'simple' contracts and 'speciality' contracts, and said that for almost all of your first-year business law purposes, you will be dealing only with simple contracts.

We suggested that the vast majority of all contracts are made verbally and don't need to be in a written form and asked you to imagine the huge number of these simple contracts which are made each year.

The necessary elements or 'ingredients' needed to form a legally binding contract were given. These include:

- offer and acceptance,
- consideration,
- an intent to create a binding contract with another person or business,
- the need for clarity of the terms of a contract, and finally
- the need for a "meeting of the minds" of the contracting parties, i.e. that they were both thinking of the same thing when forming a contract.

We pointed out the distinction between informal agreements between individuals on a social and/or domestic level and more formal legally binding contracts, between persons and businesses, or business and other businesses.

We used a minimum of case law to explain some of the main contractual ingredients and how these court decisions still apply to contractual legal disputes today.

Bilateral contacts were discussed, these normally operating between two contracting parties, and the more unusual situation of unilateral offers, which actually form an offer to the world at large.

Finally, we looked at pre-contractual situations where, although a contract may be formed, the situation may be that one person or business has been induced into entering into a contact by the use of misleading information. Then we looked at possible remedies you or your business might have if misrepresentation actually occurred in forming the contract.

Revision questions

1. Do you think it's necessary for there to be a legal system which is designed to enforce contracts, for businesses to operate effectively?
2. What are the necessary legal elements required to be able to ensure that a fully legally binding contact has come into existence?
3. Explain using case law, what the difference is between an offer for sale and an invitation to treat.
4. Do you think we still need the postal rule for acceptance or should it now be abolished?
5. In which ways can you be induced into accepting a contract when the other party hasn't told the full truth, when describing whatever it is which they're trying to sell?

4 The law of contract: Contracts in practice

Terms

The terms within a contract form the rules that both parties agree to comply with in their contractual dealings with each other.

In a written contract, these terms are very easy to recognise simply because you can read them. These are examples of *express terms*. As we will see, there may well be other terms in a contract which legally exist but they are implied into the contract by law. These are *implied terms* and no matter how hard you try to find them in a written contract you'll never discover them. Terms, both express and implied, can exist in both written and verbal contracts.

Some of the terms in a contract are legally more important than others. Unfortunately for us, we can't always tell before a case is heard in a court which are the most important terms and which are of less importance. So, if there's been some legal dispute, we have to wait for the court's decision to find out whether a term is very important or not – bear with me here and all will be explained.

Express and implied terms

Imagine that you agree to sell your car to a friend and you describe the type of car, its price and probably the registration number, colour and mileage. Assuming your friend agrees to your offer (accepts it) then whether you write down the above description and price etc. or whether this is done verbally, the details of the car as you've described it, are *express* terms which you're both agreeing to. One *implied* term in the contract, which you both probably won't even think of, is that you have the right to sell the car. That is, you actually own the car in the first place! This shows you how these implied terms tend to be a bit sneaky. They aren't always obvious and can creep up on you while your back is turned.

Another example which might be familiar to you if you have a part time job (and I encourage all students to have a part time job), is that of contracts of employment. Assuming that you have a job with a reputable employer (and not just a cash in hand job at the local chippy) then you must, by law, be given a contract of employment. In this (which incidentally isn't likely to be your full contract of employment), there will be details of your employer's name, your name and address, National Insurance number, place of work, hours of work and rate of pay, any holiday entitlement, etc. All of these are express terms of your contract of employment. If you have one, take a look at it now. It should include all the details mentioned above and quite possibly more.

What the contract of employment is unlikely to say is that you owe a duty to your employer of good faith, that you must not attempt to compete with your employer and you must not reveal confidential information about your work. But you really do have these duties whether you like it or not. This is because these duties, and many more, have been implied into such employment contracts by common law many years ago. I said they were a bit sneaky...

We'll take a look now at how implied terms can enter into contracts. They can arise in three main ways. They can come from common law (case law) as seen above. They can be implied by statute law, and they can arise by the nature of practices which have become common through long standing methods of trading and the customary way that contracts always have been made in certain localities. We'll take just a few examples of each of these but there are hundreds of examples should you wish to chase this further. I should only do this if it particularly interests you, as a handful of examples should be quite enough to explain the basic ideas.

Implied terms by case law

As we have seen above in contracts of employment, case law has implied that the employee (and the employer) have certain duties towards each other. We'll take a closer look at these duties in the chapter on employment law. Apart from employment law, there are numerous examples where the law by statute, implies various terms into contracts. Take another look at the chapter on sources of law if you want to remind yourself about this. Particularly take notice of the Consumer Rights Act 2015 and the statutory rights given to all of us as consumers when we make any contract to buy anything from a retailer.

The following case is one I always use to show the importance of the courts in implying certain terms into a contract when such a term seems, for some reason, to be missing.

The Moorcock (1889)

The facts of this case were that The Moorcock was the name of a ship carrying cargo which needed to be offloaded. To do this the ship owners made a contract with the owners of a wharf situated on the River Thames. Now, unfortunately, no one seemed to have realised at the time that the River Thames is a very highly tidal river (they've certainly realised this nowadays). So, when the Moorcock was moored alongside the jetty on the river and the tide went out, naturally the ship began to sink lower and lower into the water. Eventually the hull of the ship came to rest on the river bed and was badly damaged by a series of rocks lying along the bottom of the river.

Oh dear. The ship owners naturally thought that the owners of the wharf should compensate the ship owners in contract law for a breach of contract. Unfortunately for the shipowners, the owners of the wharf didn't agree with this at all. Now comes what the wharf owners must have thought was the clever bit. They argued something like this: take a look at the contract which we made with you. Where in the contract does it state that we are to be responsible for any damage caused to your ship by the tide going out? The contract in fact made no mention of this. We are forced to ask today, where's the sense in a wharf owner contracting their wharf out to a ship, when they must have known (or at least suspected) that the wharf wasn't deep enough to contain a ship of this size and weight?

Well of course this makes no sense at all looking at it from an objective point of view. Or, from any point of view I suspect. The court agreed with this because they implied a new term in their ruling into the contract as it stood. This term regarded the original contract as actually having to have contained a clause that the wharf was suitable for the ship to be offloaded safely. The court mentioned that the sole purpose of the contract was to moor the ship on the jetty to unload the ships' cargo. Crucially, it was inevitable that the ship would be lowered by the tide and hit the rocks.

Such a term was specified as having to be present in the contract for the purpose of 'business efficacy'. 'Efficacy', as used by L.J. Brown in *The Moorcock*, means the ability to bring about some intended result. In this case the intended result was the safe mooring and offloading of the ship. So according to the court, the original contract was to be considered to have such a term within it.

All business contracts are now considered to have such a term in them simply because they need it to make contracts work. Consider this – you get into a taxi and ask the driver "how much it will cost to take me to Buckingham Palace?" The driver says "it'll cost you £50". You say "that's fine". You sit and wait and wait and wait. Finally, you ask why you aren't moving and the driver says, "oh, we can't go anywhere because the taxi hasn't got an engine – but I'll still have your £50." So, to make contracts work, we (and the law) expect that both the contracting parties are fully able to perform what is agreed in the contract. If such a term isn't in a contract, then we know from the *ratio* in *The Moorcock*, that the term is implied in it. Such a term simply has to be there otherwise business couldn't work.

I have, at this point, to enter into a little aside and mention the role of the courts in contract law. The courts have traditionally allowed us, the contracting parties, to make our own contractual arrangements. As said before, if one contracting party is quite happy to sell her top of the range Ferrari to someone else for £1, then unless there's been some fraudulent activity, the court simply have no interest in this agreement. The phrase normally used is that the courts allow us (the contracting parties) "freedom to make our own bargains". As a result of this traditional view by the courts, you can imagine that they are very reluctant to interfere with contracts. They will only intervene in these arrangements infrequently. In a sense then, the courts merely 'police' contracts. They don't see themselves in the role of making our own contracts for us. But, in some instances, as in the case of *The Moorcock*, they obviously do intervene when they deem it's appropriate to do so. The court may also imply a term if it thinks that such a term has been in some way 'missed' in the original contract. It's important to remember that the role of the court is to discover what it thinks was the original intent of the contracting parties.

Another case where the court was asked to intervene was *Shirlaw v Southern Foundries (1939)*. I've included this because you'll be expected to be aware of the way the court intervened in the contract in this case and I also find it strangely funny.

Shirlaw v Southern Foundries (1939)

The case concerned a manager of a business (Shirlaw) who maintained that he had been unfairly treated when the company he worked for was taken over by another company. He made out that he had been removed before his original 10-year employment contract had expired. This, he said, was contrary to his original contract. The new company had altered its articles of association to allow them to remove Shirlaw. While there was nothing legally wrong with the alteration of the articles, Shirlaw asked the court if they would imply a term into the old contract so that he would not be harmed by the change in the articles.

The Court of Appeal did imply such a term into the contract so Shirlaw won his case. What I find really interesting is the method the court used to justify this change in the term. They invented a 'legal fiction' (see page 10) which has become known as the 'officious bystander' test.

To explain this, we'll just take a look at the word 'officious'. An officious person is really someone who's really nosey and interfering. We've all met them… These are the sort of people who are always 'sticking their nose' into other peoples' business – an intrusive sort of person. A 'bystander' is obviously a person standing nearby.

So, the court said, let's imagine that at the formation of the original contract there was just this sort of person present overhearing everything that was being done and said. The courts imagine then, what would this person have said if asked, "did the contracting parties intend to include such a term as Mr Shirlaw wants us to imply?" If, the court decides that this officious bystander would say, "Oh of course there was intended such a clause to be in the contract", then the court can go ahead and imply it. The court did go ahead and imply the term, so Mr Shirlaw won his case.

The reason why I find this amusing is that I can't help wondering who exactly the judges had in mind when they were asked to imagine an officious bystander. Each other perhaps? I don't know. What I do know is that whenever I think of an officious person, I can't help remembering that creepy feeling you get in a silent exam room when you think that an invigilator is hovering somewhere just behind you…

If you've read the chapter on *What you need to know* (which I hope you have), then I'm sure that you'll have realised that the officious bystander test is just an extension or application of the reasonable man, or the Man on the Clapham Omnibus test.

Terms implied by custom or by practices common to certain trades

Terms can occasionally be implied by the court as a result of the way that 'things have always been done' in certain geographical areas. It is not common for the courts to have to intervene in these more local types of contracts. However, intervention does still occur from time to time. One of the main, and one of the easiest cases to remember here is *Hutton v Warren (1836)*.

Hutton v Warren (1836)

In this case a farmer wished to end the lease he held on a farm. It was established that in the locality where the farmer lived (Lincolnshire) the normal practice was that when a farmer decided to give up a farm, he was allowed a certain compensation for the seeds he'd already planted and the labour costs involved in the planting of these. The farmer was successful in persuading the court that such a term should be implied into his transaction. I have to point out that for such a case to succeed you can't just make up something that suits you. The court must be convinced that such practices are 'notorious' in that locality. To do this you would have to bring proof to the court that this was the normal situation, well understood and normally practiced in that area.

It amuses me again that Farmer Hutton's case occurred in the Parish of Wroot. I mention this as we're all looking for ways to remember case names – any connections we can dream up are useful.

Just to conclude this section, you'll sometimes read that terms can be implied "by fact or by law". I've found that this expression causes confusion with some students and I can see why. To explain, all it means is that terms implied *by law* are terms implied by the courts or by statute. Terms implied *by fact* means that sometimes a court will imply a term into a contract where the facts of a specific case are such that a term has seemingly been missed out in the drawing up of the contract in the first place.

Having looked at how terms can be implied into contracts it's now time to open up a contract and have a look inside to expose its inner workings. I hope what we'll find will be as exciting for you as it is to me.

The contents of contracts

Exam questions and MCQs on contract law frequently tend to come concerning contractual construction (what I've called contractual 'ingredients'), implied terms in contracts, and the following types of contractual terms.

There are three possible types of term which may appear within any contract, either one made verbally or in written form. These terms are called:

- ☐ Conditions
- ☐ Warranties
- ☐ Innominate Terms

Once more we'll take these one by one and point out their relative importance. Countless contracts exist in English law at any one time. Contracts and contract law in real life really don't really concern many of us very much at all – until something goes wrong. Then suddenly it matters very much. People, myself included, generally don't pay much attention to everyday contractual activities (like buying a few tins of Carlsberg Special Brew or a flat white). But there seem to be a couple of situations when most of us suddenly take a very special interest in contracts.

These are first, when what we've bought is broken or damaged, and second, when what we are about to commit ourselves to is very, very expensive.

So, imagine that you've bought what turns out to be a dodgy second hand car. Immediately you'll be thinking about what your legal rights are. Can I get my money back? Has the car any warranty? (guarantee) These and other similar thoughts will be running through your mind. The second type of situation is when you're considering buying something very expensive (like a house). This is certainly going to force you to think about the legal implications very deeply. No doubt thoughts like, can I actually afford to buy this house, what happens if I lose my job and can't afford the mortgage payments, will be nagging at you. These thoughts certainly worried me – and still do.

Suddenly you'll think to yourself, thank heavens that I did contract law in my business studies degree. At least that's what I tell my students. I've yet to find out if it's true…

The reason why you really need to know about the above three terms and at least one case explaining how each one works, is that the legal effects of breaking (breaching) these terms are different. Also, the chances are very high that you'll need to be able to spot (in exams) whether terms presented in a hypothetical contractual situation are likely to be conditions, warranties or innominate terms. The likelihood is that such a question will expect you to explain why they fall into one of these categories. Don't worry, this isn't hard.

Conditions

Let's take contractual conditions first as this is the big one. It's a big one because if it's you that breaches a condition of a contract, you'll suddenly find that you haven't got a contract any more – not only that, but you'll probably be sued for damages as well. A term in a contract which is a condition is the most important term in the contract. Sometimes you'll see conditions being described as being, "what the contract is all about" or "a term which goes right to the heart of the contract". Both of these expressions are quite correct. This term is so important because if there has been a breach of a condition in a contract, the injured party can then treat the contract as being ended (repudiation) and also sue the party who has breached the contract for damages suffered as a result of the breach. The main case which you should be aware of for breaches of condition is *Poussard v Spiers (1876)*.

Poussard v Spiers (1876)

This case concerned a lady opera singer (Madame Poussard) who entered into a contract to sing in a theatre for a period of three months. Unfortunately, just before she was due to start, she became ill and was not able to begin her performances. She couldn't then appear for the opening night. Because of this, the owner of the opera theatre (Spiers), ended the contract and contracted with an alternative opera singer. Essentially, he considered that as he had no idea about how long Poussard was likely to be away with illness, he had every right to end the contract.

So, Madame Poussard sued Spiers on the basis that he had unfairly terminated her contract and she wanted to be paid damages in compensation for this. The question for the court to consider was whether the failure of Poussard to sing in the opera right from the opening night was fundamental to the contract or not. The court decided that it was fundamental to this particular contract so Poussard lost her case. The point for you to take away from this case is that Madame Poussard had breached a condition of the contract. Her failure to perform, according to the court, went to the heart of the contract. This was a term in the contract that was absolutely vital to its operation. The desire to end the contract by Spiers seems clear, but you can't help but feel a little bit sorry for Madame Poussard herself.

I will just mention a further option available to the innocent party where there has been a breach of condition. The innocent party can, if they wish, continue with the contract (affirmation) and also sue for damages. This is not always such a good idea as in most cases the innocent party will by this time be pretty fed up with the other party. They're unlikely to want to continue with their original contract – and who can blame them?

Warranty

Moving on to breaches of warranty, what you have to be aware of is that warranties are terms which are much less important in a contract. Warranties don't go to the heart or the root of a contract. The main case normally used to demonstrate a breach of warranty is *Bettini v Gye (1876)*. By a strange coincidence this case occurred in the same year as the leading case on breach of condition above and perhaps even more oddly, both cases involved an opera singer. (Not the same one of course).

Please note that in the current context, the term 'warranty' hasn't any connection at all to the term 'warranty', which is frequently used as a term meaning a guarantee which you'll usually get when you buy something new.

Bettini v Gye (1876)

Bettini, also an opera singer, had entered into a contract to sing in an opera. In his contract there was a term that he should arrive six days before the opening night of the opera to ensure that he could take part in the rehearsals. In the event Bettini became ill and only managed to arrive three days before the opera opened. Gye, presumably a bit of panicky artistic type, told Bettini that he wasn't going to be allowed to sing as he was too late in arriving. It seems the Gye must've been having a bit of a bad week. This in turn annoyed Bettini, because he sued Gye for breach of contract. He won his case. You see, Gye, by sacking Bettini, had (probably without even being aware of this), treated the late arrival by Bettini as a breach of condition – we can see that he must have been thinking along these lines as by sacking Bettini he had considered the contract terminated. This you only have a right to do when a condition is breached.

Now, the court said that although the term of the contract had undoubtedly been breached, the term breached wasn't a *condition* of the contract but was only a breach of a *warranty*. Breach of a warranty doesn't allow a party to treat the contract as terminated as Gye had treated the it. Breach of a warranty, as we have seen, only allows a party to sue for damages. This was what Bettini successfully sued Gye for – good for him. These highly strung artistic theatre owner types need teaching a few lessons from time to time. The court arrived at its decision by saying that the breach (being three days late) did not go to the heart of the contract. So, a lesson for you to take away here, is that it's possible to be in breach of contract by wrongly treating a term of a contract as a condition rather than a warranty. Think about this.

Innominate terms

So far so good. If all we had to worry about was breach of conditions and breach of warranties then we could all sleep soundly in our beds at night. Alas, this is not the case because in 1962 there came along another case which has the effect of making us all think again. The case is *Hong Kong Fir Shipping v Kawasaki*. Actually, the case name is a bit longer than this but the above name is good enough for our purposes – even in exams.

Hong Kong Fir Shipping v Kawasaki

In Hong Kong Fir Shipping, Lord Diplock (bless him) decided to muddy the waters for law students by introducing a third term in addition to conditions and warranties. Basically, he said that the traditional method of analysing breaches of contract (i.e. by considering a breach to be either one of condition or warranty), may not be 'safe'. He said that there should be another type of term which is an in-between, sort of a 'half way house' type of term. These have become known as an *innominate* term.

The word 'innominate' translates from the Latin as 'nameless', or as not yet having a name.

In this case, a ship was chartered (the seagoing name for leased or hired) to the alleged injured party. The two-year contract stipulated that the ship would be "in every way fitted for ordinary cargo service". In fact, the ship wasn't in a good state of repair at all, and on its first trip it broke down and needed extensive repairs. In fact, the ship was out of service for 20 weeks. During this time the party who'd paid to lease the ship decided that enough was enough and to attempted to terminate the contract. The ship owner then sued saying that this attempted termination was not legally justified.

The court had no doubt that there had been some sort of breach of contract but which type was it? Was it a of beach of condition or a breach of warranty? The ship was meant to be 'seaworthy'. It's useful here to ask yourself, how you would attempt to define what the term 'seaworthy' actually means? At one extreme, I think you'll agree, if a ship has a hole in its hull which you could push an elephant through, then it's not going to be seaworthy. On the other hand, what if you find that the ship's engine gives you trouble from time to time? In this case it's a bit debatable if the ship can or can't be used for the purpose you hired it. As we know, a minor defect is likely to be treated as a warranty only and would not allow the termination of the contract. So, should we conclude that a ship with a dodgy engine is a minor or major fault?

In Hong Kong Shipping Lord Diplock argued that there are instances where a term in a contact, if breached, could be a breach of a condition or one of a warranty depending on the consequences of the breach. This was a deviation from tradition by Lord Diplock, by saying that certain terms can't always be called conditions or warranties before a breach occurs. These mid-way terms he said will be called innominate terms. These are the type of terms that we'll just have to wait to see what the effect of the breach is, before we can classify them as a conditional breach or one of a warranty. So, this approach has not surprisingly become to be known as a 'breach-based approach'.

As we've pointed out earlier, the chances are very high that somewhere in your course of business law studies, you'll be asked to differentiate between breaches of conditions, warranties and innominate terms. So, I'm now going to tell you how to do it. What I'm about to tell you was told to me as a law student by a very likeable and knowledgeable law lecturer who, if I could remember his name, I would now mention. Pity really as he deserves a mention. If it comes back to me, I'll tell you.

What he said was that the test to see if a breach is one of condition or warranty is the following. Ask the question in each case, "has the injured party lost substantially all he or she's contracted for?" If the answer is "yes", then the breach is likely to be one of condition, if the answer is "no" then the breach is likely to be one of warranty. I didn't realise it at the time but my friendly law lecturer had borrowed and slightly altered what Lord Diplock said in his judgement in Hong Kong Fir Shipping. This proved that I didn't read the full case at the time. Very naughty I know, but it's never too late.

You can practically almost always come down one way or another using the above test. Any contractual breach can only be one of the three types. It's very likely that questions on breach will include three scenarios – one of each type of breach.

What's the breach?

What we'll do now is to take a few exaggerated hypothetical cases and apply the above test to see which type of breach it's likely to be.

In my first example let's assume that someone has always wanted to own a Rolls Royce car. We'll call her Chloe to make her seem a bit more real. Chloe's been saving up for years so that one day she'll be able to walk into the Rolls

Royce showroom and order her own car. She walks into the showroom and places her order. Let's say she pays for it there and then in cash. There's no actual reason for assuming that she pays for the car in cash other than to make the example more dramatic. After waiting three months for the car to be hand made specifically in her chosen specifications, shade of colour etc, her doorbell rings and the Rolls Royce delivery driver says, "Good morning, your car has arrived madam, I've parked it on your drive". When Chloe goes out to look, she realises that what has actually been delivered is a large cardboard box with wheels clumsily painted on each corner and "ROLLS ROYCE" painted on the side.

Ah, poor Chloe. Do we think after applying the test, that Chloe's lost substantially all that she's contracted for? Obviously, yes, so this is likely to be a breach of condition. So, as we know she can terminate the contract and claim damages (in this case the money she's paid for the car).

In my second example we'll use Stephanie. Oddly enough she also wanted a Rolls Royce and went through the same process as Chloe, paying for the car etc. When Stephanie's car arrives it's perfect in all respects but one. Although she's delighted with the car itself, she realises that the paintwork is not the exact shade of silver that she ordered.

Again, we have to ask has Stephanie lost substantially all she's contracted for? I hope you'll agree with me that Stephanie hasn't lost substantially all she's contracted for. In fact, she's got substantially all that she's contracted for. Following the same reasoning as the above, this is likely to be a breach of warranty only, so she cannot terminate the contract but only sue for damages. Damages this time are likely to be the cost of repainting the car in the exact colour which she ordered. Actually, I doubt if she'd have to sue as knowing Rolls Royce (which I really don't) I feel that they'd put this right without question.

You can have a lot of fun in class with these types of examples. For example, in seminars I often change things around a bit, asking what would be the situation if what Chloe got delivered was a three-wheel Reliant van? Well, here she ordered a vehicle and she got a vehicle – of sorts. I'll leave it to you to apply the test and see what answers you come to. Remember that you always have to back up your answers with legal authority. Here you've only got to remember two cases on these types of breach and then apply them. Easy isn't it?!

As far as middle ground sort of situations in a question is concerned, you can't do much better than use Hong Kong Fir Shipping regarding innominate terms, so you'll have to look at the effect of any alleged breach to suggest what type it's likely to be. To reinforce this: serious consequences – condition breach; minor consequences – warranty breach; middle ground – innominate breach.

The best way to answer these and virtually any law question is to explain the different possibilities. So, you state that the courts are likely to decide in one particular way if they follow the reasoning in (*name of the case*), or it the courts follow the reasoning in (*name another case*), then the courts are likely to decide in a different way. Having explained the legal situation and named the relevant cases, you then conclude by saying that in the current situation, whatever it is, the courts are more likely to follow the reasoning in: *name the case* that appears to you to be closest to whatever the question asks you.

A great way of concluding most answers to virtually any legal question having followed the above method, is to say something like, "probably the better view is that the court will follow the reasoning in…" and name the case or cases. This way you've distanced yourself from the issue and avoided saying, "in my opinion". That never looks good in an answer.

Oh, by the way, I've remembered the name of my law lecturer from all those years ago. Remember he's the person who gave me the test for sorting out whether a term in a contract is a condition or a warranty? It's Mr Baxter. Cheers to you Mr Baxter, if you're still out there.

Duress and undue influence

Note: *Duress* in this context means the unlawful threat or use of violence.

If some physical force is threatened or actually used against you in an attempt to pressure you into entering into a contract, then quite obviously there can be no real consent to the contract. So, if this is the case, then no contract will come into existence. This is so apparent that you may think that it needs no further explanation. If you look back to the previous chapter on contract law, you'll see that in the final point on contractual ingredients, I mention the Latin tag *consensus ad idem*. This translated as a 'meeting of the minds' of the contracting parties. Now this gives you a better (and more legal looking) explanation of why, if some force is used to get you to agree to accept a contract, that the contract never actually came into being in the first place.

An example of this would be where a person holds a full bottle of red wine over your head (or similar) and suggests that you if don't accept the contract (whether by signing the contact or simply agreeing to accept a verbal contract), then they'll smash you over the head with the bottle. Going through your mind at this time, I'll bet, will be two things.

First, you'll be thinking what a shame it would be to waste a full bottle of red wine and second, this is going to hurt. So, you verbally agree or sign the contract. Of course, there is no *consensus ad idem* and as we know, there is no contract.

It is tempting to say a contract of this type is voidable but it really can't be voidable as it never came into existence in the first place. If you're asked to discuss this you could add something like "contracts involving duress have no legal effect"

Economic duress

Originally in the early development of English common law, acts of duress were confined to threats of the use of violence, or the actual use of physical violence. Not so long ago, at least in the history of contract law, the courts recognised that duress could be applied in other ways than just physical violence in contractual situations.

So, the courts began to accept that what is called 'economic duress' could be used to force a party into agreeing to a contract. This was quite a move forward in law so that certain commercial situations then began to come under the heading of economic duress. This is why this area is important to us as economic duress can easily occur in business transactions. Economic duress is actually the same concept as financial duress.

As a hypothetical situation, let's assume that Bruce, who is CEO of Shove Ltd, has been dealing with Tara, the CEO of Surrender Ltd. They have been contracting with each other for many years quite happily. Bruce becomes aware that Tara's company has no other sources of supply of the goods his company sells to Surrender Ltd. As a result, Bruce, without warning, triples the price of the goods his company supplies to Tara, regardless of what the contract between them says. Well, this is the type of situation where the courts may find that there has been economic duress.

The difficulty with these types of situation is that the court has to decide in each instance whether this might be just an ordinary example of commerce in operation, i.e. the cut and thrust of business generally. Or does such a hypothetical action (by Bruce) go further than this? The court has to be sure that such an action amounts to actual economic duress and is not caused simply by the operation of supply and demand i.e. not just the natural actions of market forces. To do this the court has to identify commercial situations where it appears that some actual and often unusual, financial pressure has been used. This is not an easy thing for the courts to be sure of.

Remember, the existence of economic duress does not automatically make the contract void, but just makes the contract voidable. So, in the case of Bruce and Tara above, the contract can be ended (voided) by Tara if economic duress is found to have been used. The reason why the contract isn't automatically void is that Tara may, for reasons of her own, want to continue with the contract until she decides to make an application to have the contract voided. She may elect to carry on with the contract until it suits her to bring it to an end. She may think that as Bruce has increased his price so much, she'll try to find an alternative supplier and then void the contract. It's her choice.

As has become clear from case law (and it's pretty obvious really), if you want to start an action under this heading the sooner you do it the better. If you, or your business, think that some element of economic duress has been used against you in a transaction, then it's no good waiting for a couple of years before you do something about it. If you wait too long, the court is likely to assume that it couldn't have been very important to you in the first place.

A good case to illustrate the operation of economic duress is *D & C Builders v Rees (1966) 2QB 617 (CA)*. Incidentally this case shows the operation of several different aspects of law so it's a great case to have in your 'case bank'.

Undue influence

Remember the concept of 'equity'? If you don't remember take a quick look back at Chapter 2, *Sources of law*. As a swift reminder, the law of equity is based on the use of fairness and integrity/morality in law. When you look back, you'll find that we talked of equity as being a gloss or sheen on the common law and that it developed to 'fill in the cracks' in the common law, which tend to lead to some 'rough justice' at times. We noted that this is still true today.

The concept of undue influence is based upon equity. It may be used where it can be shown that one contracting party has used their greater authority, power or knowledge to influence another party to enter into a contract. So undue influence may occur when one party has been shown to be exploiting the vulnerability (weakness) of the other party.

Unfortunately for ourselves, undue influence itself splits into two categories. (Is there no end to this? Don't worry I'll be showing an easy exercise to remember the whole area). Anyway, to continue, one of these categories is called *actual undue influence* and the other is known as *presumed undue influence*. It is the latter category which is the most common one, that we see today in business or our ordinary transactions.

Actual undue influence

This type of undue influence occurs when a person has had some pressure brought upon them which prevents them from making a properly independent judgement in some transaction. This includes contractional situations. In a relatively modern case, *Daniel v Drew (2005) EWCA Civ 507*, a nephew, who by many accounts was a 'forceful' character, was found to have obtained his aunt's resignation from a family trust by using undue influence. The aunt was 85 years old and was "particularly vulnerable". She stated in court that she had difficulty in attending family trust meetings because her legs ached. She also appeared to show signs of confusion when giving her evidence.

The cases of actual undue influence have declined in recent years owing to the widening of the areas where the courts have found duress (above) to apply. Nowadays then, actions under actual undue influence are likely to be brought only when there is strong evidence that some unacceptable or unfair pressure has been used to influence a person when entering into a contract. Remember that here we are in the area of equity, meaning that the court will look at each case on its own merits. The court will act at its own discretion as to whether or not it will award a remedy. So, a contract where it can be shown that actual undue influence has been used is voidable at the request of the injured party.

Presumed undue influence

Unfortunately, again, there are two types of presumed undue influence.

Special relationship

The main type is where there is some special relationship between the two contracting parties. This is deemed to be in situations where one of the parties is in a position of much greater knowledge or power than the other party. So, it's where there is some kind of extra trust or confidence between the two parties – a 'special relationship'. This type of special relationship is not easy to define. We have to leave it to the courts to tell us where it exists. Cases here have involved banks and their clients, lawyers and clients, medical practitioners and patients (the list is much longer than this – take a look). All the cases of this type cover the relationship between a professional and an ordinary person. Here the ordinary person goes to see the professional precisely because they haven't got the same level of expertise that they expect the professional to possess. If this area of law is on your university course specification then have a really good look at the surrounding cases on this. There are plenty of them out there to find.

The really interesting thing here is that in all of these cases there is no need to actually prove undue influence in a dispute. This is because the law presumes that there is real undue influence in such transactions. That's a bit startling don't you think?

What this means is that if you go to see your bank manager, for example, and later have some kind of dispute, then it will be up to the bank manager to prove that he/she didn't use undue influence! You won't have to prove that he/she used undue influence – the court will start for the presumption that he/she did.

I think that's really great for the ordinary person. What this means in practice is that in any financial transaction nowadays (the financial institutions caught on to this pretty quickly) you will be strongly advised verbally to obtain independent advice before going ahead with any agreement. Also, any printed material you get from the bank/building society or insurance company etc. will have similar advice printed on it – "we strongly advise you to obtain independent financial advice before making any decision to carry on with any transactions with us".

That's their get-out clause. I'm pretty sure that many hours of training are spent by these institutions ramming home the fact to their workers that they'd better make damn sure that this message gets through to all of their customers.

Recently I had to go to my bank to get a small extension to the mortgage on my house. A bank employee asked me to sit through a half hour video explaining just this. I protested mildly saying truthfully that I teach this stuff every other day. It didn't do me any good as I was told that if I didn't watch it, we could go no further with our negotiations. These institutions are taking this very seriously, for good reason.

Abuse of trust

The second (and last, thankfully) type of presumed undue influence is rarer. This can occur when there is, on the surface at least, none of the above conditions of 'special relationship' that we'll find between, say, a lawyer and client.

Here it has to be shown that one party has, in some way, placed confidence and trust in the other party. The 'injured' party believes that this trust and confidence has been abused.

In these cases, it used to have to be shown until recently that the wronged party had been put "at a manifest disadvantage" by the other party. However, in *Royal Bank of Scotland v Etridge (2002) UKHL 44*, this test was updated. Since this case, it now needs to be shown that such transactions "call for an explanation". It is up to the claimant to make this assertion. Each case is different and whether a call for explanation is successful will depend upon the specific facts of every case.

If the alleged offender can show that the other party entered into the transaction completely of their own free will, then there is no case to answer. It has often been pointed out that the more extraordinary or unusual the transaction, then the more persuasive and convincing the answers must be. Contracts made under these circumstances, again, are voidable by the wronged party.

Privity of contract

This concept was mentioned briefly in the previous chapter. It's worth a closer look because the issue of third-party situations in contract law tend to be a favourite area for law lecturers to ask questions in exams.

As you'll remember, the term 'privity' if just another way of stating the privateness of a contract. So, for example, A offers to sell something to B. But C (who is nothing to do with the contract at all), tries to accept the offer by A. Well he can't because C isn't 'privy' to the offer. To extend this, the saying is that a person who is not privy to a contract can take no action under the contract and cannot benefit from such a contract. Another way of looking at these situations is to say that C can't be in a contract because he provided no consideration to the contract. We know from contractual ingredients, that simple contracts require 'good' consideration to make them enforceable. So, C is not privy to the contract and additionally has provided no consideration.

This is an age old concept and *prima facie* seems to makes sense. At least is seems to make sense in the illustration above (I hope) The difficulty is that the concept of privity has caused many a great deal of criticism coming from the judiciary themselves, academic writers and business law students, to question the fairness of some the decisions in certain cases. I'll just give you one case to illustrate this alleged unfairness. See what you think.

Tweddle v Atkinson (1861)

The case of Tweddle v Atkinson (1861) shows some of the problems associated with privity. Here there was an agreement between the father of a groom and the father of a bride-to-be, to each pay the groom money upon the occurrence of their marriage. The groom's father was to pay to him a sum of £100 and the bride's father was to pay him £200. Unfortunately, before the £200 was paid, the father of the bride died, leaving the £200 unpaid. The now married son, sued the representatives of the deceased father of the bride for the unpaid money.

His action failed (and I bet you can see why). The now married son was not privy to the contract between the two separate fathers. To give you part of a quote from the case, "third parties to a contract can't derive any benefits from such a contract nor are they subject to any burdens imposed by such a contract".

I don't know if you think the outcome of this case is unfair or not. My students usually seem split about 50/50 on this.

What it actually means is that, say you and I, for some reason want to make a contract for the benefit of someone else. It could be a mutual friend or even a mutual relative we have in mind. Well, by using the simple form of contract as we just saw in Tweddle, we can't do this. This is the bit that most of my students, and me, find rather silly. Why they say, can't two adults with the intention (full legal intent) make a contract for the benefit of another person? After all, we're obviously in full agreement on this otherwise we wouldn't be thinking of doing it at all.

To cut a very long story short, the above type of question occurred to many individuals for a very long time in the course of legal history. Many exceptions to this rule began to be used by the courts to get round it often by the use of legal fictions. I'll just give you one well known exception to the rule which I use regularly in seminars. I ask, is anyone a driver here? Usually in a group of say 20 students, nearly half will put their hands up. Then I ask, in order to legally drive, what is it that you need – apart obviously from a car? Of course, MOTs will be mentioned along with road tax. Eventually someone will come up with the fact that the law needs you to have your car insured. Of course, this is true. Then I ask what is the minimum type of vehicle insurance you have to have by law? 'Third party' will be mentioned. The penny drops.

Students are usually aware of this as they understandably tend to have the minimum required car insurance.

What you are doing when you get your car insured, is to make a contract with your insurance company to protect a third party to the contract. The third party is the one you hope you'll never meet. The person you've contracted to insure yourself damaging, is the person you may accidentally run into with your car – the third party.

If this isn't an example which flies in the face of the concept of contractual privity then I don't know what is? On the one hand you've got the law telling you that it's a criminal offence to drive your car without insurance and the civil law of contract saying you can't make a contract for the benefit of a third party!

The Tweddle case we looked at above is really just the tip of the iceberg. There are plenty of other instances when the strict application of this rule of law caused a certain raising of the eyebrows – just take a look. After many years of debate and criticism, Parliament decided to pass an act allowing in certain circumstances third parties to be able to benefit under a contract which they have some interest in. This act is the Contracts (Rights of Third Parties) Act 1999. This act can be used to confer contractual rights upon a third party as long as you follow the wording of the act closely. The act covers a great many different contractual situations but also excludes some contracts which aren't covered. So, beware if you need to use the act, that you construct your contract to be within the powers which the act gives you.

How contracts come to an end

Up until now we've looked at how a legally binding contract comes into existence in the first place. We've also taken a look inside the contract to see what type of terms are likely to be *express* within the contract, and which type of terms may be a bit more hidden away– these of course are the *implied* terms. We also took a look at conditions, warranties and innominate terms.

Now it's time to look at the main types of ways in which a contract may come to an end. Actually, we've looked at a few of these already in passing because we had to in order to explain other points. But now we'd better treat this a bit more formally because that's exactly what you'll be expected to do in an exam answer. There are a number of ways by which a contract can be ended or terminated. Generally, this area is called *contractual discharge*.

Contractual discharge

Performance

The first and most common way for a contract to end is said to be by performance. This is very straightforward: all that is means is that both parties have performed all the obligations which they contracted for under the contract and everybody walks away happy. The contract is over and done.

Agreement

Just as a contract comes into existence by the agreement of the parties involved, it can also be ended by agreement. If both parties to the contract agree to end it before any of the provisions stated in the contract have yet happened, then again all is well and there are no further legal consequences.

Unfortunately, sometimes some performance may already have occurred. This is referred to a *part performance*. Here as long as the other party agrees to end the contract on this basis, some compensation may be payable from the 'losing' party to the other party. The amount payable to a losing party is evaluated on what is known as a *quantum meruit* basis. This Latin tag simply means as much as deserved in each case. I advise you to get this phrase in as much as you can – it looks great, I think you'll agree!

Breach of contract: A reminder

We've talked a lot about breach of contract when we were discussing the effect of one party not properly performing a condition, a warranty or an innominate term in a contract. We saw that these terms were of differing importance:

- ☐ If one party breaches a *condition* then the other party could consider the contact ended and additionally sue the offending party for compensation (damages). Here should the victim wish to continue with the contract he/she is also able to do this.
- ☐ A breach of a *warranty*, as it's of lesser importance, only enables the aggrieved party to sue for damages and not be able to consider the contract ended.
- ☐ With an *innominate* term we have to wait for the court to tell us whether the breach is one of condition or warranty. Only then can we tell what the legal result might be.

Don't forget please that a *counter offer* (Hyde v Wrench) terminates the offer but doesn't terminate the contract as there never existed a contract in the first place.

Frustration or impossibility of performance

A contract may become impossible to carry out because of the occurrence of some future unforeseen event. This area is a study in itself. Whole books can and have been written on this area of discharge alone. As ever, check in your course handbook and in your course specification as to whether this area is covered and how much detailed knowledge you may be expected to have. In general, you will be expected to be aware of contractual frustration but it's possible that your course tutor may want you to cover this in more detail. Ask yourself, did we cover this quite deeply in a seminar? Were practice questions set on contractual discharge? If so, the chances are that a question which may include frustration may come up in your final exam.

Traditionally the view taken by the common law was that the parties to a contract ought to have been able to anticipate future events and consequences and incorporate these into their contracts. The courts began to recognise that it is possible that future events may occur which could not be foreseen by either party which may act to make the performance of the contract impossible.

A very early example of the courts beginning to recognise the possibility of a contract being frustrated is *Paradine v Jane (1647)*.

Paradine v Jane (1647)

In this case, Paradine sued Jane for rent owing on land which he leased to Jane. This was during the Civil War and Jane had his land occupied by the army which was invading. This apparently happened to quite a lot of larger houses at the time. Who's going to argue with an invading army? The army were of Roundheads, fighting against King Charles 1st. (You don't really need to know this but I think it's interesting). Jane asked the court whether he could continue to hold back the rental payments to Paradine. The rent was three years overdue. The court said that Jane was within his rights to do this. They gave the example, "if a house be destroyed by tempest or by enemies, the 'rent' is excused". They seemed to think that the situation was out of the control of Jane. I wonder if he ever paid it back?

There are several possibilities where the courts have agreed that to enforce such a contract would be unreasonable. Frustration may be allowed where events occur which are outside of the sphere of control of one or other of the contracting parties – as shown by the above case. The main situations where this may occur are, for example, when something which was necessary to the contract no longer exists. This happened in *Taylor v Caldwell (1863)*. Here there was a contract for the hire of a hall for a concert. Before the concert could take place, the hall was burnt down by fire. Frustration may also occur where an individual is contracted to, for example, give a live performance and becomes too ill to perform on the night.

Where the contract has already been made but a law is changed making it illegal to carry on with the contract may also lead to frustration. This occurred after the outbreak of the 2nd World War where it was made illegal to trade with the enemy. Many British businesses had their existing contracts with the Axis powers frustrated.

The above are just guidelines as to where the courts have found frustration to exist. Each case is looked at individually on its facts to see if frustration can be allowed.

Possible outcomes if frustration is allowed

The Law Reform (Frustrated Contract) Act 1943 allows that if a contract is discharged by frustration:

- Any money or property changing hands before frustration may be recovered
- Any party who has experienced expenses may recover these out of any sums already paid or any money still payable
- If a party gains some value from work completed before frustration, the court may award a reasonable sum in compensation for this. This sum will be determined by the court at its discretion.

Electronic commerce and the law of contract

I often have to point out here to most of my students that trading on the internet by means of emails and the use of websites is, legally speaking, quite a new area. Probably very few readers of this book won't be able to remember a time when it was really easy to just 'borrow' you mum or dad's credit card, have a quick visit to Amazon (other trading websites are available) and buy a couple of nice things for yourself. Unfortunately, I wasn't able to do this when I was growing up because the internet didn't exist. I can't tell you how much of a feeling of sadness and regret this gives me.

The point for us to think about here is that is there isn't much by way of decided case law yet for us to make fully informed statements about the internet and how contract law may apply to it. As the years go by of course there will appear more and more cases which will give us a clearer picture. For now, we'll just have to take a look at the rules and regulations which have already been passed in an attempt to regulate internet trading.

The main piece of regulation in English and Welsh law in this area is the Electronic Commerce Directive 2002. I think a little aside is called for here. When you consider the necessary ingredients needed to form a legally binding contract (of a non-internet type), which we looked at in the previous chapter, we mainly have offer/acceptance, consideration, and the intent to form a contractual relationship. Well, in the main, the law surrounding any contract exists has to have these elements included, otherwise there is no contract. We won't have to take a new look at consideration as using the internet this will almost always just be money changing hands. We can assume that there will be an intent to create a legal relationship with the buyer because otherwise whatever you're attempting to buy wouldn't be advertised and you wouldn't be trying to buy it. So, we're really just left with the questions of communication of the offer and the position of when and how the acceptance was made.

Luckily the above Directive gives us some help here by stating that orders made electronically, are deemed to be received when the parties to whom they are addressed are able to 'access them'. So, the position when you send an order to a website seems to be that you are responding to an advertisement by filling in the online form with your email address and any other information they may ask for, together with your payment details. An advertising website then, much like most other forms of advertising, has simply issued an invitation to treat, i.e. it's asking for you to make the offer which the online company can accept or reject as it wants to.

The electronic acceptance side of things is arguably a bit more difficult. The only thing which seems to make sense as a communication of acceptance of your offer is a return email to you stating that the seller of the goods has received your order and is in the process of dealing with it. In my experience this is what normally happens with every website I've ever dealt with.

I can foresee a lot of new case law appearing in future years regarding at which exact moment a contract made electronically becomes binding. Electronic systems might be very clever but they do crash from time to time. It might well happen that a computer receives your order but is unable to send you an automatic email response. How can you tell if your order was correctly received? How can you tell if you've actually got a legally binding contract at all?

These and many other problems await the courts to sort out. The courts do have some older cases and associated precedents dealing with 'instantaneous' transmissions which they are likely to look and apply in an attempt to modernise the law concerning e-commerce.

Summary

We got through a fair amount in this chapter. We started by digging down into the heart of a contract and we said that are three main types of term which can be within a contract. These are, conditions, warranties and innominate terms. These terms haven't all got the same importance as each other and different legal consequences occur by breaching (breaking) any one of them.

Then we looked at the effect on a contract by someone forcing you to enter into the contract. This force can be physical, or it can be non-physical but unjustified influence. The use of such unjustified influences may make the contact either void (ended) or voidable, where you as the 'injured' party, can end the contact if it suits them to do so.

The main ways that a contract can come to an end was looked at next. This is the area of contractual discharge. It can include where both parties to a contract have done whatever the contact asks them to (performance), where both parties want to end the contact and agree to do so (agreement), where some fundamental term of a contract has been broken by one or other of the parties (breach of contract) and where there has been some change in external circumstances which means that it has become impossible for the contact to go ahead (frustration).

After looking at this, we took a quick look at the effect of modern technology on contacts. This is the area of e-commerce and communication by the use of emails and business websites. Remember that this is very much a developing area of contract law so all that you can be expected to know will be that which is currently in the textbooks. That doesn't mean that by keeping an eye on the currently developing area of electronically communicated forms of commerce, that you can't include in an exam or coursework situation, things which haven't yet reached the textbooks. This is the sort of thing which shows that you've done your own research. It also tends to lead to much higher marks.

Revision questions

1. What may be the legal consequence when a party to a contract has breached one of the terms contained within the contact? Please use the relevant case law in your answer.
2. Using decided case law, explain how a court would be likely to deal with a case where a bank manager has forgotten to give you advice as to consulting an independent financial advisor before you, on behalf of your company, enter into a disastrous agreement with the bank.
3. Rachael, over lunch in a university canteen, offers to sell her phone to her friend Michael. John overhearing this says, "ah thanks Rachael, I'll take that". Is John within his legal rights to try to enforce what he thinks is a binding contract? If not, why not?
4. What would be the legal effect if a limited company makes a contract with another limited company for the purchase of a container of cotton wool and unknown to either company, the container has been lost at sea before they attempted to contract for its sale?
5. Do you think if you see something advertised on a website, that the advert is likely to be an offer for sale or an invitation to treat? Explain using case law which of these you think it is likely to be.

5 The law of tort

How the law of tort affects you and your business

Tort law, like contract law, is a civil area of law. This area of law is extremely important to you and your business. It is quite possible to make yourself and/or your business liable to be sued in tort for negligent acts done by you or done at your instigation by your business.

Some of the many areas based on tort law which you have to be especially aware of when running your own business are:

☐ Making sure that you do not allow any defective products to be sold to your consumers;

☐ Ensuring that employees are kept safe and supplied with the correct protective equipment;

☐ Making sure that any plant and equipment used by employees is safe and correctly maintained;

☐ Making sure that any references you supply to an employee are correct and factual (employees are beginning to look a bit of a nightmare);

☐ Making sure that any business premises, and private property you may have are kept in a safe condition for anyone coming into them (including trespassers!);

☐ Making sure that, if you are in the business of supplying advice to clients, that this advice had not been issued carelessly.

Of course, this list is not exhaustive but at least it'll give you an idea of the wide range of business activities where the law of tort comes in. Luckily for you as a business law student, not all these torts will be covered intensively on your course. In the main, what you will have to look at closely on an undergraduate business law course is, the background to tort, that is, the general principles of tort, the tort of negligence, negligent advice and occupier's liability. So, that's what we'll do.

The basic principles

As is the case with contract law, torts are civil wrongs. For our purposes, we can say that a tort is any civil offence which is not covered by contract law. I'm aware that sounds like a cop out but it really isn't. So, a tort is a civil wrong that has been normally performed by one person against another person. It doesn't amount to a criminal offence against the other person. It involves a breach of a duty which you owe to another person or some unlawful intrusion of the rights of another person. Tort cover a vast area of law. Just to give you an idea of how far reaching tort is, it covers amongst other things:

- **Trespass:** See example below.
- **Negligence:** This where someone owes a duty of care to other people, are careless as to their actions and cause damage to others which is directly due to their careless actions. An obvious example here is that a driver of a vehicle has a duty of care not to injure other road users. If a driver is careless when driving a vehicle and causes damage to other road users, then he is likely to be sued by anyone damaged by his actions.
- **Occupier's liability:** A duty to protect the safety that an occupier of 'premises' has to visitors to their premises. This duty of care to others, which all occupiers have, operates in your own home or any offices, shops or buildings that might be used by your business including outbuildings and any land occupied by you or your business.
- **Nuisance:** There are two types of these – private and public nuisance. An example of private nuisance might be you playing the Rolling Stones at full volume every night for eight hours at a time, disturbing the old lady who lives in the flat above you. This is a tort. A public nuisance is where you disturb a great many people all in one go. An example might be where you hire a sound stage on Wimbledon Common and turn up all 40 of your amplifiers to distortion level and the noise you make can be heard in Belgium. This is a tort and a criminal offence. Particularly criminal if you are playing anything by Barry Manilow.
- **Defamation:** Saying/writing/publishing some untrue information which is intended to injure the reputation of this person.

Luckily for us, in business law, we only have to look closely at three torts. Namely: negligence (this has two aspects – *negligent acts* causing physical harm and *negligent statements* causing financial loss to others) and *occupier's liability*. We do come across the idea of tort again, in passing, in employment law with something called *vicarious liability*. But for now, as an explanation of what a tort is, we'll have a quick look at trespass to land. This should give you an idea of what the law of tort is all about.

Trespass to land – a quick example

Trespass is probably the oldest and most wide ranging of torts. As such it provides a good background to the torts we do have to cover. Trespass to land is based on a person intruding onto the property rights of another person. Trespass actually covers *interference*, not only to land, but also interference physically to another person (bodily interference) and interference with another person's property.

The tort of trespass to land is particularly easy to understand and the concept will be familiar to all of us. For example, let's suggest that someone starts to walk across your garden every day because it's a quick way to get to the local shops. We'll assume that although they keep walking across your lawn, they don't cause any real damage apart from squishing a few leaves of grass. So, no real harm done? Well not really. But do you really want to have some unknown person walking over your garden every day? I suspect you wouldn't, as neither would I.

In this tort of trespass to land, someone is trying, in a sense, to take over the rights which you personally have over your own property. These are often called your 'proprietorial rights'. After all, you own your own garden and if you haven't given any other person the right to walk all over your lawn then they have no right to do so.

This is the basis of all torts – someone has invaded your personal rights in some way and you don't like it! The behaviour explained above is not in itself a criminal offence, however annoying it might be when you look out of your window. But, if whoever it is that walks over your lawn went further and started kicking your garden shed as they went by, then this would almost certainly become a criminal offence (probably criminal damage). Torts can often overlap with criminal law and in certain instances can result in both civil actions and criminal actions being taken simultaneously. As we don't need to study criminal law in a business law course, we'll exclusively restrict ourselves to the civil side of things.

So, if trespass isn't a criminal offence then it must be (and is) a civil offence. Just as with contract law, as it's a private offence, it's up to you to take your own legal action (to sue) to put this situation right, Annoying I know, but unless this trespasser starts pinching your petunias, there is not much more you can do to put things right apart from taking them to court yourself. Of course, if a trespasser does start damaging your property then you can call in the police.

The tort of negligence

All of the torts we have to look at occur in situations where one person owes a duty of care to another person or a duty of care to group of people, as mentioned above. In some way that duty of care has been broken by a wrongful act which causes that other person or group of people some kind of injury or loss or damage to themselves or their property. Interestingly, you can also commit a tort by not doing something where you are under a duty of care to do (this is a breach of duty by omission).

To explain this, let's assume that you've made a domestic agreement between your family, that every Wednesday you'll take your elderly aunt's medication to her as she's upstairs lying in bed at death's door. One Wednesday you forget all about her, and go instead to see the latest Star Wars film. As a result of you forgetting to take her medicine up to her, thereby breaking your duty of care, your aunt dies. Boy, are you in a lot of trouble now! Because you haven't done what you've agreed to do (omission), this means that you're now liable to be sued in the tort of negligence – you're probably also liable for manslaughter and possibly also liable for breach of contract. I'll tell you what, The Force sure ain't gonna help you out here, brother.

The main aims of the law of tort is to compensate the person you have injured by your action (by paying out damages). It's said that this will act to deter other people from committing the same sort of negligent acts you have. If they commit similar negligent acts, then they will also have to pay damages. Personally, I think that the deterrence argument is a similar type of argument which says, the longer time which you put a criminal in prison, the less crime there will be. I really wonder about this: I'd love to see the evidence backing it up.

The tort of negligence splits into two parts: Negligent physical acts causing damage to others; and statements made negligently, which other people (or other businesses) rely upon and in so doing lose money. Case law deals with these areas in a slightly different way. You will need to know both of these areas very well unfortunately…

Negligent physical acts (or omissions)

Like Carlill's case in contract law, negligence also has a well-known central case which gives us the start of the 'modern' law of negligence. This case is by no means the start of all of the tort of negligence in English law. The key phrase for you to *always* use in any work in this area of law, is the 'modern law of negligence'. The following case can be seen as the start of this 'modern law of negligence'.

Donoghue v Stephenson (1932)

Now this is a very interesting case not least because it is not its real name. The actual case name is M'Alister (or Donoghue) (Pauper) v Stevenson. It seems that Mrs Donoghue somewhere during the start and finish of her case, had married and then split up with her husband. Her first name was May and after the case was finally decided, she became known by a variety of different names. She may have been trying to avoid publicity due to the fact that she became, for a short time, a national celebrity and was trying to evade the attention of the newspapers. She was a 'pauper', meaning that she had little or no money of her own. (A feeling not unknown to many of us).

Anyway, on Sunday evening, the 26th of August, 1928 she and her friend agreed to go to the Glasgow Fair for a little bit of fun and entertainment. On their way to the fair, the two friends agreed to go into the Tally Café at Wellmeadow Place in Paisley, Scotland. Interestingly, The Glasgow Fair is still up and running today.

All went well for a while. Mrs Donoghue's friend, whose name we don't know, but we do that know he was a man, ordered and paid for their refreshments. Mrs Donoghue had a dish of ice cream together with a bottle of ginger beer.

Apparently, at the time this was a fashionable dish to have. The idea was that you pour some ginger beer over the ice cream as you eat it. My students tell me that this peculiar sounding activity is still fashionable today – I wouldn't know as clearly; I don't get out enough. The bottle of ginger beer was made of dark opaque glass meaning you couldn't see through the glass so you couldn't inspect its contents.

Everything at first went well by all accounts. Mrs Donoghue's friend poured some ginger beer over her ice cream and they started eating. Shortly after this Mrs Donoghue went to pour some more ginger beer into her glass and out popped (or plopped) a snail which was partially decomposed. Yuk! Some authorities say it was a slug not a snail. Either way, Mrs Donoghue got a very unwelcome surprise. I think most of us would! Whether it was a snail or a slug, poor old Mrs Donoghue suddenly realised that she had just eaten a sizable portion of something which was slimy, decaying and nasty that she didn't very much like. Who can blame her being a little bit upset?

It happened that she was a bit more than just a little upset. She suffered from shock (what we would now call psychiatric injury) and also had to be treated for gastroenteritis by a doctor. I'm reminded here of the old schoolboy story of someone who bites eagerly into an apple only to see half of a worm still wriggling inside it…

Naturally, after Mrs Donoghue had recovered, she was looking for some kind of recompense and this is where the legal trouble started. You see, the first thought she had (or her lawyer had) was that she should sue whoever had manufactured the bottle of ginger beer for breach of contract. She thought, quite reasonably, that she had got less than she bargained for (or more depending on how you look at it) Unfortunately, she couldn't sue for breach of contract as she had no contract with either the ginger beer manufacturer or the café owner, because she didn't buy the bottle – her friend did.

So, her friend most likely had a contract with the manufacturer of the ginger beer and the café owner, but Mrs Donoghue didn't. Oh dear, what could she do? The manufacturer had clearly been negligent in allowing a dead and decomposing snail (or slug) to enter into the bottle of ginger beer and clearly Mrs Donoghue had been injured as a result. But trying to use the law of contract just wouldn't work.

At the time the law only recognised negligence by a manufacturer which went on to harm a person in a very limited way. If a manufacturer had acted in some fraudulent way and by doing so had harmed another person, then there would've been a good legal basis for taking the case to court. But there was no question of fraud in this case. It was only due to Mrs Donoghue's solicitor, a Mr Walter Leechman, (a very good name given the circumstances) who was very persistent, that the case was heard at all. Mr Leechman had already lost two similar cases before this one. Brave man.

So, thanks to Mr Leechman, eventually the case landed up at The House of Lords – the then equivalent of the now Supreme Court. The House of Lords had to decide first, was there a course of action at all, and second, how to decide the case if there was. The fundamental question for the court to decide was whether a manufacturer of a product should owe a 'duty of care' to ensure that the final user of the product was not injured in any way by what they produce? The court decided that, yes, manufacturers do indeed owe such a duty of care to their customers. Nowadays of course, this won't come as come as much of a surprise to us.

I have to go into a little aside here. Pretty much all of us who have grown up subject to English law, have assumed that manufactures have always had duty to protect us as consumers. This principle has been ingrained into us almost from childhood so we rarely think to question it. It has become so much a part of our culture that we seem to naturally assume that if a product harms us in some way, well, we can sue the company that made it. We expect that the manufacturer will almost automatically recompense us if their product causes us harm. This is the importance of Donoghue v Stevenson as this case is where the above principle of law, or *ratio*, was first clearly set out.

This concept has also over the years been included in various bits of legislation. Take another look at Chapter 2 (page 19) on statutes and consumer protection if you want to remind yourself about this. To put you out of your misery, yes, May Donoghue won her landmark case and was awarded £200 in damages. Using my trusty online Bank of England Inflation Calculator again, the £200 awarded in 1932 is worth £13,750 today. Once more I wonder what she spent it on? As a pauper this must have been like winning the National Lottery.

I must remind you as a student of business law that you must take a close look at this case. It is vital to you to have a good knowledge of this area if you want to do well. You must know the principles of the case and the case law which surrounds it, if you want to impress your examiners. I'll remind you of this again later, many times.

Lord Atkin made a speech in the case which you will need to take a look at. (You can find it here: https://www.bailii.org/uk/cases/UKHL/1932/100.html.) This speech has become the foundation of the modern law of negligence. I won't reproduce all of it here as you can simply look at it in any textbook or go online to read it in full. What I will do here is to explain it. Just to make sure that we're all singing from the same song sheet. The speech centres on the sentence: "You must take reasonable care to avoid acts or omissions which you can reasonably foresee would be likely to injure you neighbour."

Lord Atkin went on to explain what he meant by 'neighbour'. I've found that the word 'neighbour' as used by Lord Atkin has caused some puzzled looks in seminars. This is because the word immediately makes us think of the person who lives next door. I've found that a few students think that this *ratio* only covers and protects people living either side of them. There's nothing really wrong with this because it can indeed include the person who lives next door to us. But, as Lord Atkin went on to explain, he meant neighbour to actually mean anyone we should reasonably have in mind who might be affected by our acts or omissions when going about our daily life.

The use of the word neighbour by Lord Atkin seems very old fashioned to us today. But then it meant 'any fellow citizen'. So, activities like driving a car, riding a bike, shopping or walking your dog would all be covered by the term 'neighbour' today. In fact, it covers pretty much anything you do where it is possible that through your own careless or negligent actions (or inactions) you may cause loss or injury to someone else in close proximity (near you). So, the possibilities are nearly infinite. I will leave you to think of possible occurrences where you could harm someone by your careless actions or inactions.

Now, the word 'proximity' normally means closeness physically of one person to another, but as we will see shortly, it doesn't just mean physical closeness. As a hint, it could well be that you might pay a building surveyor to give you a report on a house you are interested in buying and you could have never personally met the surveyor. You'll probably just read the report. Here the connection between you and the surveyor, might well be 'proximate' enough to meet the Donoghue criteria. So 'proximity' can mean both physical proximity and legal proximity. All it takes for liability to exist in the two instances, is for the court to rule that in either of these cases (physical or legal proximity) that some duty of care existed and this has been broken.

Where Lord Atkin uses the word 'reasonable' he is referring to the reasonable man test – the Man on the Clapham Omnibus test (see Chapter 2 on this). As we have seen this refers to the ordinary person in the street. Would the ordinary person in the street, in the same circumstances, have foreseen that the actions by you would've caused the damage that they did? If the reasonable man would have foreseen these consequences, then as far as the court is concerned, so would you. Therefore, you are liable in the tort of negligence. Notice, once again, the court isn't in any way interested in asking what you were actually thinking at the time you caused the damage – this would be a subjective test which as we now know, is very rarely used in civil law.

It must be shown in each case whether a person actually owes a duty of care to another person, whether some breach of this duty has occurred and also whether some injury has been caused by the breach before any court action can be taken. We certainly don't owe a duty of care to everyone. Each case must be looked at individually as they occur.

Having said that, over the course of years, the courts have established some instances where they have decided that there certainly is a duty of care.

Some of these instances include the following:

- ☐ As seen above, a manufacturer owes a duty of care to the consumer of the product.
- ☐ Employers have a reasonable duty of care to make sure that that their workers are safe.
- ☐ A driver has a duty of care to other road users.
- ☐ Parents have a duty of care to make sure that their children are given food and kept safe.

Professional people and professional firms – solicitors, banks, surveyors and accountants etc. have a duty of care to their clients in providing services to their clients which have not been negligently performed. This is the area of negligent misstatements – see below.

A local council has a duty of care to anyone using a public toilet which is meant to be repaired by them – I put this case in for a bit of light relief. It is absolutely true though. See *Sayers v Harlow (1958)*, outlined on page 128. I've never worked out whether Mrs Sayers got any light relief while she was locked in the toilet. We'll take a closer look at Mrs Sayers' unfortunate case a bit later on.

Where a doctor bought some pairs of underpants and contacted dermatitis (a nasty itching of the skin and blistering) after wearing them, the manufacturer owed a duty of care – see *Grant v Australian Knitting Mills (1933)*. I feel his pain every time I think about his case.

The list is practically inexhaustible so you can see that the tort of negligence covers a very wide number of possible occurrences. The original tests for negligence as to whether there is a duty of care, was set out by the court in Donoghue's case. The court requires that all of these three tests should be applied to see if a case would succeed in each case of negligence. The answer to each of these questions must be "yes".

1. Is a duty of care owed in the first place?
2. Has this duty of care been breached (broken)?
3. Has some damage been caused directly as a result of the breach.

As it is impossible for the court to foresee every possible new situation where negligence may arise, the courts have more recently decided to take an 'incremental' approach. This means a 'bit by bit' approach to new cases which may occur. They look at new cases and decide whether the case may already fit into a previously decided case via precedent.

If the facts of a new case fit the precedent set by an older case then all well and good. A decision can then be reached following the *ratio* set in the previous case. If a new set of circumstances occurs in a later case, then the court would decide the new case by applying the above three tests to the new case to discover whether a duty of care exists or not, has it been breached and has some damage been directly caused by the breach? Of course the court will be using the reasonable person objective test.

It is sometimes said that this is the beauty of the Donoghue case, that it is capable of being extended to cover any new cases which may later occur. The principles of the case have certainly been extended to cover a huge variety of different areas of negligence up to modern times.

In *Caparo Industries V Dickman in 1990* (don't worry I'm not going to include too many more cases here) there was developed an even 'more modern' way for the court to decide whether a duty of care exists in new each case coming to the court. This is called the Caparo test which deals with the first Donoghue test in a more up to date way.

The Caparo Test: does a duty of care exist?

The test is now the following:

- ☐ Was the damage foreseeable? – this is just the reasonable man test again!
- ☐ Was the relationship between the parties 'proximate' enough? (closely enough connected) for the court to conclude that a duty of care exists?
- ☐ And the final Caparo test is, and this is the really new bit, is it 'fair, just and reasonable' to impose a duty of care in this new case?

This new bit was added because the court foresaw that there could be circumstances where it might be unfair to impose such a duty of care on someone. This is an area of public policy which has always had an intimate connection with negligence. A good example here is the infamous case of the Yorkshire Ripper murders, where it was alleged that the police should be liable in negligence for failing to catch the murderer of the women. Naturally, the court would have none of this at all, public policy again – there's no getting away from it.

Taking stock of all the above

Over the course of many years I've had countless students coming up to me saying that they're really confused with all these separate tests and rules concerning how the courts actually try to determine whether a person may become liable in the tort of negligence. Bear in mind it's highly likely that you will have at least one question in your exams which will be directly related to this area of law.

I can quite understand how confusing this all this looks. I actually had a someone fairly recently who came to me in tears asking me to explain all this to him. I didn't mind in the slightest, but you don't normally expect this sort of thing from a fellow university lecturer. In an attempt to drive a path through all this apparent muddle, let me try to make the position clear.

The tests for liability in negligence was first formalised in the *Donoghue v Stevenson* case. The case gave us the basic three-stage test. The court will ask the following:

1. Is it established that the person being sued in negligence had a duty of care to the other party?
2. If the answer to 1 above is yes, then has this duty of care been breached?
3. If the answer to both above is yes, then has the damage has been directly caused as a result of the breach of the duty of care?

The answers to each of the questions must be yes. If one answer to the three questions is negative, then there is no liability.

Where the Caparo test comes in is only in number 1 above. In Caparo, the court broke down the first part of the Donoghue test as to determine whether is a duty of care exists. They broke the test down into questions of reasonable foreseeability and proximity.

The first part is now concerned with how reasonably foreseeable was it that damage might be caused? (the objective Man on the Clapham Omnibus test). The second part of the test asks is the relationship between the parties proximate (close) enough.

'Proximate' simply questions whether the parties involved in the case were close enough physically in the case of physical damage for a duty to exist. For example, it's no good if someone accuses you of knocking them off their bike in London and you can prove that at the time you were in Beijing. In the case of relying on a negligent misstatement (particularly for finance students – see below), this 'proximity' relates to whether it can be shown whether a 'special relationship' exists between you and the other party. If so, it

> must be shown whether this special relationship is 'proximate' enough. So 'close enough', here becomes 'legally close enough' and has nothing to do with physical closeness.
>
> The third part of the Caparo test asks whether it "fair, just and reasonable" to impose a duty of care in each case (public policy again).
>
> Finally, in modern cases, if a duty of care has been established, the court will move back to Donoghue again to ask the last two questions:
>
> 1. Has it been breached?
> 2. Was the damage which has been caused a direct result of the breach?
>
> Remember that Caparo only really comes into play in the first of the tests established in Donoghue case. It does this in establishing whether or not there is a duty of care in the first place in terms of foreseeability and proximity. It then imposes the fair, just and reasonable test. Only then does the court move back to the last two other Donoghue tests.

Phew! I hope that I've shown you how to clear the way through this seemingly jumbled area. Don't forget that you must collect some cases to back up the concepts of 'foreseeability', 'proximity', and 'fair, just and reasonable' to get the higher marks. Ideally you need to look at contrasting cases where the court has decided where there is sufficient proximity and where there is not, where there is foreseeability and where there isn't and the same with fair, just and reasonable.

That means you must have Donoghue and Caparo covered. You will then need a minimum of two contracting cases for each of the tests. That doesn't seem too difficult, I hope.

The situation where a duty of care may exist (or not) was brilliantly described by Lord Esher in *Lievre v Gould in 1893*. He said the following: "The question of liability for negligence cannot arise at all until it is established that the man who has been negligent owed some duty to the person who seeks to make him liable for his negligence". He went on to say, "a man can be as negligent as he pleases toward the whole world if he owes no duty to them".

This is as true today as it was then. You owe no duty of care to anyone, legally, until the law says you do. The obligation of a duty of care in the tort of negligence is imposed upon us by law. The situation is entirely different from contract law where we have to agree to enter into a contract. The duty of care obligation in tort, is one which has been dumped on us by law, like it or not. Please make a special note of this crucial difference between the two areas of law.

It might seem odd but there is no 'Good Samaritan' rule in English law. So, if you're walking through your local park and see a young child that you have no connection to, drowning in a shallow paddling pool, you are under no legal obligation to rescue the child no matter how easy it may be to do so. As you have no connection to the child, the law says that you have no duty of care towards him or her. Morally you might well have a duty of care, but legally you haven't. Mind you, I expect we would all go a little bit out of our way to pull the child out of the pool. But legally we could walk away.

A practical example

Having put you through all of the above, it's time to give you an example of how all this stuff works in practice. I will be using just one case here. This a case which I love because it shows us so much. I don't like what happened in the case, but it shows the application of the rules regarding the tests for negligence. I use it in many lectures and more so in seminars where students get more of a chance to answer me back for once. The case is:

Barnett v Chelsea & Kennington Hospital (1969)

As is often the way, the facts of this case are quite simple. Imagine the scene: we have three night watchmen (the sort of big men who look after factories at night – usually in uniform and often with a torch and a large dog like an Alsatian). Well, they of course had been drinking tea on and off during the night – they were English after all. At sometime around 8 in the morning they visited the emergency department of the Chelsea Hospital complaining that they felt very ill and had been sick after drinking their tea. Apparently one of them, Mr Barnett, felt particularly ill. The nurse at the hospital couldn't find the on-duty casualty doctor as the hospital was so busy but she managed to reach him by phone. This was a Dr Banerjee. The doctor advised over the phone that the men should be told to go home and see their own doctor as soon as they could. He didn't personally examine the men.

Unfortunately, Mr Barnett died at around one o'clock that day. The other night watchmen although feeling ill for a while, recovered completely. An investigation later showed that the tea they had all been drinking had been inexplicably mixed with the deadly poison arsenic. Presumably Mr Barnett liked tea more than his workmates. (Note: Stick to hot chocolate if you ever become a night watchperson).

Mrs Barnett quite rightly felt more than a bit upset by this turn of events and sued the hospital for negligence in their treatment of her ex-husband. This is where it gets exciting because naturally the court applied the three tests from Donoghue. At this point in my seminars I hope to 'get one over' my students because I reckon that they haven't read the case.

So, I say the court will have to apply the three Donoghue tests here to establish if there is a case for negligent liability, so let's do this now.

The first test is, "does a hospital have a duty of care to its patients?"

The answer always comes, "yes of course a hospital has a duty of care – common sense". Correct!

Then I ask, do you think the hospital (the duty doctor really), had breached the duty of care by not examining the night watchmen? Again, the answer is almost always "yes" and again this is correct.

I follow this up by asking, did this lack of the duty of care by the doctor lead to the death of one of the night watchmen? The answer the students give usually depends upon whether they've been doing the reading I've set them. Most say, of course, that the death was due to the resident doctor not examining the patients.

Here I spring my big surprise.

No, it wasn't. Why? Well, because:

The three workmen had all ingested the arsenic so it was in their blood system. By this time, it was too late for any doctor to do anything about it. The amount of arsenic taken by the workman who died would have killed him regardless of anything the doctor could've done. The doctor was almost certainly negligent in not going along and examining the men. But, had he examined them, one of them would have died anyway.

This behaviour by the doctor doesn't fit the third part of the test as directly laid down by Donoghue: Had the doctors' negligence directly caused damage? No, in this case it hadn't. The deceased night watchmen's wife therefore had no claim. Seems a little bit unfair don't you think? This part of the concept also involves the what is often called the "chain of causation" – it'll benefit you to look this up and absorb yourself in it.

> The Caparo test obviously didn't have to be asked here as Caparo came along over 20 years later. Actually, it really probably wouldn't be relevant to ask is it fair, just and reasonable to expect a hospital to have a duty of care to its patients as the answer it too obvious.

Before we leave negligence of this physical type, I must just again say a word about the Caparo concepts of foreseeability and proximity. These concepts are closely related to each other. Naturally, in the physical world at least, the closer (proximate) you are to another person the more foreseeable it is that you may harm that person by doing something really stupid. You must have a few case law examples of where this relationship has been examined in your case law memory bank. It's a very examinable area, believe me.

Economic loss and 'pure' economic loss

Ordinary economic loss is relatively easy to claim. So, if someone runs into your car denting it badly and also causing damage to yourself, it is quite well accepted that you are able to claim compensation for damage to your car.

Personal bodily damage compensation to yourself is also commonly awarded You can generally claim monetary loss you may have suffered as a result of loss of earnings because of the other person's negligence, i.e. you may be in hospital and lose pay. It has also become more common to be able to claim for psychiatric damages, assuming that you can prove to the court that actually have this type of damage (remember Mrs Donoghue on this?).

But, and I hate to have to say this here, particularly to students of business law, you cannot ordinarily claim for what is called 'pure' economic loss. So, what is pure economic loss? It's sometimes called 'loss to the balance sheet' so it's really an accountant's sort of loss. The best way to explain this is by looking at one of my favourite cases in this area of tort. It's a really good case but my bet is that you aren't going to like the *ratio* very much. The case is:

Weller v Foot and Mouth Research Institute (1966)

In case you haven't heard of it, foot and mouth disease is caused by a very nasty virus which mainly affects cattle. It is highly contagious and is nearly impossible to contain in one geographic area. The disease breaks out only occasionally in agricultural areas and when it does, the whole locality has to have an exclusion zone set up around it (usually by the army). Car tyres and people's shoes are doused in the strongest detergent when anyone is trying to enter or leave the area. The cattle within the area are killed and burned in an attempt to stop the virus spreading. It's the stuff of a farmer's worst nightmares.

In the above case, the institute was conducting research into the disease trying to find a cure and any possible treatment for infected cattle. The research institute were negligent in allowing the virus to escape from the institute. That negligence had occurred was not an issue as previous cases against the institute taken by local farmers who'd had their cattle destroyed because of the leak of the virus, had been successful.

The issue for the court to decide here was could a local cattle auctioneer bring a case for damages against the institute for negligence as he had lost practically all his business owing to the virus escaping?

The answer the court gave was no, he could not claim damages. The court decision was based on legal proximity. Given that negligence was proven, the auctioneer was legally too far removed from the source of the negligence to be able to claim. Keep following and all will be revealed. At first sight this seems to be grossly unfair – the auctioneer had had his business practically destroyed by the effects of someone else's careless act and he could do absolutely nothing about it.

> It does seem to most students that this decision is unjust, particularly so if you're thinking of running your own business. But, let's take a closer look at what might happen if the auctioneer's action had been allowed. If the auctioneer had succeeded in winning his case, ask yourself where might other possible legal actions stop?
>
> If the auctioneer had won his case and received compensation, then presumably any customers of the auctioneer (or any other local auctioneers) would be able to claim that they also should be paid damages. Perhaps local butchers could claim that as they were now unable to get their supplies of beef, they should also be paid compensation. Perhaps restaurant owners or café owners could claim that they now couldn't buy beef for their businesses from the butcher, meaning that they were also losing money. Perhaps the customers of the butcher could claim damages as they couldn't now have their Sunday roast?
>
> This kind of argument underlies the concept of pure economic loss – that's why it's often called balance sheet loss. It's also called the 'floodgates' argument. Once you open the floodgates. . . Bit hard on the poor old business person though don't you think? Do you not see public policy hiding here again?

Negligent statements or negligent misstatements

(We can treat these two expressions as the same thing for our purposes)

So far, we have only been talking about acts which have been done negligently; someone knocks you off you bike or the sort of situation where you get hit hard on the head by a group of young boys playing basketball in a supermarket with a pumpkin. There was no intention to hit anyone but it hit me. It hurt I can tell you. Ah well, it was Halloween. But what about where someone who should know better gives you some advice which you rely on and the advice turns out to be negligent advice? As a result, you or your business lose money because of this?

It's surprising to think that until not too many years ago – in the eyes of the law – if your bank manager gave you advice regarding the investment of your money and that advice was negligently given and you lost money because of it – well there wasn't very much you could do about it. This was because the law of negligence at the time mainly only covered negligent physical acts. You couldn't, back then, expect the courts to award you monetary compensation if you took advice which was negligent and you or your business lost money because of this.

This advice could come from any 'professional' person – doctor, surgeon, building surveyor, car salesman, estate agent or law lecturer. Many people at the time thought that this was ridiculous. It was. Then came along another game-changing case concerning the giving out of negligent advice. After this case if advice was given negligently, received and acted upon and that advice had the effect of causing financial loss to the party receiving it, legal action was now more easily available. This decision was none too soon in my opinion.

This an area you really must get to know in order to get into the higher marks as it is fundamental and highly examinable. It's an area which covers non-physical loss, i.e. financial loss caused as a result of taking some professional advice which turns out to be bad advice. This is particularly important to you if you're studying accountancy or finance as part of your business studies degree. This could be in your first or second year of your degree.

Negligent misstatements are an area where at least one exam question is likely to be based. Before we get into this, I want to state clearly that the sort of situations we will be taking under this heading do not involve contract law at all. If in real life, for example, you go to see a solicitor with a case you hope she will take up for you, the paperwork you will have to sign will invariably involve you in a contract with her and/or with her law firm. If she gives you advice which turns out to be negligent, then the best and easiest form of action (and therefore the cheapest) for you to take is to sue for breach of contract.

A little exam tip here; if you see a question in an exam paper which is on negligent advice (you think), take a closer look to see if the question says something like, "X, a bank manager, advises Y (or company Y) about the best place to put Y's money. Acting on this advice leads Y to great financial loss" – there should be somewhere in the question either directly said or heavily implied, that there is no contract between X and Y. If the question states that there is a contract between X and Y then obviously you know you're in contract law and probably being asked to write about breach of contract. However, if the question states that X and Y have no contractual relationship, which it ought to do, then you know you are in the area of negligent advice. Off you go.

The central case in the area of negligent advice is *Hedley Byrne v Heller & Partners (1964)*.

Hedley Byrne v Heller & Partners (1964)

I'll just give you an outline of the facts here. Hedley was an advertising agency. They were considering whether or not to do business with a new client. They asked the new client's bank, Heller and Partners, for a credit reference. Heller stated that this new client was good financially, "for its ordinary business engagements". As a result of this, Hedley went ahead and took on the new client but lost a great deal of money as the recommended client soon folded. Hedley attempted to sue the bank for the financial losses caused as a result of the bad advice they were given. The claimant actually lost the case as the advice given included a disclaimer clause. It is the *ratio* which came from the case that is important. This *ratio* began to be applied to new cases in this area of negligent misstatements. So, the question for the court to resolve was: did the bank owe a duty of care when issuing financial statements or not?

This for us is the important bit. The court decided for the first time in English law that in certain circumstances the answer was yes, a duty of care was owed when making statements that others were going to be relying on.

Lord Reid's statement in the case said that the rules coming from Donoghue's case (for physical harm) couldn't on their own be used for cases of negligent advice causing financial harm. This is because, negligence causing physical harm is generally a 'one off' situation. i.e. you generally only knock a person off their bicycle once by negligent driving (we hope). If you do it again at some time in the future then you're probably an idiot. So, physical accidents tend to stop once the accident is over. Then when the victim gets out of hospital, they'll start legal action against you.

Lord Reid said that this is not often not the case with verbal statements. No one knows how far this type of information will travel. Gossip, rumour - "I heard it through the grapevine". How many times has someone said to you, "can you keep a secret?". How many times have you told a secret just to one person? Lord Reid went on to say that for a claim for loss caused by a negligent statement to succeed, there must be a "special relationship" to be found to exist between the parties involved (more on this shortly).

Lord Reid also went on to state that even if the person who is making a statement which normally, we might be expected to rely on, makes that statement in a social setting, we really can't be expected to rely on it in those circumstances. So, if we meet our bank manager at a party where he may well have had too many wine gums, we can't hold him or her responsible for any financial advice he may decide to give out to anyone who is listening. Also, if you hear some interesting statements in a party/social setting and then pass this on to someone else, they also cannot rely on the information. Even if you're given advice in a proper business setting and pass this on to someone else, they cannot rely upon it. This would be second hand information which is often changed in the retelling quite inadvertently.

So, to establish whether a duty of care exists between the person or business making the statement and the person or business receiving the statement, certain questions must be answered:

- ☐ First, does the person making the statement have some kind of expert or 'special skill'? This means does this person know, or should they know, exactly what they are talking about – examples to follow.
- ☐ Second, could the person hearing the statement have "reasonably relied" on the statement?
- ☐ Third, does the person making the statement know that it is very likely that the person hearing the statement, would follow this advice?

Each case is looked at individually to see whether this kind of special relationship exists or not. Essentially this relationship exists where someone has some kind of specialist knowledge in an area – knowledge which you haven't got and which is why you asked for their advice in the first place.

Now, the person giving the advice can have this knowledge or, as we will shortly see, may have assumed this special knowledge and not denied that they actually have no such knowledge. Most of the situations where we might expect there to be a special relationship are obvious. So, case law has shown us that there is a special relationship between bank managers and customers, a medical person and patients, estate agents and clients, building surveyors and clients, even employers and employees when the employer issues a reference in a negligent manner. You need to know some of these cases. As ever, the more cases you know, the better.

The one case I'll use here to demonstrate some of the principles is *Chaudry v Prabhakar (1988)*.

Chaudry v Prabhakar (1988)

Here we have two close friends, Mrs Chaudry and Mr Prabhakar. Mrs Chaudry was looking for a nice second hand car. Mr Prabhakar was well known and had a reputation in the area, as knowing a fair bit about the buying and selling of used cars. In real life he worked as a grocer so he couldn't have been a super whizzo 'professional' second hand car salesman (though he appeared to like to think he was). Mrs Chaudry asked him if he could look out for a "nice car" for her to buy.

The only thing Mrs Chaudry said was that she certainly didn't want was any car that had been involved in an accident. Mr Prabhakar had a look round and reported back that he had seen a nice car that would suit what she wanted. No money was exchanged between the two friends as Mr Panabaker undertook this at the favour to a friend.

The car Mr Prabhakar recommended was a VW Golf that he said, looked nice. Notice that I haven't mentioned anything about a contact between the two people. As mentioned above, this is extremely important in this area. If there's a contract then we're unlikely to be talking about negligence.

Anyway, Mrs Chaudry took Mr Prabhakar's advice and bought the car. Shortly after buying and of course driving it, she discovered that the car had been in a serious accident and been badly repaired. You know, "a bit of filler here a splash of paint there and nobody'll know the difference". Mrs Chaudry sued Mr Prabhakar for financial loss because she alleged that he had issued negligent advice to her. She won her case and was awarded damages against Mr Prabhakar for supplying negligent advice leading to her financial loss. Once more the court used the objective reasonable person test. So, it didn't matter what Mr Prabhakar was thinking, only what he had factually done.

We are really also in the law of agency here, but you can easily use this case as an example of voluntary assumption, considering that you have knowledge or experience that you really haven't got. Someone relies upon this which leads to their financial loss. This loss caused by your 'authoritive' statement(s) could be suffered by another person or a business. You can use it as a warning to yourself to be very careful about what advice you give to friends.

In terms of any business law course you will be expected to have a good working knowledge of *Hedley*. Admittedly it has been severely criticised over the years by lawyers and the legal profession in general ... it would be, lawyers make their money from giving advice. One thing that we can be fairly sure about, is that Mr P and Mrs C are not so friendly as they used to be...

An occupier's liability for premises

You will be pleased to hear that in relation to all the above, the concept of occupier's liability is relatively easy. Occupier's liability stems from the wider tort of negligence but it has a narrower focus as it deals with the duty of care which an 'occupier' of 'premises' may have to visitors to these premises. There are only two Acts of Parliament which operate in this area. These are:

☐ The Occupier's Liability Act 1957, and
☐ The Occupier's Liability Act 1984.

The earlier act deals with 'lawful' visitors to premises and the later act deals with 'non lawful' visitors (mainly trespassers). The 1957 Act defines premises as, "any fixed or moveable structure, including any vessel, vehicle or aircraft." As the Act mentions not just fixed objects but also moveable ones, we now know from case law following the Act, that the definition of premises can also extend to any buildings, including outbuildings, lifts, chairs, ladders and even scaffolding. I was asked recently whether a submarine might be included here. I suspect the answer is yes, as a submarine is a vessel. Unfortunately, neither Act gives us a full definition of who an 'occupier' actually is, so once more we've had to rely on decided case law to give us some satisfactory definitions.

Luckily the two areas above, (occupier and premises) are the only tricky issues you are likely to find with occupier's liability. We'll deal with these shortly. Let's start with the duty of care the earlier Act tells us we have to visitors to the places where we live, and to any business premises we might be using.

Section 2 (1) of the 1957 act states, "an occupier owes the same duty, the common duty of care to all his visitors except insofar as he is free to and does extend, restrict, modify or exclude his duty to any visitors by agreement or otherwise."

The next section S 2 (2), gives us the character of the duty itself, "to take such care as in all the circumstances is reasonable to see that the visitor will be reasonably safe for the purpose for which he is invited to be there."

Under the 1957 Act an occupier who doesn't make sure that his premises are reasonable safe may make himself liable for physical injury to a visitor and any damage to the visitor's property.

Notice the use of the word "reasonable" here? This once again, is the objective reasonable person test. This means that the duty of care to visitors is not normally a particularly troublesome duty. The use of common sense is invaluable here. If you know that a visitor is coming to see you, then your duty is to see that they don't come to any harm because of the state of your premises. This relates to any premises that you may use for business and also to where you live.

So, if you've been decorating, you'll have to make sure that there are no paint tins lying around for someone to trip over, or stepladders in the way, or loose carpet at the top of the stairs causing your visitor to break their neck. But if you know that your parrot swears in front of visitors, you won't have to move his cage to another room. Common sense again.

Who is a visitor?

A lawful visitor at your home could well be someone you have invited round for a drink or a meal or a chat. A lawful visitor at your business premises might include anyone you have invited for a business meeting or customers coming into your shop, if you have a retail outlet. These people have a right to be on your premises because you invited them. There are other possibilities where someone has an implied right to be on your premises. This includes the postman, Amazon delivery person, or milkman. (I was pleased to hear that milkmen are currently increasing in numbers recently, said to be largely due to David Attenborough's series, *Blue Planet*). Anyway, we cannot treat these people with an implied right to visit our property, as trespassers.

Of course, we have implied permission to enter shops for the ordinary purpose of spending our money. Very rarely is there anyone standing at the shop doorway inviting you inside to do your shopping and hoping sincerely that you have a good day – unless you live in the USA, where they are called 'greeters'.

Some potential visitors to your property have a statutory right to be on your premises even when you're not there. This includes members of the emergency services, e.g. the firefighting force and the police if they suspect you're hiding a Columbian drug baron (or a folk singer).

If you've bought a ticket to the cinema, then you are in the cinema (premises) by contract. The contract was made when you bought the ticket. You are then a lawful visitor. This allows you to view the film but you may well turn yourself into a trespasser if you see the film and then bed down in your sleeping bag in the toilets – however temping this may be.

If you are in a shop and you open and step through a door which says 'staff only' then you've turned yourself from a lawful visitor into a trespasser.

Other people who might be on your premises might be tradesmen. Tradesmen could be, for example, a firm of decorators which you have hired under contract to do repairs and repaint your house. Assuming that these decorators are competent (you should obtain references from them to show that you have checked them out) then if some visitor gets injured by something the decorators have done or failed to do, you as the occupier will not be liable. It's a good idea to check and assess any work by the contractor yourself as far as you're able. This is just a bit of extra protection to yourself just in case.

The situation is different where you employ 'specialist' independent contractors. If, for example, while you are doing some repairs to your house you suddenly discover asbestos in the ceilings, you are not allowed legally to remove this yourself. This because asbestos (an old-fashioned insulator) is a severe danger to health. Then you will be forced into getting a specialist firm to deal with this hazard. If as result of negligence caused by such a contractor, leaving your premises in a dangerous state, then you will not normally be liable for this but the contractor will be.

Finally, under the 1957 Act, you as occupier have a greater responsibility if your visitor is a child. Once more this this is common sense. As adults we should know that children have an almost irresistible attraction to things left lying around which may hurt them. They can't help it. It's in the nature of children to be attracted, for example, to a garden pond or sparkly glass ornaments on a low shelf. Anticipation is the key to making your premises safe for both adults and children. In this way you can remove any obvious (dangerous) items which children may be attracted to.

Who is the occupier?

As the Act concerns an occupier of premises but doesn't define exactly what an occupier is, it was left to subsequent case law to provide us with a working definition. One case you will have to be familiar with is *Wheat v Lacon (1966)*. In this case Lord Denning gave us the definition of an occupier (or occupiers) of premises which is used by the courts today.

Wheat v Lacon (1966)

The case involved the Wheat family staying as guests (visitors) at a pub. Mr Wheat was attempting to descend the stairs in the pub. Near the bottom of the stairs the handrail was broken and the lightbulb was not working. Mr Wheat fell and injured his head, and died as a result.

A legal action was taken under the Occupiers Liability Act 1957. Lord Denning in his decision, said that a person or persons with "sufficient degree of control" over the premises is an occupier. It is sufficient that a person has some degree of control over the premises and this control can be shared with other people. As control may be shared with other people, two or more people can be occupiers. In Wheat v Lacon the responsibility for the injuries to Mr Wheat was shared between the pub managers, Mr and Mrs Richardson and the pub owners, Lacon.

What this decision means to you is, for example, that if you share a flat with other students, you will be deemed to have enough of a degree of control over your premises to be an occupier. You could then be liable under the Act for not making sure that your flat is reasonably safe for any visitors you or your student colleagues invite to your flat. Obviously, you will have a greater 'control' over your own room, but you will all be jointly responsible for any common corridors and entrance ways. Under case law, you don't have to be an owner of your flat. If you are renting this is good enough. During the period of your rental, as far as the law is concerned, you and your fellow students are occupiers.

Occupier's Liability Act 1984

This seems to be a more contentious area if my seminars are any guide. What some students dislike is that this Act gives some protection to people who are trespassers on your property. A broad definition of burglary is that a burglar is a person who enters your property as a *trespasser*, with intent to steal.

Quite a few students are at first outraged when they first come across this concept. I've had students saying, "why on earth should I have to make sure that my property is safe for someone who's trying to break in and steal my stuff?" I can understand this point of view completely. The 1984 Act does, at first sight, seem to a little bit unfair to the occupier.

What we have to understand is that there was quite a change in the attitude of society to property between the dates of the two acts. Before the introduction of the 1957 Act the view of society regarding property seems to some extent to have still been based on the old saying, "An Englishman's home is his castle". This saying is still heard today occasionally but seems to have been first stated about 400 years ago. The meaning of the phrase is that people should be able to do anything they might want to in their own house once they've shut their front door. In earlier days this often involved setting man traps in gardens and threatening any uninvited guests with guns or guard dogs.

Gradually this attitude began to be seen as becoming a little outdated and a new spirit of humanitarianism slowly developed in society. The idea that you could do just about anything to a trespasser slowly began to change. Alongside this, it also began to be realised that many trespassers were children. Eventually the thought began to grow that surely, we ought to owe some degree of protection to individuals on our land even if they have not been invited? Perhaps we should owe some protection if a trespasser is a child who may not even be aware that they are trespassing? I expect most of us would agree with this to some degree after a little thought.

An influential case came along in 1972 which further brought to the attention that perhaps some duty of care should be given to trespassers. This case was, *British Railways Board v Herrington*. In this case a 6-year-old boy had strayed through a fence belonging to the Railway Board onto an electrified railway line. He was electrocuted and burnt very severely. The Board were aware that there was a hole in the fence and had done nothing about this. They were also aware that children had been seen playing near the electrified line.

The court found that the Railway Board owed "a common duty of humanity" to trespassers and were therefore liable. This was something of a landmark decision. This case and other similar cases ultimately led to a Royal Commission Report which in turn influenced the introduction of the Occupiers Liability Act 1984.

This later Act deals with 'non-visitors' (this generally referrers to trespassers). An occupier has a duty to trespassers under this Act if he is aware that there is some danger on his premises or has reasonable grounds to know that there is some danger, and he is aware or has reasonable grounds to be aware that non-visitors are or may be within his premises. In these circumstances, the potential risk to a non-visitor is such that the occupier may reasonably expected to extend some protection to the non-visitor.

OK, now we have looked at the two acts governing who are lawful visitors to our property and who may not be lawful visitors. Let's now take a look at what we can do to eliminate, or at least reduce our, liability. These are called 'defences'.

Avoiding liability

The first and most obvious thing to do is to is to take a good look around your home or business premises to make sure that there is nothing that you've left lying around which could harm anyone. This is not a hard thing to do and could well prevent any legal action being taken against you in the first place. I did say the whole thing is mainly common sense. Remember that if you may have children coming, take extra care.

Signs may be used to warn of any potential danger as long as they are clearly written, properly placed and easy to read. "Danger Deep Water. No Swimming" or similar sign may be used near to a pool in a park, for example.

Exclusion clauses may be used. A good example here is often seen in car parks. Take a look at the car parks around your university. You're bound to see signs stating something like, "All cars parked at owners' risk. No liability is accepted for loss or damage". When you park your car in the university car park, you are entering into a contract with the university whether you realise it or not. As it is a contract, the terms used in the above sign is an exemption (or exclusion) clause in the contract. The clause is obviously designed to exclude the liability of the university towards anyone parking their car. As these types of signs are contractual, they are subject to the Unfair Contract Terms Act 1977. Under the Act they have to be written so as not to be 'unreasonable'. Placing of such signs is also important. A sign attempting to exclude car parking liability in your university is unlikely to have much effect if it's written on a postcard and stuck three metres high on a fence.

Consent to the danger is also available as a defence. So, for example, imagine that you've gone out of your way to point out to a visitor that there's something particularly dangerous on your property and they choose to ignore your warnings, go ahead and damage themselves anyway, then they can be said to have consented to the danger. You are very unlikely to be liable in this situation. This defence has the Latin tag of *volenti non fit injuria*. This translates as, "to one who volunteers, no harm is done". The same effect would occur if you were to voluntarily step into the boxing ring with the current world heavyweight boxing campion, who I have it on good authority, is called James 'Bonecrusher' Smith. When you wake up, you can hardly moan to the referee that Bonecrusher smacked you "a right nasty one on the nose" when you weren't looking.

It is possible to obtain occupier's liability insurance from most insurance companies. This would be relevant for business premises and it is surprisingly inexpensive. However, you may need to give this some extra thought before deciding to go ahead with it. As with most insurance policies, the insurance company will try to wriggle out of many claims made to them. So, if your business decides to take out some occupier's liability insurance and you make a claim, the insurance company will investigate whether you had gone through all the processes of ensuring that you premises were safe in the first place. But assuming that you've already done all you can reasonably do to ensure that your premises is safe, why would you need extra insurance anyway? Maybe the answer is just extra peace of mind.

Contributory negligence

It is possible for someone to contribute to their own injuries caused by someone else's negligence. Common examples here are when someone is a passenger in a car which crashes owing to the negligence of the driver. If the passenger couldn't be bothered to fasten their seat belt and as a result is damaged more severely then they have by their action, (or in this case inaction), contributed to their own misfortune. Again, if you are riding a motor bike without a crash helmet and a car driver crashes into you causing additional injury because you weren't wearing your crash helmet, then, it's very likely that you're partly to blame as you've contributed to your own injuries.

The Act governing contributory negligence is easy to remember as it called The Law Reform (Contributory Negligence) Act 1945. Under this act the court may reduce the amount of damages payable to a person claiming depending on the assessment by the court of to what extent did that person help in causing their own injuries.

A favourite case I use here is one I've already mentioned above. It is really a bit of a sad story. The case is *Sayers V Harlow Urban District Council (1958)*.

Sayers V Harlow Urban District Council (1958)

The facts here were that Mrs Sayers entered a public toilet which was owned by Harlow Council. The toilet block was supposed to be maintained by the council but hadn't been properly kept in good order. As a result of a faulty lock on the toilet door, Mrs Sayers unfortunately got locked in the cubicle. She was late for her bus and tried calling out for help. As no help came, she decided to try to climb out without waiting for help to arrive. In order to escape she put her foot on the toilet roll holder. Unfortunately, toilet roll holders are not really designed for climbing on and the holder twisted on the wall. Mrs Sayers fell and broke her ankle.

The court found that the local council were liable for negligence but Mrs Sayers was partly to blame for her own injury. The damages she received were reduced by a quarter. One of my students once said that she was glad that the damages weren't reduced by 1p. A sorry tale indeed for poor old Mrs Sayers. I bet after this she made sure she went before she left home.

How this relates to occupier's liability is that a visitor can, in some circumstances, also contribute to their own injuries. Let's assume that you, as an occupier, are aware of a particular danger on your premises. You've put up plenty of warning notices which are designed to warn of this danger. If you have a visitor, say an adult, you might even have given this person a verbal warning as well saying watch out for the deep hole in the garden. You've also roped off the hole just in case.

Your visitor by now is very well aware of the danger but if he foolishly leans over the rope just to see how deep the hole is and falls down the hole. Well there is a strong case here to believe that he is a little short on brain power. In a claim against you for damages, it's highly likely that the court will take this sort of behaviour into account in the claim. Even if damages are awarded against you, they are likely to be substantially reduced.

Summary

We introduced this chapter by mentioning some of the ways by which the law of tort can affect you and your business. We explained that a 'tort' is a civil matter as opposed to a criminal offence so in matters of tort, for example trespass, the police have no part to play and it's up to the person suffering from some tortious activity to put the matter right themselves by taking the other person to court to hopefully gain compensation.

Then we moved on to the three areas of tort which you'll have to be aware of as a business law student. These are, negligence of a physical nature which goes on to cause someone harm, the effect of a business which by its nature commonly gives out financial or other advice which may been produced in a negligent manner and, occupier's liability where you may have some business premises which have been left in a dangerous state.

We looked at the leading case where the rules governing the 'modern' law of negligence and also looked at a later leading case where these rules were updated.

We then took stock of all of the above and applied them to a case which shows how the courts will apply the rules given in the two leading cases in practice.

We looked at the concepts of 'economic' loss and 'pure' economic loss. We mentioned that the first of the above losses is relatively easily claimable but the second one is not.

We moved on to look at the second main area of tort which you need to have a good knowledge, of particularly if your course title includes the word 'finance' or 'law for accountancy'. This is the area of loss caused by you or your business by issuing statements, mainly of a financial nature, which have been prepared in some negligent way and relied upon by another individual or business. We looked at some steps you can take to ensure that your business can avoid possible liability here.

The third area which you're highly likely to need to have a good knowledge of was introduced next. This is the concept of occupier's liability where you may become liable in negligence if either an invited person and an uninvited person (trespasser) injures themselves on your residential or your business premises. We mentioned some sensible steps which you can take to minimise you risk here.

Finally, we saw how a person can contribute to their own damage by entering premises which have been negligently allowed to become dangerous to visitors. We saw how a visitor to premises can, through their own actions, essentially make matters worse for themselves. If they do contribute to their own damage this will reduce any monetary compensation payable.

Revision questions

1. Explain what constitutes a 'tort' in civil law and give some examples of these.
2. Describe the main rules which a court will apply when considering whether a person is or is not liable in the tort of negligence.
3. Explain the difference, using case law, between economic loss and pure economic loss suffered by a person or a by a business.
4. You run a limited liability company. As a result of acting on advice given to you by your company bank about the financial status of a company you want to make a contract with, your company suffers severe financial losses. You discover that the advice you were given was completely wrong as the bank negligently mistook the company you were enquiring about with another similarly named company. Explain what legal rights are likely to have.
5. Your company owns and runs a garden centre open to the public. What 'reasonable steps' might you take to protect your company from being sued by customers for any harm they may suffer on your premises?

6 Types of business

This may well be an area of business law that you will be comfortable with. If so, good. Any student who's taken A level or equivalent in either Business Studies or Economics will have covered the main forms of business formation before. The difference is that here we will not only cover the main types of business, but also the formation and legal implications of each of these.

It's unfortunately true that unless you're aware of these legal implications you can get yourself into a whole lot of trouble with the law. You can, in some cases, lose just about everything you own. The worst-case scenario is that if you don't know what you're doing, you could end up doing a stretch at Her Majesty's Pleasure in a (with luck) open prison.

Self-employment/sole traders

The obvious place to start here is to look at working for yourself. The self-employed type is the oldest and easiest way for you to start a business. It's quick and cheap to set up and requires little paperwork at the start. The income tax and VAT (value added tax) authorities have now been combined into one authority – HM Revenue and Customs (HRMC). Officially you have to inform the HRMC what you're doing, but in fact very few people do this at first, but wait for the tax people to catch up with them. Obviously, I can't recommend you doing this yourself but let's just say an awful lot of people do. Depending upon your estimated business turnover, you may have to register for VAT (Value Added Tax) at HMRC, but currently your business turnover has to be more than £85,000 before you have to bother with this. It's doubtful if you are going to have to worry about this in your first-year trading as a self-employed person

According to the Office of National Statistics, at the time of writing there are 4.93 million self-employed people in the UK. I'm not going to argue with the Office of National Statistics, but the figure for self-employed is a very difficult thing to measure – people dodge in and out of being self-employed on a regular basis. This is because it's so easy to do. One week you may be working for yourself as a bricklayer, and the next week a builder may offer you a job working for his building firm. Now you are no longer working for yourself but part of the 'employed' section of the National Statistics. The total figure for the self-employed then can't be much more than an estimation. Even so it's a pretty big figure representing around 15% of the total working population.

The sole trader form of business organisation is popular for several reasons. You often don't need very much by way of capital (money) to start your own business and, as said above, there is little formal setting up needed. Self-employment has traditionally formed the basis of many occupations such as bricklaying, plumbing and hairdressing. Market traders and small 'jobbing' builders and handymen also tend to be self-employed, as are most window cleaners. Many of these occupations are not always carried out by people working for themselves but they often are.

If you are currently fed up with what you're doing, you could set up as a sole trader tomorrow morning. You could, for example, get a pitch at a local market for very small outlay per day or week. The difficulty is choosing something to sell on your stall. Existing market traders are very protective of their own businesses and not too keen about the idea of someone else setting up and selling the same goods as themselves.

So, what are the main attractions of this form of business organisation?
- Low cost of setting up;
- Being your own boss and making all the decisions yourself;
- Keeping all the profit (assuming you make a profit);
- Cheap and easy;
- Flexibility;
- Being you own boss – you can employ workers if you want to but you have to pay them of course;
- Privacy – you don't have to publish your accounts so competitors can't see what you're doing.

What may put you off?
- As a self-employed person you won't have a contract of employment so you can't expect the benefits of holiday pay or employers sick pay.
- Difficulty of raising capital if you want to expand. Bank managers tend not to like the self-employed.

- ☐ Usually you have to put in extremely long hours as you generally not only have to organise your business yourself but also be your own administrator, accountant and marketing person etc. etc.
- ☐ You will have to pay twice for any holidays. First the cost of the holiday itself, and second the loss of earnings while you're relaxing in Tenerife for a month each year. Depending on the level of competition, you might also be very worried that you may have lost all your customers by the time you get back.
- ☐ Also, what's going to happen if you get ill and can't work?
- ☐ You are responsible for calculating and paying your own income tax and possibly Value Added Tax (VAT). This means that you're going to have to deal directly with HM Revenue and Customs. The people at HMRC do not take prisoners. Particularly with the self-employed. The tax authorities are going to be much happier when (and if) we move to a completely cashless economy.
- ☐ Personal liability – this is the really big one. Should your business run into trouble then you are seriously in danger of losing any assets you may own: this includes your house, your car, your furniture and everything else you used to call your own. Interestingly, if you go bankrupt, as a self-employed person, you are allowed to keep the tools of your trade. So, a plumber, for example, is able to keep any spanners and wrenches and so on which would be needed to carry on as a plumber. Presumably a private sector doctor would be allowed to keep his or her stethoscope and needles needed to keep on practicing. Would you take your old granny to a bankrupt doctor go to get her course of vitamin B12 jabs?

I think you get the point. Working for yourself is great when things are going well but can be really bad when your business takes a downturn. Unfortunately, unless you have someone to leave your business to when you die, your business also dies along with you. On a happier note and having said all this, lots of people have operated in this way for many years without any trouble. Don't let me put you off but just keep in mind the danger. The real danger, just to remind you, is that you have complete personal financial liability should things go wrong!

Legal requirements for the self-employed

As said, there are just a few legal requirements to be considered when going on your own, or working for yourself. You are instructed to tell HM Revenue and Customs what you are going to do. They will inform you that you must keep "records of all sales, purchases, expenses and earnings". Depending on what business you are intending to start, you may benefit from taking up some public liability insurance – this is not too expensive and may cover you should you damage a member of the public or someone's equipment while you're working.

You do not have to register your business with Companies House, but you might consider registering the name that you're going to be trading under with the National Business Register. This is because if you come up with a brilliant name for your business, you don't want anyone else pinching it. Have a look at hairdresser's salons or barbers the next time you're out and about. They're very good at this sort of thing: 'Curl up and Dye', 'Hair Port', 'Dye Another Day' are some examples. My personal favourite is 'Anita Haircut'. Also, and this comes in just about everywhere, you have to think of the Health and Safety regulations that may govern whatever you are planning to be doing. Obviously, there will be more Health and Safety regulations for you to be aware of in some activities than in others.

If, for example, you're running a market stall, the law says that, "you must clearly display your business name and address to which legal documents must be sent". This stipulation of your personal name and address also applies to, receipts, invoices, orders and any correspondence used in the course of your business. Have a look the next time that you're at a market and you'll see that the majority of market traders try to get around this by putting a postcard size notice up with their postcode only written on it.

Although many market traders do this, it doesn't actually comply with the law. Some traders don't even bother doing this this until they're told to. You may also need a market traders' licence but this depends on the area you are intending to trade. Remember that Tesco, Marks and Spencer, Innocent Drinks, Dunelm and Poundland all started as market traders. There is then a good deal to be said for starting your business in this way. By the way, the person who sees to the day to day running of markets and collects the rents is called the 'Toby' – so that's who you ask for on your first day. Keep in with the Toby. Although called a Toby this can be a woman or a man.

> **Partnerships**
>
> Traditionally, the next business type introduced at this point, is forming a partnership with one or more people. But we'll look at these later, for reasons which will become clear. For now, we will concentrate on a safer way of conducting a business than becoming self-employed and this means going through a legal process called incorporation. This is the process of forming a limited liability company (Ltd) or a public limited company (PLC).

Incorporation

The concept of incorporation is a real game changer. Once you go through this legal process, your company now is not simply just you, as it is when you are working for yourself. After incorporation, the business is legally 'born' and takes on a separate legal existence of its own (often called a 'legal entity'). Now although no doubt you will want to keep control of your business, the company is legally separate from you and you are no longer normally responsible for most debts run up in the name of the company.

The business now can go into liquidation, and if your company has no assets, you are personally protected against being liable for these company debts. You, as the business owner, are said to have 'limited liability'. Your own liability for the company debts is normally limited to the amount of capital (or money) which you decided to invest in the company when you started it up.

Please note that it is you personally, as the business owner, who has limited liability for the company debts. The company itself doesn't have limited liability. This means that if debts have been run up in the name of the company, then the company itself may be sued for these debts and the company will have to repay them if it has sufficient assets. You however, as long as you have not been using the company for fraudulent purposes, will not be personally liable. How good is that!

You can see now why this was a paradigm shift.

The legal ruling which is generally said to be the start of the idea of this separation of you from your incorporated business, is usually attributed to the decision in the case of *Salomon v Salomon (1897)*. This is the case which your law lecturer will expect you to quote. In fact, this case was not the first appearance of the notion of separate legal existence upon incorporation, but is better seen as a later affirmation of the legal concept. After this case it became clear that an incorporated company exists in law nearly as much as you do.

As an analogy to human beings. it has been said is that an incorporated company is, 'born' just like you were. When the company becomes incorporated it has a brain (directors), it has arms and legs (employees), and it dies (if and when it's 'wound up' under the Companies Acts).

Obviously, you can't marry it, but you can do pretty much everything else with it. The company can sue and be sued in its own name. It can borrow money, it can lend money, it can employee staff and managers and it can sack workers if they've done something at work which they really shouldn't have.

Most people realise that a company has its own legal existence without really thinking about it. If, for example, you walk into an Asda store and you slip over on a broken bottle of tomato sauce which an employee has been told to clean up and has failed to do, then you are likely to want some recompense (damages).

Now, you could sue the negligent employee, but it's more likely that you wouldn't. This person is not likely to be insured for this sort of thing, and anyway they are unlikely to be able to pay you much. You wouldn't sue Mr Asda because there isn't one. You would sue Asda the company. If Asda has a dispute with say Guinness, then Asda would sue Guinness the company, or vice versa.

Note that an incorporated company has by law to have the words Ltd or Limited after the company name. In the case of the usually much larger type of limited company, the public limited company has by law to have Public Limited Company or PLC after the name of the company.

This is to ensure that anyone dealing with the company is warned that the company and its members including the shareholders have the protection of limited liability. It is intended to make you aware that if perhaps you supply goods to either of these types of company, and the company runs into severe financial difficulties, then your ability to get your money back is dependent on whether that company has any assets to sell to pay you back. If it hasn't sufficient funds then it would be pointless to sue the company for your money.

I often think that seeing the abbreviations Ltd or PLC has become so common that it is easily possible to forget this is a written warning. If you do forget this you could well find yourself a lot worse off financially should things go wrong.

The two main types of limited liability company

A private limited company

This form of business is by far the most common of all limited companies in the country. Remember that this is the company with Ltd after its name. They are called private companies as, although they issue shares within the company, they cannot sell these shares to the public by means of the London Stock Exchange. A PLC by contrast can sell its shares to the public via the Stock Exchange. This ability is the reason for starting a PLC in the first place. Hence in general a limited company is much more restricted in the amount of capital (money) it can raise for investment and/or expansion. This is why a private limited company tend to remain much smaller than a PLC. Out of interest there are approximately 2 million actively trading limited companies at the time of writing.

How do you start a private limited company?

The current piece of legislation governing companies is the Companies Act 2006. This is a real whopper of an act. You can pull muscles in your back trying to pick it up. I very much doubt that you will be asked to look at the original, but if you decide to look at it, remember to ask a friend to help you lift it down from the library shelf just to be safe.

The process needed to set up a limited company used to be quite involved both legally and financially. At one time to start such a company involved paying a solicitor and/or accountant to do it for you. First, you have to get your company registered with Companies House together with the proposed company name. Nowadays this is much easier to do. You can approach Companies House by post, but the easiest way is to go through the process online. It really is just a matter of a day or two to get your limited liability company up and running. The government website boasts that this process can normally be completed within 24 hours.

The best place to start is Gov.uk "Set up a Limited Company: step by step" This gives you an excellent cost-free introductory guide to getting your company registered at Companies House and setting up the process of incorporation. The main documents which you're going to have to send to the registrar of companies to get a *certificate of registration*, are the *articles of association* and the *memorandum of association*.

The articles of association are the documents which deal with the internal rules and regulations of the company, such as what powers the directors have and how the share capital is to be allocated, etc. The memorandum used mainly to deal with the external regulation of the company, such as the object(s) for which the company was formed. Much of the information which was contained in the memorandum has, since the Companies Act 2006, been shifted to the articles, making nowadays the articles the most important company document.

Currently a private limited company only requires one director.

Now of course if you want to start such a company, you're going to need a company name. This is going to be quite important to you, so it's worth checking whether the name you might want is available. This is where you can have a bit of fun. To find out if a particular name is available you simply go to one of the (free) websites which check whether the name you come up with is or isn't available. Some words are 'restricted or excluded', presumably rude words. I had half an hour of happy Googling the other day by searching something like "free company name checks".

Let me tell you some of the names I was allowed and some that I wasn't. Allowable company names I found were, Spindly Legs Ltd, Plonker Ltd, Dodgy Ltd and Plagiarist Ltd. I was not allowed Trump Ltd, Limited Ltd, Toilet Ltd, Micky Mouse Ltd and Plastered Ltd. I only wish I could tell you the rude names I was and wasn't allowed. I urge you to have a go yourself – it's a real giggle. I only stopped when my wife asked me what I was doing, when she heard a wild giggling sound coming from my study and I realised that I was engaged in a very juvenile activity. What fun it would be I thought to start a publishing company called Plagiarist Ltd.

A public limited company (PLC)

A public limited company is fundamentally the same as a private limited company with the key difference being that a PLC is able to offer its shares for sale (in this country) on the London Stock Exchange. The setting up of such a company entails a few more legal processes to be overcome and, as of today, you have to raise £50,000 of share capital to go ahead. Normally you would attempt to raise this capital by advertising in various newspapers or online, saying that you're going to be setting up a PLC and what the purpose of the company and its objectives will be. This is the called the *company prospectus*. You are inviting prospective purchasers to buy shares in your new business or promise to buy shares in the near future.

When you have reached or exceeded the magic £50,000 you can obtain a trading certificate and off you go.

The setting up of a new PLC involves a few more steps than I have outlined here, but I'm sure that you get the idea. As with a private limited company, the process is fairly straightforward. Once more the Companies House website gives further details of the setting up process of a PLC. All the larger companies you can think of are PLCs – Barclays, Ford, Tesco, Microsoft, W H Smiths, to name but a few, are all public limited companies.

Some of these have grown so large as to become international operations, taking advantage of their ability to raise capital by the sale of shares in many different countries. As with a private limited company you'll need to obtain articles and a memorandum of association and get issued with a certificate of trading. Currently a PLC requires a minimum of two directors. A PLC also requires that you appoint a qualified company secretary. This person has many responsibilities and is charged with ensuring that the company complies with all its duties as laid down by the Companies Act 2006.

The sole purpose of the PLC is to take advantage of the much larger availability of capital which comes possible from the sale of shares on the London Stock Exchange (in the UK). As large amounts of investable capital become available, PLCs can use this money to invest in their businesses, allowing them to grow to a vast size and thereby take advantage of scale economies.

This process, we are told, can bring the average costs of production down and these cost savings can then be passed onto us as consumers. This is only the case, of course, as long as the PLCs have competition. A glance at the amount of money the average household currently spend on food as a proportion of their income, for example, shows that these cost savings have been very substantially achieved. The same cost reductions have been achieved with just about everything which is mass produced and sold in every modern economy throughout the world.

How to simplify the process of setting up a limited company or PLC

This is how to set up your own incorporated company whether a private company or a PLC very quickly and at a small cost. Since traditionally setting one or other of these companies was a relatively expensive and long-winded process, other firms began to undertake this process themselves. So, they would (and still do) set up ready-made incorporated businesses which don't yet actually trade. They then sell these 'off the shelf' companies to whoever wants to buy such a company.

This is entirely legal and can save a lot of time and worry about whether you've filled in all the forms correctly. It's called buying an 'off the shelf' company as it's the same as buying a suit of clothes from a shop rather than going to a tailor and getting a suit of clothes made specially for you. The cost of buying a ready-made company is surprisingly low. I checked the other day and the price for a fully formed private limited company online varies from about £15 to £99 depending on the package you might want. For example, with the higher priced companies, as part of the package, you would not only get a fully formed company but also the use of a London address for a given time. Various other packages offered a company bank account being already set up for your company as part of the deal.

You can use exactly the same process to buy a ready-made public limited company, although this will cost you more as the legal requirements are more complicated. The cost is actually surprisingly small. Go online and check out the current costs.

In principle you could buy one of these companies online and use it to set up and sell your own ready-made companies. I think you would find the competition quite fierce though.

Piercing/lifting the corporate veil

It's worthwhile taking a look at this as it's a favourite area for questions to arise in business law. Let me explain. Think of a wedding ceremony taking place and imagine the thin piece of material which covers the face of the bride as she goes through the wedding ceremony itself. What the bride is wearing is, of course, a veil. Now, writers and practitioners of law (and business people) have realised for a long time that as the process of incorporation produces an entity which is entirely legally separate from the person or people who set the organisation up in the first place, this is an ideal vehicle for fraud.

I really don't want to give you ideas which may well get you into a great deal of trouble, but imagine the following made up example: I decide to set up a small private limited company. I may do this online to save time, but whichever method I use, I end up with a limited company which we'll call, 'Paul Bates Co. Ltd'. Now I am able to trade by using the company name.

I rent a large warehouse and I get on the phone and call up every manufacturer and wholesaler of electrical good I can think of. I ask, "can you supply me with computer equipment, TVs fridges, freezers, toasters, microwaves and washing machines please?"

The normal method of paying for such items is by using what is called trade credit. This means that you are able to get hold of these items but only have pay for them 30 to 60 days after you've taken delivery and sold the goods. So, I have at least 30 days before anyone will want to be paid for anything that they've supplied me with. Now I wait three weeks as my warehouse fills up with goods. About three days before I have to pay for any of them. I announce, "Massive Sale. Everything must go!" I sell everything in my warehouse for cash as cheaply as possible. As soon as I have the cash, I disappear to somewhere that I am unlikely to be found (I hope). Probably Cardiff because Cardiff, I hear, has a very low incidence of crime.

The crucial point here is that if I am found by the police, I simply say, "sorry officer, I certainly didn't do it, do I look like a villain? My company may have done it but not me – honest".

What I'm trying to do here is an attempt to "hide behind the corporate veil". I'm using the concept of the incorporated company, having a completely separate legal existence from me, to take the blame for my illegal activities. This is intended to take the blame away from me and direct it to the company itself: using the company as 'front' to hide behind.

Please let me point out again that these sorts of activities are very likely to end up with me becoming a guest of Her Majesty at one of her more private 'rest homes'. I'd probably be out of circulation for about 10 years. Who's going to feed my cats?

Now the concept of piercing or lifting the corporate veil, is where the court may look at alleged attempts by anyone who has set up a limited company for just the sort of purposes as described in my example above. In this example it is highly likely that the court would conclude that I was trying to use the concept of incorporation to hide behind the corporate veil (I was). They can then "lift the corporate veil" and very likely find me guilty of fraudulent activities. Perhaps surprisingly, the courts won't do this as often as you might think.

One explanation for this reluctance by the courts is said to be that it must be shown, very clearly, that these people are actually trying to use the incorporated company format specifically in a fraudulent way, and are not a just complete halfwits trying to run a business – I've met a few of these types – the sort of people who have difficulty with tying up their own shoelaces but tend to start limited companies by the lorry load.

Another reason behind the hesitancy of the courts to intervene in corporate matters, it's been said, is that to overdo court intervention would strike at the heart of capitalism. So, to follow the argument through, too much interference might well frighten off budding entrepreneurs. This might act to reduce the number of new business start-ups and thereby might slowly reduce GDP. The real reasons for the courts rather cautious approach are quite likely to be a mixture of both of these explanations.

As this area is so examinable by people like me, it's worthwhile for you to attach a few cases to this. Check your course specification before you do this and only go ahead if this area is covered in your particular specification (it is quite likely to be).

One good case to remember here is *Guilford Motor Homes v Horne (1933)*.

Guilford Motor Homes v Horne (1933)

Here the facts were straightforward. Horne worked for Guilford Motor Homes Ltd and agreed that when he left this company he would not attempt to 'pinch' any of the customers from Guilford Motor Homes. This was stipulated in the terms of his contract of employment. But when he left Guilford Motor Homes this is exactly what he tried to do. He formed his own limited company and started to contact the customers of Guilford Motor Company asking for their business for himself.

When sued by his ex-employer for doing this, he made out that the promise not to attempt to take custom away from his old employer, applied to him only and not his new company. The court didn't agree and said that Horne had tried to use his new company as a "cloak or sham to engage in business". Effectively then, the court lifted the corporate veil that Horne tried to hide behind.

Depending on the focus of your particular course, this one case may be enough to cover this area. If your course is heavily based on company law then you are going to have collect some more cases. Being able to quote this one case certainly proves that you understand the concept.

When a company becomes a PLC either from the outset or by growing from a smaller private limited company, there are various expressions used to describe the process. Don't worry, they all mean the same thing.

It can be called 'going public', 'obtaining a listing' (adding your company name onto the stock exchange list of PLCs) or 'floating' the company.

Why start A PLC?

The first and most obvious reason for running a company as a PLC is that you're able to issue and sell shares in your company to the public. This means in theory that the amount of capital you can raise is increased enormously compared to a private limited company. Remember that a private limited company does issue shares, but these shares cannot be offered on sale to the general public (this is why it is called a private limited company).

Now, a PLC is theoretically not limited to the sale of shares in its home country. Some of the largest companies in the world issue shares for sale internationally. These are multinational companies (multinational PLCs). Coca Cola is a good example, as my bet is that everyone on the planet has heard of Coke. So, if you are able to sell shares throughout the world, the amount of capital you can raise, whilst not infinite, is gigantic. For any economists listening, this means that potential economies of scale available are unbelievably vast. However, all is not sweetness and light for most PLCs. There are some drawbacks to running a PLC which need to be thought about before going public.

What may put you off of going public

There are several new problems that you will have to face when you are running a public company. One of these is that under company law you must now disclose a great deal of information about the company to anybody who might want to look. This is mainly financial information and information about the proposed future direction of the company. This is for the benefit of existing and prospective shareholders so that they can make informed decisions about whether to buy shares or keep them if they are an existing shareholder. This is fine and is as it should be but, in disclosing all this extra information, you may well be telling your competitors exactly what they want to hear.

Oh yes, we mustn't forget, that now your shares can be bought and sold on the stock exchange, your company could be taken over and you may well be left with nothing to show for all your effort! Shame.

One of the main concerns you may well have as a CEO (chief executive officer) of a PLC is that now you have shareholders to look after. There are many different types of share that a PLC can offer for sale to the general public but the most important to us are called *ordinary* or *equity* shares. The two terms mean the same thing and can be used interchangeably. The term 'equity' you will remember, means fairness. These shares are called equity shares as each share that you own of this type means that you are entitled to one vote at the annual general meeting of the company. This in theory means that you can have some influence on company policy and also on the choice of members on the board of directors – or in principle, the removal of directors.

How much influence you have depends upon the number of shares you hold: one share, one vote: a million shares, a million votes

In practice, of course, as an individual shareholder it's highly unlikely that your individual votes will have much (or no) effect on the outcome of any company decisions. This is because probably you will be a minority shareholder. Majority shareholders who can make a real difference to company decisions, are normally PLCs who often buy shares in other PLCs, or what are called *institutional shareholders*. Institutional shareholders are mainly other large PLCs such as pension funds and insurance companies. So, even if you have a couple of thousand shares in a PLC, institutional investors may hold millions or billions of equity shares. It's easy to see that in any vote you are very likely to be easily outvoted. You don't stand much chance as a small shareholder against the really big boys.

By now you might well be asking, just how 'equitable' are equity shares? You may also be wondering why should anyone bother to buy ordinary shares in a PLC at all?

The answer to this is simple. Equity shares pay a *dividend*, you hope, in each year that they've had a successful trading period. This is a pay out to each shareholder, the amount of which is decided upon by the board of directors. Of course, in bad times it's quite possible that there will be no dividend paid. In these circumstances the company will normally write to each shareholder explaining why they are unable to pay a dividend in the current year, and they will try to encourage you not to sell your shares.

Normally they will say that this is just a temporary situation and they will make up for not paying you any dividends this year, by announcing increased dividends in future years. Whether you believe this is up to you. You may choose to sell your shares and buy shares in a different PLC which is paying dividends. On the other hand, you may decide to hang onto your shares a bit longer. It really depends on your personal view on the future of the company and its previous history of dividend payments.

The other main reason for buying shares is that you hope that if you hang on for enough years, the share price will rise. This is called *'capital gains'*. The history of the stock market tells us that if you buy and keep shares in a reputable company (or better still a number of reputable companies) over a good period of years, their share prices will rise and you can sell them at a later date at a profit. The trouble with this is that some of us just can't wait that long.

Now it's time to take a short, but vital, 5-minute tea break here to explain the importance, in terms of business law, of equity shares. You see as an equity shareholder, you haven't just invested your money in the company by deciding to buy an equity share. Of course, by buying equity shares, you have invested your money in the company. But, as a buyer of an equity share you have legally truly become a part-owner of the company! So, legally, the owners of a PLC are the sum total of all the equity shareholders.

For example, if you buy 5% of the equity shares of a PLC, you actually own 5% of that company. If a PLC has one million shares issued, and you buy one share, then you own one millionth of that company. If it has a billion shares issued and you own one share then you own billionth of the company The commonly held belief that if you can acquire more than 50% of the equity shares of such a company, then you have a controlling interest in that company, is quite true. Hopefully you can see the advantages a majority shareholder has over minority shareholders. Now comes the trouble: as the equity shareholders of such a company actually own the company, how come they don't have much (or no) say in the running of the company? This leads us to the following, admittedly arguable, concept regarding all PLCs.

The divorce of ownership from control

OK, we've now seen that the legal owners of such companies are the equity shareholders, but the people who actually do the day to day managing of the company are the Board of Directors. These people are also responsible for the overall decisions regarding the direction and long-term strategy of the such companies. The trouble, many people argue, is that the directors are responsible for managing millions (sometimes trillions) of dollars or pounds, however you want to measure it, of money which doesn't belong to them. They are using the legal owner's money – our money, if we've bought equity shares in the company. Is this fair?

The answer, as ever, depends on your own point of view. One argument is that all equity shareholders should have some say in running a company of which they part own. Can you see any problems arising here? I can. Let's take an example. PLCs are involved in the production of just about anything you can think of: from cars to ball point pens, mobile phones to toilet paper, clothing, paint, shoes, trousers and gold, coal, oil, diamond and uranium mining.

That's ignoring the service industries such as banking, tourism, insurance (home, personal, car and shipping, to name just a few). That's an awful lot of different products and services across the world I think you'll agree.

Now let me ask you a question: what do you actually know about the production and mass marketing of trousers? Or ladies' underwear for that matter? Be truthful. (Actually, forget ladies' underwear – I don't want to know.)

Anyway, I'm willing to bet the answer is not a lot – same here. So, maybe if we're interested in buying shares in a company which makes and supplies ladies and gents clothing, we should leave it to people who do know what they're doing? i.e. appoint people to the board of directors who have knowledge and experience and proven track record of success in this area. Incidentally, I wouldn't be much of an asset to a company involved in producing toilet paper either (and I have been approached).

The term *divorce of ownership and control* is sometimes written as the *separation of ownership and control* and also (commonly by economists), as the *agency problem*. All three terms mean exactly the same thing. The term agency problem is probably the most appropriate, but you may decide to avoid it as it may not be a term all your law lecturers will generally use in this context. If you do decide to use it, it's probably best to explain what you mean by it. The agency problem arises when you appoint other people to act on your behalf (agents). If you do this, can you always be sure that the appointed people are always acting in your own best interests? Probably not. What many individuals ask is that, can we as shareholders in a large corporation always be sure that directors have us in mind when making their operational decisions? Well, there's plenty of evidence suggesting that indeed they have not. See the chapter on corporate governance for more detail on this.

The shareholder 'problem'

Remember that as a PLC, you now have shareholders in your company. You are under some responsibility to pay these shareholders dividends, often annually or half yearly. The trouble is that this costs your company money. You, as CEO, together with the other members of the board of directors, may prefer to use this money as retained earnings to reinvest back into the company. You're thinking long term – hoping to grow the company in the future. Unfortunately, your shareholders may not be thinking the same thing. It has often been argued that shareholders tend to think only about the short term. Can we really blame them?

Many shareholders rely on the dividends coming from the companies they invest in as part of their annual income (particularly retired people). If they see that their dividends are going to fall then they don't like it. This doesn't apply necessarily to all shareholders, but is does apply to a significant number of them. Enough to worry some PLCs. The question is, can such a large company convince enough shareholders to hold on to their shares in times in which the trading year has been poor, or times when the company may want to keep some of its earnings within the business to inject back into the company? If they can't convince the shareholders of the advisability of doing this, then there may well be a mass sale of shares and the share price will fall hugely. Oh dear...

A question which has occasionally come up in my seminars (and it's a very good question) is, why does the company care at all about its own share price? Just this question was asked by a student a couple of years ago – and you'll remember who you are if you're reading this. Her argument (leading to the question) went along the lines of "If I sell my car to someone for a certain amount of money, I don't really bother if it's resold at some later time for more or less than I sold it for. So, why should a PLC care about its share price once the shares have been sold?" Well the answer is, the company cares a great deal about its share price because if the price becomes very low, it becomes far more difficult to raise future capital. If, for example, the share price is £10 per share then the company only has to sell one share to get £10.

If the share price falls to 10p per share then 100 shares have to be sold to get the same amount of funds. So, no PLC likes to see its share price fall. Simple.

From around 2005 onwards there began to be speculation in the financial press that Richard Branson of the Virgin Corporation may well have been speculating on aspects of the shareholder problem.

Let me quote from the financial expert Robert Peston from his blog "Peston's Picks", 2nd July 2007. He was speculating about the Virgin Media part of the Virgin Group. Robert Peston was, and still is, a highly respected and knowledgeable financial journalist and media presenter. The possibility at the time was that this part of the Virgin Group at least, might be removed from its listing on the stock market and turned into a private limited company.

Peston stated in his blog that if this part of that Virgin Group did become private then, "They would be freed from the onerous requirement to make quarterly announcements of earnings and could be less fettered in the way they invest in the business." On the same point, Elon Musk (boss of Tesla) has been reported as experiencing "enormous pressure from his 'public' shareholders", pressure to take decisions that may not be "necessarily right for the long term" (Steven Vines' 2018 blog, Aug 15th 2018).

An ongoing worry for many large corporations, then, is trying to keep shareholders happy. I think we'll leave them to it, after all we don't get paid to worry about their troubles.

Let's return to the types of business structures where no one loses any sleep over money-grabbing shareholders. These are the types of businesses which you'll remember we left out at the start of the chapter. They are the various types of business partnerships which can be formed. The reason I left this alone before is that one of these types of partnership (which is a relatively new one) includes the process of legal incorporation described above and wouldn't have made much sense to anyone new to this concept.

Partnerships

Forming a partnership seems to be a natural extension to your business for anyone who is self-employed. After all, a partnership seems to offer a great number of attractions. It's not our place here to go into all of these attractions as this is more the province of an economics text.

However, it's normally pointed out that forming a partnership with one or more other people, can increase the possible amount of capital you can inject into your business. It can also increase the amount of expertise available. So, for example, you might know an awful lot about bricklaying but nothing at all about roofing, electrics or plumbing. Put together a partnership and you might well, between the four of you, be able to build houses and sell them. All well and good so far. But textbooks on economics almost always go on to say that by forming a partnership you are reducing your risk by spreading it amongst all of the members of the partnership.

Now in an economic sense this may well be a reasonably accurate statement. But in another sense (legal) you may not be sharing risk at all – in fact you may well, with two partners, be doubling your risk. Equally with three partners, you might well be tripling your personal risk. In a legal sense (and a mathematical one) there is a direct relationship between the number of partners you have and the personal risk you are exposing yourself to.

All will be explained in due course and we shortly take look at a way to protect yourself legally in a partnership arrangement.

I'm not trying to put you off the idea of forming a partnership at all if you happen to fancy it. All I'm pointing out is that if a partnership is your thing then that's absolutely fine. But just be very careful about the type of partnership you choose to form and how you choose to do it.

I once, just a few years ago, had a student who was by all accounts a very entrepreneurial person. He was always quite keen to let us all know in class the latest whizzo deals he'd put together and how much he stood to make. At this time, we were just starting the legal aspects of partnerships, he was very keen to learn. He told us that he'd just formed a business partnership with someone. As we went through the various types of partnership and the legal implications of each, he suddenly stood up, and truly, looking as white as a sheet, excused himself. He mumbled to me that he'd just realised that he'd made a bit of a mistake and could he could he "pop off now" and try to put it right? As far as I know he succeeded in undoing the damage he'd unwittingly done. I hope so. If only he'd waited a week or two…

Ordinary partnerships

We'll start with the most basic (traditional) form of partnership which is variously called an ordinary partnership or a general partnership. This type of partnership is governed by the Partnership Act 1890 and if there is any dispute within the partnership, it's the provisions of this act that the court will apply to settle any disagreements. This type of partnership does not need any formal documentation to set up – so it's very easy to make an agreement with one or more persons and start trading straight away. You could for example decide to go into partnership with someone over a pint in the pub one night. The agreement to start such a business with someone else forms a legally binding agreement – in this case a verbal contract.

But a much cleverer way is to have written agreement (contract) with the other person just as a record as to what you've actually agreed to with your new partner. This forms what is called *using partnership stationary*. If any future disagreement occurs (and believe me it will) then you have written record of, for example, who put what into the partnership, how any profits will be shared out amongst you, and when and how the partnership will become dissolved. Ready-made partnership agreement forms can be downloaded free from the Web.

The big trouble with this form of partnership is that it's not incorporated. Remember we looked at the trouble with not being incorporated earlier? It means that you have no protection at all if and when the business runs into financial trouble. The legal position for each partner is exactly the same as if you are all sole traders. So, you can lose everything you own including your house and any other personal possessions. It gets worse…

In this type of organisation each partner is said to be *jointly and severally liable*. 'Severally' is just a posh word for separate liability. Why this is so dangerous is not only are you as a partner personally liable for the debts of the firm, but any partner can make any other partner liable for any debts run up in the name of the firm. A partner then, unknown to you, could order and get delivered, say 50 Rolls Royce cars, sell them and then disappear with the proceeds. Now you're in big trouble. You'd be left with a rather large and unexpected bill to pay.

If these cars have been ordered in the name of the partnership, then it would be left to you and any other partners to pay for them. This is what I meant when I was wondering earlier whether a partnership really does spread risk. Of course, the term jointly and severally liable only applies to activities done by a partner in the course of the partnership. If a partner personally forgets to pay the mortgage on his or her house and as a result loses it, they can hardly blame the other partners for this.

I expect you can guess by now the type of partnership my rather ill-looking student must have formed – an ordinary one.

Having said the above, there are certain tax advantages to trading as a partnership. If you are trading as a limited company, the company will have to pay corporation tax on profits before the company pays you your salary. You'll then have to pay income tax on your own pay. An ordinary partnership, not being a corporate body, avoids this extra tax. So, the partnership itself isn't taxed, just the members.

Originally the number of members of a partnership was limited to 20. It seems that the thinking behind the original 1890 act was that if a business needed more than 20 members then the more appropriate form of business would be that of a limited company. This 20-member stipulation has now been removed in 2002 by the Regulatory Reform (Removal of 20 Membership Limit) Order. Actually, there were many exceptions to the old rule anyway, so the new ruling is unlikely to make much difference.

In this type of partnership each partner acts as an agent of each other partner. This means that each partner has what is called a *'fiduciary'* duty to each other partner. The term fiduciary really means a special duty of trust, or if you prefer, partners have an ethical duty of trust to one another and to the partnership as a whole.

Partners' main duties are stated within the 1890 act and there are three of them.

- First, all partners have a duty to account to the other partners details of all activities and financial accounts which may affect the partnership as a whole.
- Second, a partner must not obtain any hidden benefits from the partnership which are undisclosed to all of the other partners.
- Third, a partner must not start any other business enterprise which competes with the partnership. This we would refer to today as making sure that there are no conflicts of interests in your business dealings.

It must be said that regardless of the seeming disadvantages of the general partnership business format, many of this type of partnership were set up many years ago and are still successfully running today.

As we have seen, the main disadvantage to the more old-fashioned type of partnership is that it offers no personal limited liability. Putting this another way, just for emphasis, as a partner you have completely unlimited liability. Quite frightening when you see it put this way isn't it? This must be what my student suddenly realised in class and so suddenly did a disappearing act. Consequently, the business risks are very considerable. The risks are at least those of simply trading as a sole trader, but now the risk is in reality magnified by the fact that any other partner can drop you in it. And they can do this without you knowing anything about it – until it's too late.

As a consequence of this, and after much lobbying by numbers of large partnerships, Parliament introduced a new 'hybrid' type of partnership in the form of the Limited Liability Partnership Act in 2000. This is known by the letters LLP which must appear after the partnership name. (In reality English law followed a similar form of partnership introduced in the US some years before).

The limited liability partnership (LLP)

This form of partnership offers a great number of attractions. It is a cross between a limited company and the more old-fashioned traditional partnership form of organisation. Many general partnerships have elected in the years since the act was introduced, to transform themselves into LLPs. This is mainly because by doing so they can take advantage of the huge benefits of limited liability but still retain much of the advantages of the less rigid organisation required of a full blown private limited company. It seems, at least to me, that in those general partnerships which haven't as yet made this transformation, it is quite likely to be due to the fact that they simply haven't yet heard of the possibility of doing so. It looks to make little sense for the majority of traditional partnerships not to make this switch, as it seems an ideal half way solution.

So how do you start an LLP? Well, once again you have to become registered with the Registrar of Companies. The easiest way to get your LLP up and running is online, as with a limited company. Visit the "Set up and run a limited liability partnership (LLP)" page at the government website, gov.uk. It tells you all you need to know and contains a list of easy to follow instructions. Not surprisingly you'll find that you need a minimum of two members and you will need "an LLP agreement that says how the LLP will run". Once established the LLP becomes a separate legal entity. That is, it has become *incorporated*. This means that partners, in most instances, have limited liability nearly exactly the same as do members of a private or public limited company.

There are very many advantages to the LLP form of doing business. Apart from getting away from the huge downside of personal liability, an LLP has the same tax advantages of a traditional partnership in that it does not pay corporation tax but each partner pays only income tax. Being incorporated means that the LLP has perpetual succession which means that it won't end if a member leaves or dies. This is exactly the same as in the more traditional incorporated business.

In short if partnerships are the sort of business organisation which takes you fancy, then what's to lose with an LLP?

Limited partnerships

Finally, with partnerships, we have to mention the limited partnership. This form of partnership is regulated by the Limited Partnership Act 1907. This is a rare (but still existing) form of partnership. Partnership of this type permit one or more partners to have limited liability, but stipulates that at least one partner has unlimited liability. A limited partner is not allowed to take part in the management of the partnership but must contribute an agreed amount of capital.

The liability of the limited partner extends only to the amount he/she has contributed to the partnership. Such a limited partner is also often called a silent or 'sleeping' partner (careful, I do the jokes). Limited partnerships, not surprisingly, are required to register with the Registrar of Companies. There is still some use for this type of partnership in some areas of finance, we're told but as of now they're pretty thin on the ground. This doesn't come as much of a shock as it's so easy these days to establish your business as an LLP or as a private or public limited company. So, the need for this type of partnership has steadily declined over the years.

Please make sure that you remember this rather unusual type of partnership - once again I'm thinking of possible MCQ questions.

Summary

We started this chapter by looking at the oldest and easiest way of starting your own business – by becoming self-employed. Some of the advantages of starting this type of business were given together, with the huge risk this can involve – if your business goes wrong you stand to lose virtually everything which you own.

Then we looked at the legal process of incorporation and how you can start a private limited company or a Public Limited Company (PLC). We said that by going through the process of incorporation you can reduce your business risk to an absolute minimum.

We looked at the legal process of incorporation and how to start your own limited liability company. Then we looked at how you can avoid the legal process of incorporation by buying a ready-made company 'off the shelf'.

We looked at the problem of the ease of using the process of incorporation for fraudulent purposes and what might happen to you if you attempt this. This is the area where the courts might 'lift the corporate veil', and lock you away safely for the good of society and other businesses.

The concept of the 'divorce of ownership from control' was examined and alleged shareholder 'short-termism'. This is often called the 'shareholder problem'.

Finally, we looked at ordinary partnerships, and a much more modern form of partnership, the limited liability partnership. We said that this form of business organisation offers the advantages of ordinary partnerships and that of the safety of a limited liability company.

Before leaving, we took a brief look at limited partnerships, a business format that is little used nowadays.

Revision questions

1. Can you ever see yourself starting your own business on a self-employed basis? If so, why?
2. Why is the process of incorporation vitally important to modern business? Which piece of case law is thought of as producing the most important decision which allowed incorporation to occur in the first place?
3. What is meant by the expression 'divorce of ownership from control'? Do you think this divorce is a problem for modern businesses?
4. What is meant by the 'shareholder problem'?
5. Describe the main types of partnerships and which type would you choose for you own business?

7 Outline of the English and Welsh system of courts

Civil and criminal courts and the tribunal system

The English and Welsh main court systems are split down the middle into two separate structures. There is the civil court system and the criminal court system. As we've mentioned many times before, in business law we concern ourselves almost exclusively with the civil side of things. Having said that, you will be expected to have some knowledge of the workings of the criminal court system. This is because you may well be asked to single out some differences between the two systems. Once more here I have in mind MCQs, where it's easily possible that a question may ask you to pick from three or four possible answers as to whether a named court is a civil or a criminal one. I often set this sort of question, because it's so easy to do.

You'll only be expected to have a working or broad knowledge of how the court systems are organised. The study of law at least in this country, interestingly and perhaps a bit surprisingly, can start at GCSE level. Students start their GCSE law course at the age of 14 years and they take their final exams at 16 years. At this early stage students are often expected to be able to reproduce diagrams showing the hierarchy or pyramid-like structure of the court systems accurately. It's very doubtful if you'll ever be asked to do this on any first-year business law courses. You're just expected to have an outline knowledge about which are the more important courts and which are of lesser importance in the system. You'll also be expected to have a working knowledge of the appeal system. The court structure is based on the system of precedent and sets out clearly which courts are able to tell which other courts what to do. Essentially the structure shows which courts are bound to follow precedents set by courts higher up in the system.

Talking about the appeal system, it's true to say that many students assume that if you don't get the result you wanted in the court of first instance (where your case was first heard), you have an automatic right to appeal to a higher court to try to get the decision changed. This is by no means the situation I'm afraid. What you have to do is to ask the higher court for permission to appeal. This in technical language is called asking for 'leave to appeal' and you might not get this permission. The court acting as an appeal court in this situation, may not agree that there are any grounds for an appeal, e.g. there may be no new evidence to support an appeal.

A favourite question which your lecturers may ask is to get you to explain, in a longer piece of work, what are the main differences between the civil and criminal law systems. A question such as this is likely to be an exam type question or a piece of coursework. As we shall see, there are quite a lot of differences between the two systems. Later I'll give you a list of these main differences. We'll start with the system of civil courts and take a look at the hierarchy (level of importance) of these courts and then we'll take a quick look at the criminal court hierarchy.

Ah yes, we mustn't forget the system of tribunals used in English law. Tribunals are mainly administrative bodies created by acts of parliament and are used mainly to take the pressure off of the more formal and older civil courts.

To demonstrate the system of the hierarchy of the courts, usually law texts will give one or more diagrams for illustration. I've found that such diagrams, although you'd think they would, don't interest students very much at all. They can be pretty complicated looking. However, if you like diagrams and find them a useful way of learning, I'll give you the following website to look at: www.judiciary.uk.

If you click onto this website and follow the links, you'll find excellent charts of the Courts Systems of England and Wales and a diagram showing you the Tribunals Structure Chart. Of course, the website is free to access which is always a very important consideration to me. If you find these charts useful you can print them off and stick them up on the wall of your bedroom.

I don't think that you'll make too many new friends by doing this though, particularly if you've made room for it by tearing down your poster of Status Quo or the Manic Street Preachers.

I have supplied a very simplified couple of these diagrams later in the chapter, as a kind of visual summary. If you need, or want to know in more detail, about court structures, then as I say, log onto the above government website.

One of the areas which is sometimes confusing is that some courts have both a civil and a criminal function. Other courts have a purely civil or purely criminal role. In addition, certain courts can act as what is called a 'court of first instance' and the same court can act to hear appeals from lower courts.

A court acting as a court of first instance is a court in which a particular case is heard for the first time. As we go through the court system, I'll point out the functions which each court can take – they can act either as a court of first instance and/or act as an appeal court.

The Supreme Court

Starting at the very top of the whole court system stands the Supreme Court. Until 2009, the highest court had been the House of Lords (or more exactly, the Appellate Committee of the House of Lords), as the senior judges were members of the House of Lords – the so-called 'law lords'. As members of the House of Lords they could have a hand in framing new laws, which as judges they would then have to apply. There was a 'separation of powers' issue here (see Chapter 1). Creating the Supreme Court and removing the law lords from the House of Lords resolved this. It also resolved any possible confusion, if someone was talking about the House of Lords, as to whether they meant the highest court in the English legal system or a division of Parliament – the one which is sometimes called the 'Upper House'.

You'll still see many references to House of Lords cases, which means that the case you're looking at was heard in highest court at that time. More modern and very important cases since 2009, will be called Supreme Court cases. All you just need to remember is that the two are exactly the same court.

The Supreme Court is often called the final court of arbitration in England and Wales. This simply means that a decision made in this court is the concluding one. There is no higher court to which you can appeal. After the Supreme Court rules on your case, you just have to accept their decision whether you like it or not.

The Supreme Court has both civil and criminal jurisdiction so whether you've been accused of murder or been involved in a multi-million pound business contractual dispute, this is the court which will finally decide your fate. That is, if your case gets this high on an appeal. The Supreme Court only deals with the most significant of cases. Interestingly this, the highest court in the land, used to be bound by its own previous decisions. As a law student I used to think that this was a little bit silly. After all, I used to think, how can it be that this court was forced to follow its own rulings even though some of its decisions were made hundreds of years ago? Where's the scope for flexibility and the ability to change with the enormous transformations which took place in society during hugely long period of time?

Well, in 1966 things changed; the House of Lords issued what was called a practice statement which said that in future the House could change its mind where was deemed, "right to do so". Great. Of course, this now applies equally to the Supreme Court.

At the same date, the ability of the Court of Appeal (see below) to be able to change its mind in certain circumstances, was allowed. The Court of Appeal, however, is not allowed as much flexibility as the Supreme Court in its ability to deviate from its own previous decisions.

The date that practice statement was issued has always been an easy one for me to remember because this was also the year that England finally won the football Word Cup. By all accounts it's also likely to be the last one.

The Court of Appeal

Standing directly below the Supreme Court is the Court of Appeal. In 1966 the court was split into two divisions, the criminal division and more importantly for us, the civil division. The civil division hears appeals on points of law (see Chapter 2) and on questions of fact from cases previously heard in the lower civil courts (the High Court and the County Courts). Effectively, the Appeal Court goes through all of the evidence which was presented at the court of first instance. The court is able to reverse a decision of the lower court, or it can order there to be a retrial in the lower court. The decisions of this court are binding on all lower courts but obviously not upon the Supreme Court – because the Court of Appeal is lower down in the pecking order.

The criminal division of the Appeal Court may hear appeals from the Crown Court (see below) and may *quash* (reject as invalid) a previous court decision or it may substitute a different verdict if it thinks it's necessary to do so. It can also directly hear appeals from the High Court in civil matters. This route of appeal from the High Court is called the 'leap-frog' system. This is because cases occasionally, are allowed to bypass the Court of Appeal and be heard directly by the Supreme Court. These types of cases are extremely rare and only occur on points of law and where the case is "of public importance"

(The leap frog procedure as a possible MCQ do you think?).

The High Court of Justice

Below the Appeal Court is the High Court of Justice. This court is normally referred to just as the High Court. If you use the name 'High Court' only, everyone will know which court you mean.

This court is composed of three divisions:

☐ The Chancery Division – this division deals mainly with company law and the law of tort;

☐ The Family Division – dealing mainly with such matters of adoption of children, divorce matters and matrimonial cases; and

☐ The Queen's Bench Division – which deals (amongst an awful lot of other matters) with very 'serious and sensitive' criminal matters.

Here is another source of confusion, because High Court judges sometimes sit with Appeal Court judges to hear certain cases. When High Court judges are acting in this capacity, they wear red robes – nice!

The High Court also has a supervisory jurisdiction over the public bodies (often local authorities) and tribunals (see below).

Let's take a breath here just for a couple of minutes... I hope you're beginning to see why it's very doubtful if you'll ever be asked to reproduce the structure of the courts in exam conditions – and we haven't finished yet.

We'll move on with the courts which you'll be expected to know a bit more about. These on the civil side are County Courts and on the criminal side, are the Crown Court and the Magistrates' Courts.

The County Court

This is the court you'll be most likely to find yourself in if you, for example, have a contractual dispute or some other civil disagreement with another person or business. The County Court also deals with bankruptcy cases, landlord/tenant disputes and divorce cases (and a whole lot more). At the time of writing, cases in the County Court with claims up to £10,000, are dealt with by the small claims track of the court; claims up to and including £25,000 are dealt with by the court under the fast track system; in cases where a claim may be above £25,000 the multi-track system is used. Remember that this is the court which will hear the vast majority of civil law cases and it is civil cases which you'll be exclusively involved in your business law course.

In cases which are very complicated legally, or the amount of the claim is currently £100,000 or above will be heard in the High Court.

The Magistrates' Courts

This court deals with criminal offences of a relatively minor nature. So, cases of shoplifting (theft), minor assault and most driving offences will all be heard here. Interestingly, it really doesn't matter what criminal offence you've allegedly committed – murder, manslaughter, shoplifting or driving without insurance, the Magistrate Court is where your case will start. If the Magistrates Court feels that it doesn't have sufficient power of sentencing the offender, then the case will be moved up to be heard in the Crown Court, which has virtually unlimited powers of sentencing.

Currently the maximum sentence that can be imposed by magistrates is limited to 12 months in prison. That is, six months for one offence. If you're found guilty of two offences, then the total becomes 12 months. Financially, the maximum you can be fined is £5,000. Clearly these maximums seem acceptable if you've been found guilty of stealing a box of Smarties from your corner shop, but they don't look too good if you're found guilty of murder (or even a series of murders). This is why if you happen to be accused of something as bad as this, the magistrates will automatically refer your case up to the Crown Court.

Magistrates deal with over 95% of all minor crime each year. Obviously, this leaves around 5% of crimes to be referred up to the Crown Court where the case will be heard by a judge and a jury. The magistrates deal with what are called *summary* offences. The word 'summary' here really just means offences considered to be of lesser importance. These include minor assault on a person, most road traffic offences, most shoplifting and "offensive behaviour in public places", whatever that might mean?

Indictable offences are much more serious wrongdoings and are automatically heard by the Crown Court. Examples of some of these would be murder, manslaughter, armed robbery and grievous bodily harm amongst many others. Worth noting is that there are a range of 'middle of the road' offences, which could possibly be either a summary or an indictable offence depending upon its severity. An example here could be theft. Shoplifting is an offence of theft, but you could be accused of stealing a packet of 20p mints from Asda, or theft of £10 million in gold jewellery from a neighbour who happened to have it lying around their house.

Where such offences occur, it's the value of the stolen items which can determine whether you're likely to be tried summarily by a magistrate or by the Crown Court on indictment.

In a few cases you, the accused, can have the choice of being tried by the magistrates or by judge and jury in the Crown Court. If this happens to you, you have a lot of serious thinking to do. "Why should this be?" I hear you ask. Well, statistically if you choose to be tried in the Magistrates' Court, you're far more likely to be found guilty. But remember that the powers of sentencing are quite restricted in a Magistrates Court. If you elect to go the Crown Court route, to be heard by a judge and jury, you're far more likely to found innocent. But, please don't forget that if you're found guilty in this higher court, their powers of sentencing are practically unlimited.

The statistics speak for themselves. I suppose your decision about which route to choose might well depend on whether you actually did commit the offence or not. These half-way offences are often called hybrid offences. I've added the above paragraph for your personal interest and information because it's the Magistrates Court that most of my students seem to find themselves in most of the time...

In more recent years, magistrates have been able to deal with a range of civil offences in addition to their criminal function. So nowadays the court is able to deal with family and marriage disputes, adoption of children, granting licences to pubs and restaurants, etc. You'll also find yourself facing the magistrate if you've put off paying your council tax for too long.

Below are two diagrams showing the English law court systems. I really have tried to trim these diagrams back as far as I can while hoping that you can still grasp the overall system.

It's worth me repeating myself here, in that no sane law lecturer at this level is going to expect you to get out your pencil box and draw accurate diagrams of the court system. Any law lecturer is, however, likely to be really annoyed if you think that the Supreme Court comes before the County Court when you're accused of some civil offence. I really think it's enough for you to get a visual imprint of the following two diagrams or any similar ones that you like the look of. In reality the whole system is immensely complicated as you will see if you take a look at the gov.uk website.

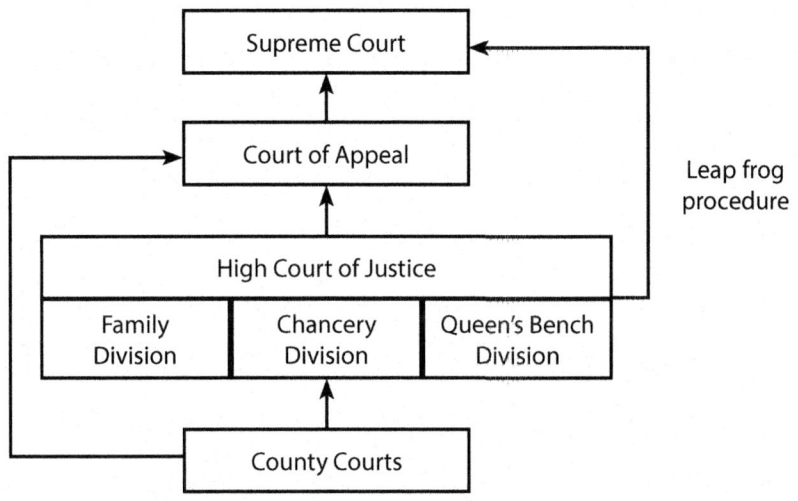

Figure 7.1: The main civil court appeal system

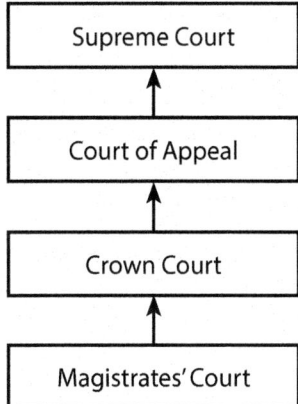

Figure 7.2: The main system of appeals in the criminal court

Note: In both systems, precedent flows from the highest court to the lowest. The arrows show the main appeal routes

Superior and inferior courts

Let's finish off with the court systems by stating which are the so-called 'superior' courts and which are the 'inferior' courts. You'll also need to know which courts make precedents, which must be followed by lower courts and which don't. Then we'll point out the major differences between the civil and criminal systems. This should cover you, or at least give you a good starting point, for the civil/criminal legal distinctions, as this is very popular area for exam questions.

It's not good enough for a student to answer such a question with what one of my students once wrote, "well if you don't know the differences by now, I'm certainly not going to tell you". Sometimes I just wonder…

The superior (or Senior Courts) are the Supreme Court, the Court of Appeal, the High Court and the Crown Court. These courts make precedents which must be followed by the courts lower in the hierarchy.

The inferior (or Lower Courts) are the County Courts and the Magistrates' Courts. These two courts don't make precedents. I feel a bit sorry for them sometimes – it does seem like a bit of a shame for them don't you think? After all, they undoubtedly put a lot of effort into their work.

Some of the main differences between the civil and criminal systems

A. The case names are different. In civil law, one person is *suing* another person or business. In criminal law, a person or business is being *prosecuted* by the state. The case names in the civil system are those of the person or business suing and the person being sued. So, you'll see a case name such as *Robinson v Jones (2020)*. In a criminal case you'll see *R v Adams (2020)*. Here 'R' stands for *Regina* or *Rex*, meaning 'Queen' or 'King' depending on who is currently reigning. Of course, the Queen or King doesn't do the prosecuting, as this is left nowadays to the CPS (the Crown Prosecution Service). For business law purposes, you can largely ignore any case with an R at the start of its name. Don't bother trying to look up the above two cases – I made them up.

B. The whole principle behind the two systems is quite different. In civil cases the object of a court is to discover whether one party is *liable* or not. If a person or business is found liable, the main object is to ensure that the 'injured' party gets appropriate compensation. In a criminal case the purpose of the court is to discover whether the party prosecuted is *guilty* or not. So civil law is designed to ensure that a person or business have their rights upheld. The purpose of the criminal law is mainly to punish the offender.

C. The outcome of a civil case will normally be a payment of damages (monetary compensation) to the party found liable. Other equitable remedies may be available such as specific performance, etc as discussed before. In a criminal case a guilty party may be sentenced to a period of time in prison or a fine (or both).

D. A civil case will take place within the civil law court system which will usually start at the County Court. A criminal case will be heard within the criminal court system. All criminal cases will start at the Magistrates Court and depending on the seriousness of the case may move up to be heard at the Crown Court.

If you're aware of the above points, this should be enough to get you through most questions on civil/criminal differences. As ever, of course there is more to this than I'm able to give you here, so again keep your eye on any hints (and there will be hints) that your lecturers may give you in the revision period leading up to your exams.

Overview of the tribunal system

After the end of the Second World War, there began to be a fundamental change concerning how society should regard itself. Starting just after the war in Europe ended, we saw successive governments becoming more and more involved in the internal workings of society. The old *laissez faire* attitude of governments, which really meant leave it alone and it might sort itself out or, even better, problems might go away altogether, began (thankfully) to change in a fundamental way. This new attitude had been voiced even before the war finally ended.

A leading light in the new labour party was Aneurin 'Nye' Bevan, who was the Labour Minister for Health. In the 1945 general election the Labour Party won a landslide victory, which upset Winston Churchill a fair bit by all accounts. The incoming Labour Party government began to introduce far reaching social policies, the like of which had never been seen before in this country.

These included the introduction of the National Health Service – mainly as a result of Nye Bevan's activities – and the expansion of state funded education for all. This was the start of what has now become known as the 'welfare state'. Apart from these fundamental changes, we saw for the first time, acts of parliament covering town planning and acts concerning housing and rent restrictions. In a sense it was a wide-ranging reversal of governmental *laissez faire* attitudes towards society, which had been in existence for a very long time.

Each of these new areas, which the government saw fit to introduce into society, needed a system of regulation and a system of resolving the considerable number of disputes which were bound to occur. This is the period which saw the growth of administrative tribunals, which were put in place to deal with disputes between ordinary individuals and the sections of government which were administering the new acts. Obvious example here, and those which almost everybody has heard of, are the Employment Tribunal, Rent

Tribunal and the Asylum and Immigration Tribunal. All of these tribunals, and very many more, are nowadays very active on a daily basis.

Why were they needed?

One obvious point which many students quite rightly make is that couldn't all these new types of civil disputes be dealt with by the ordinary civil law system of courts which we already had in existence?

The answer is that yes, they could be dealt with by the ordinary civil court system. But the main counterargument is that if we allowed the existing courts to deal with the unavoidable increase in dispute resolution, all we would do is to clog up the civil court system. This it was argued, would lead to huge backlogs in court hearings which may lead to collapse of the system.

So, the system of tribunals was set up to take the pressure off of the civil court system. They were introduced in a very much 'as needed' approach, so very few tribunals are organised in exactly the same way as every other tribunal.

Structure of tribunals

The essence of tribunals is that they're normally comprised of a panel of three individuals (the 'tri' bit of the name gives this away). One of these three will be legally qualified and the other two will be experts in the area to be examined. A tribunal is much less formal than an ordinary court, but usually Legal Aid (government funding of legal services for lower-income people) isn't available.

There is a *first-tier* of tribunals where a case will first be heard, and an *upper* tribunal which act to hear appeals from the first tier. Tribunals are said to have certain advantages over the more formal civil court system in that they are able to make decisions much more quickly and are not bound by their own previous decisions.

Tribunals are subject to control by the High Court (Queen's Bench Division) by a process called *judicial review*. Judicial review is sometimes referred to as supervisory jurisdiction which allows the High Court, in certain situations, to overturn a decision of a tribunal.

Oh, I'd better also point out that the tribunal system is relatively cheap – always an important factor where law is concerned.

Summary

We first noted that the English and Welsh court system is split into two areas of jurisdiction: the civil system and the criminal system.

It was noted that although you'll be expected to have a working knowledge of the court systems, it's doubtful if you'll ever be expected to reproduce diagrams of the complete system, especially under exam conditions. A government website address was provided through which you can access complete diagrams of the civil and criminal court systems and of the system of tribunals.

We noted that one of the complications of the court system was that some courts can act as courts of first instance and/or as appeal courts when hearing different cases.

We then considered the most important court in the land. This is the Supreme Court which replaced the Appellate Committee of the House of Lords in 2009. Since the Practice Statement of 1966, this court has been able to deviate from any of its prior decisions. This introduced more flexibility in the system than was possible before 1966.

Then we looked at the Court of Appeal which stands just below the Supreme Court. The Court of Appeal was split into the civil and criminal divisions, also in 1966. This court is able to reverse lower court decisions, substitute a different verdict from the earlier one or order there to be retrial.

We worked down the hierarchy and next looked at the High Court of Justice (normally just called the High Court). The High Court has three divisions, each with its own jurisdiction. The High Court also has a supervisory jurisdiction over tribunals and public bodies.

We then mentioned the Crown Courts which dealt with the majority of serious criminal cases, with a judge and a jury. We followed with a look at the Magistrates' Courts which deal with around 95% of all less serious criminal offences, and the County Courts which deal with civil cases concerning contract law and tort (the areas which interest us).

We gave a short comparison of the civil and criminal court systems as this is a highly examinable area. Some of the main differences between the two systems were given.

We finished with an overview of the tribunal system which was introduced after the end of the Second World War. This was because governments of the time began to take more of an interest in the welfare of society, and introduced more acts of parliament than ever before which affected ordinary individuals. Disputes between ordinary individuals and the new state bodies needed a more specialist, quicker and cheaper system of resolving disputes. Tribunals, it was said, would be more efficient than the ordinary civil court system which would have been quickly clogged up by the increasing amounts of disputes which were emerging and which required speedy decisions to be made. Examples here are the Rent Tribunal and the Employment Tribunal, which acts as a form of arbitration between employers and employees.

Revision questions

1. What is the function of the Supreme Court in English and Welsh law?
2. Do you think that it's important that the Supreme Court should be able to deviate from its previous decisions? If so why?
3. Give four differences between the courts and cases heard by the civil and criminal courts.
4. What types of cases are the magistrates court able to hear?
5. Is it possible to appeal a decision from a first-tier tribunal?

8 Employment law

Employment law is a big element in most, if not all, first-year business law courses. This area is best approached by viewing it as being split into two sections. The first section concerns the nature of the agreement between the employer and the employee. This forms a contract (the contract of employment), so your knowledge of general contract law is useful to you here – including express and implied terms in contracts, etc.

The second section concerns the very many rules surrounding such things as the difference between unfair and unlawful dismissal, what may happen if you're subject to redundancy, and so on. Most of this area is now governed by statutes, of which the most important is the Employment Act 1966. Disputes are generally heard by Employment Tribunals rather than a standard civil court. Disputes within the area of employment law may involve the use of case law in a civil court regarding such areas as breach of your contract of employment, or the application of statutory law by an employment tribunal.

The first section, concerning the type of contractual relationship you may have (or not have) with your employer, is the area where you're most likely to be asked to produce an essay or answer a longer written question in an exam. This is where you have to know some case law. As always, the more you know the better. The second section is, by the nature of the many different rules and regulations involved, the area which is most suited to multiple choice questions. Here unfortunately, you just have to keep reading and re-reading the information and hoping you've managed to remember enough facts which may come up in an MCQ exam for you to do well. I hate to have to say this but MCQs are really not much more than a memory test…

Most law lecturers, for reasons given in an earlier chapter, are likely to give you some hints about which areas to concentrate for the longer questions in the exam but it's difficult to give hints about MCQs. This is because it's so difficult to give any hints here without giving away specific questions.

Unless you're doing some specialist type of business law, which is unlikely in your first year, unfortunately you'll have to be pretty familiar with both of these sections in the exam. Once again let me remind you to check your unit handbook which should give you the breakdown of how your exams are set out to see if you're likely to face MCQs which might include employment law.

Because of the nature of the second part of employment law, this is where you're likely to face the more intricate questions of the different types of dismissal and so on. These types of questions still exist, because it's so easy for your lecturers to set MCQs which can test very far reaching areas of knowledge. At least that's why I do it. Also, MCQs are so easy to mark. Particularly if marked electronically.

It's worth mentioning that a great deal of the modern law surrounding employment has come from our previous membership of the European Union. Pretty much all aspects of this law have been merged into English law, but questions have arisen as to what the effects might be on employment law once we fully leave the European Union. As virtually all aspects of European law have now been integrated within English law, most authorities suggest that for the greater part that's where it will stay. We won't be likely to see any more changes coming from Europe from now on. Changes in this area of law in the future will come from new acts of parliament or from changes made by English case law.

Section 1: Contracts of employment

It may seem strange, but you might be working in a full or part time job thinking that you are an employee, only to discover that if this is ever tested in court, in fact you are actually not an 'employee' at all. I'd better explain that one of the first difficulties is that, for a long time, the idea of whether you are an employee in the normally accepted understanding of this word or not, was rarely questioned. But, with the rise in more modern forms of employment such as job sharing, zero hours contracts, the whole issue of the gig economy and so on, the question of which type of worker you might be, has come more into question.

A current trend within employment is the so-called gig economy which has brought its own legal problems. If you haven't heard of the gig economy yet it's pretty certain you soon will. For example, a topical question is what employment status does an Uber driver have? Often individuals working in these newer forms of employment are referred to as 'atypical' workers. This term would also cover people who work from home and people who work for various agencies. There has been a recent resolution, of sorts, of the situation regarding the worker status of Uber drivers – in 2021, the Supreme Court decided that they are 'workers' and entitled to statutory rights as employees. My guess is that this story is far from over. Keep your eye on the newspapers for further developments in this area.

Under the Tribunals, Courts and Enforcement Act 2007, employment disputes are now heard in a first-tier employment tribunal. As with most tribunals there is normally a right to appeal your case in an Upper Appeal Tribunal. An appeal is normally heard on a point of law, and legal aid for these appeals is normally available. A 'point of law' is a question to be decided as to what the law actually is on the particular issue at hand and how should this law be applied to the facts of a current case. Most of the case law which we'll use in this chapter was decided well before the advent of employment law tribunals but the decisions of these earlier cases are still major precedents in this area of the law today. This is why we continue to use these cases, as they remain exceedingly relevant and are highly influential in employment law tribunals.

Why does it matter as to what type of employment relationship you have, you may well ask? Well it matters a great deal because, depending upon what type of employment you may be deemed to have, legal rights and protection afforded by the law could be quite different from that which you thought you might be entitled to. Traditionally your employer is responsible, amongst other things, for collecting your income tax through the Pay as You Earn (PAYE) scheme and collecting your National Insurance payments (NI).

Most of us have probably never had to be involved with any of this at all – probably never given it a thought apart from wondering why so much income tax is taken from our pay packets. Depending on the type of employment you have, your employer may (or may not) be responsible for your holiday pay, redundancy payments and any sickness pay which may be due to you and/or maternity and/or paternity leave.

This is why it's so important to discover exactly what an 'employee' actually is – the answer may affect your legal position if you're threatened with redundancy (with or without pay), the position if you become ill – will you be paid sickness pay or not, and should you receive holiday pay or not?

The main act covering employment law is Employment Rights Act 1966, the ERA. This act gives a definition of what an 'employee' is. The trouble is that this definition is quite wide ranging and therefore needs interpretation in many cases. This is where the older common (case law) comes in. The courts have, for many years, been involved in attempting to decide in individual cases whether a person is actually an 'employee' or not for the reasons given above.

Let me give you an example of the difficulty involved here. Assume that one day you find that your cold-water system has suddenly sprung a leak. Water is spraying everywhere covering your pizza and chips or curry and chips (you're a very multicultural student). Oh, dear what to do?!

Well, what you'll probably do if you've got any sense, is phone a plumber. How long you'll have to wait is anybody's guess. Eventually a plumber turns up and after 10 minutes fixes your leak. Now, the question is, is the plumber working for you or not? Certainly, while the plumber is in your house fixing the leak, he/she is in a sense working for you. Does that make you an employer? I think you'd be a bit surprised if the plumber said, "right chief, the leak's all fixed that'll be £500. I've also added £50 on top towards my holiday pay". The £500 for 10 minutes of a plumbers' work probably wouldn't surprise you. In fact, you'll probably feel you got off lightly. The extra £50 added to go towards his holiday pay might well cause you to raise your eyebrows just a little bit.

These are the sort of difficulties facing the courts. Our plumber, for example could be self-employed or could be in a full-time employee relationship with a firm of general builders. That same firm of builders might equally employ full time bricklayers and plasterers. This ambiguity also appears in many other occupations – university lecturers for example.

Both plumbers and university lecturers can quite easily be employees or independent contractors working for themselves. A lecturer can in fact work for several different universities – so called 'doing the rounds'. If a lecturer does this then he/she is much more likely to be self-employed. Others lecturers are employed solely by one university. The same principle holds with supply teachers. Are they self-employed or employed by an agency? It's not always easy to tell.

Employed or self employed?

The example above illustrates the need to emphasise the crucial difference in law between an employee of a company and that of an independent self-employed contractor. An employee is said to be employed under a contract *of* service(s) whereas an independent contractor is said to be employed under a contact *for* service(s). There have been many marks lost (particularly in MCQs) for not knowing the difference in the above sentence between the '*of service*' and the '*for service*' elements in the sentence.

Our plumber then, is quite likely to be an independent, self-employed person. I only say this because most plumbers tend to prefer to operate on a self-employed basis. This is an example of the question of whether this person is actually being employed under a contract *for* service rather than under a contract *of* service. We'll see later how this difference, which is seemingly quite a minor one, turns out to have a vital importance in employment law disputes, and liability for careless acts done while at work. It is also a fertile area for exam questions and assignment work in employment law.

The main tests the courts have been forced to develop in an attempt to try to work out if a person is 'employed' are given below. This is where the case law comes in – you'll be expected to know at an absolute minimum one case for each test. Sorry to repeat myself, but as you know, I always say: you cannot know enough case law – (actually I'm not really that sorry).

Tests to determine whether a person is or is not an employee

- The **control** test – how much control does the employer have over the employee while they are at work?
- The **integration** test – how much work does the employee perform which its integral to the business?
- The **multiple** test – where the court looks at all the factors in each case including both of the above. This is the more modern approach and is sometimes called the '**economic reality**' test.
- The **mutuality of obligations** test. This looks at the question of whether the supposed employer and supposed employee have established a level of obligations towards each other sufficient to establish that there is actually is a full employer/employee relationship.

We'll take each of these one by one and add in some other and observations as we go.

The control test

This is historically one of the oldest approaches. In the 1800s the approach to employment was based on the age old 'master and servant' relationship. This had been the nature of the employment relationship for most people from time immemorial. The approach to all modern employment law is essentially still based on this old master/servant relationship.

To explain, for centuries, as you will know, the economy was mainly an agricultural one. In each area there would be the Lord of the Manor and the rest of us would be workers, often called 'serfs'. Serfs were the underlings, the common people who did the manual work. The master ultimately would be the Lord of the Manor (or Squire). The Lord of the Manor would tell us, the serfs, what to do and we would do what he said. He would, at least while we were working for him, be our lord and master. Incidentally, we will be seeing this relationship appearing again below under the heading of *Vicarious liability*.

Out of this rather old-fashioned arrangement springs the control test. We were under the control of the lord. The idea is that during the period when the industrial revolution started to happen and workers began to move from the country to the new towns and cities to work in factories, we were still under the 'control' of our new employers.

So, the concept of master and servant was transferred from agricultural workers to workers in factories. Depending upon whom you work for, this master/servant relationship still seems to exist, at least in the minds of some employers, today. Many of you may know this to your cost.

One of the very earliest of cases on the control test is seen *Yewen v Noakes (1880) LR6 QBD 350*. Here it was said that an employee "is a person subject to the command of his master as to the manner in which he will do his work". At the time the judge made this statement it made sense. However, as attitudes towards work and the nature of work itself developed over the years, this test began to look a bit outdated, to say the least. As mentioned, do we really like to still think of our employers as our masters and being under their control?

As time moved on an updated form of test began to be called for. This was provided by Lord Denning in *Stevenson, Jordan & Harrison v MacDonald & Evans (1952) 1 TLR 101* (it is enough to refer to this case as *Stevenson v MacDonald*).

The integration test

The integration test was first introduced in *Cassidy v Ministry of Health (1951) 2KB 343*. This case is actually one involving vicarious liability. We'll be looking at vicarious liability later in this chapter.

Lord Denning stated in this case that a person is to be seen as an employee if he "is employed as part of the business and his work is done as an integral part of the business". He went on to say that a person would not be an employee if his work is not integrated into the business but is only "accessory to it". I think I can see what Lord Denning meant here – sort of at least.

The trouble was that in later cases other courts didn't seem to be able to work out what Lord Denning actually meant by these statements. Unclear statements are never a good thing when they come from a judge, but are by no means uncommon. Actually, it is a bit uncommon for Lord Denning, who was normally known for his extremely clear reasoning and pronouncements in hundreds of other cases.

Anyway, although this new test was *prima facie* an improvement on the older control test, it was soon realised that it was going to be a bit difficult to apply in practice as it seemed so subjective. For example, what does "integrated into the business" actually mean? Integrated into the busines is quite a difficult thing to quantify. Also, assuming we could measure aspects of this integration, how far integrated into the business would a person have to be to be deemed an employee?

The integration test began fairly rapidly to fall into disfavour, mainly because of the evolving employment and changing working practices which were occurring. So, the use of flexible, part time and supply workers which increased greatly since this time (and still is increasing) raised questions as to whether these types of persons are sufficiently "integrated" to legally become employees? After all it was argued, the use of these newer types of workers must be vital to the operation of the firm, otherwise firms wouldn't use them.

It was, and still is, argued that all that firms are doing here is an attempt to reduce their overhead costs in terms of their administrative outlays by the use of such workers. In addition, it was quickly pointed out, these types of workers have much reduced legal rights and duties compared to full blown employees. Using this type of worker was seen then as simply a devious method by which firms could reduce their costs. Importantly, trade unions didn't like it one bit.

Largely owing to the difficulty of implementing the test, it wasn't adopted widely by subsequent courts. The whole concept of integration as a test of the status of an employee was heavily criticised in the next case, which we'll look at to describe the more modern approach taken by the courts.

The mixed test or the economic reality test

The leading case on the mixed test is one you really will have to get to know. The case is *Ready Mixed Concrete v Ministry of Pensions and National Insurance (1968) 2 QB 497*. The reason why this case is so illuminating is that here the court pointed out that there were many more issues that have to be looked at rather than simply concentrating on aspects of control and integration. The whole of the circumstances of each case must be considered before a court can declare its decision.

The case is highly relevant to us in modern employment law. The court had to decide whether drivers used by the Ready Mixed Concrete Company were actually employed by the company or were self-employed. There was a tax implication involved here so you can be sure that the Ministry of Pensions and National Insurance were willing to chuck as much money at their lawyers as possible to get the result they wanted (don't mention this in an exam).

The company decided that they would introduce a new scheme for drivers where the drivers would become owners of the lorries which they used to deliver concrete to the customers of the company. This was called their new 'owner driver' scheme. To achieve this, they effectively got the drivers to agree to be sacked from their original jobs and then, after they had bought their lorries, to be employed under a new contract with the company (can you see trouble coming here?)

Now, under the new contract the drivers all had to agree to wear a standard company uniform and to pay themselves for the cost of keeping their lorries in good roadworthy condition. In addition, the drivers were to be allowed to choose which route they could take to each customer and were even allowed to pay for another alternative driver to take over their shift if for some reason they couldn't or didn't want to work that particular day. They could also decide for themselves which hours of work suited them.

The question for the court to decide was this: were the drivers now self-employed of were they employees of the company? The trouble was that some aspects of this new contract made it look as if the drivers were employed by the company and other aspects seemed to look like they were now independent contractors (i.e. self-employed) – what would you decide? It's a tough one.

The court decided that the lorry drivers were in effect running businesses of their own. Therefore, they were no longer employees of the company. They decided this on a number of grounds. Importantly for us, the court said that although an element of control was important it was not the only factor that needed to be considered. The element of control was evident in that the drivers had to wear identical uniforms but there was also a great importance to be put on the ability of the drivers to be able to substitute replacement drivers should they want or need to. Company risks were also to a large extent now transferred to the drivers as they had to pay for the costs of running and repairs of their own vehicles.

Crucially then, the court decided that contract was better viewed as a contract *of* services rather than a contract *for* services. Therefore, the drivers were no longer employed by the company but had become self-employed.

On this exact point I became friendly with a milkman a few years ago. He's called Gary. He's a lovely bloke and he tells me that he really enjoys his job as milkman. Why he's lucky is that he, unusually, has skills which most milkmen don't have. He's qualified as a blacksmith. The dairy which employs him, which I shouldn't really name, were trying to get him to become self-employed and buy his own milk float. He really didn't want to do this and actively resisted it.

He was quite happy working as an employee and didn't want any changes. His employer was trying to force him into this unwelcome change of employment. He's currently fighting this action by the dairy in the employment tribunal and as yet doesn't know what the outcome will be. He tells me that if he's forced to become a self-employed milkman, he'll simply quit the job and start on his own as a blacksmith. He and his union are taking his case to the employment appeal tribunal and I wish him all the best with it. As you can see, this stuff is really law in action.

The truth is that there are huge monetary and legal advantages to companies encouraging workers to become self-employed rather than to be employees and to remain on the company payroll. It can reduce company costs and reduce the legal obligations of the company. This is the main reason that we're seeing the rise of so many 'alternative' forms of so-called employment, some of which we've mentioned above.

In several later cases there developed a new method the court may choose to use in order to try to settle the question of employment status. A good case to use here on this point is *Carmichael v Natural Power PLC (1999) 1 WLR 2042 (HL)*. In this case the concept of a 'mutuality of obligations' which may exist between the alleged employer and employee is questioned.

Here two ladies worked as tour guides in a power station, (this actually sounds like an interesting job). They were employed on a "casual, as required" basis. The arrangement was that they worked when the hours of work were offered but only when they chose to work. So, they could accept work or reject it as suited them. They weren't paid any holiday or sickness pay but the law at the time didn't then specify that these types of payments had to be made. The arrangements I'll think you'll agree were very flexible.

A dispute arose because the ladies insisted that they hadn't received full written particulars of their jobs as required under The Employment Rights Act 1966. The ladies bought their case to an employment tribunal but then appealed their case to the House of Lords. The House of Lords decided that as there was no obligation on the ladies to accept work if they didn't want to accept it, they were not employees. In this case the court decided that there wasn't sufficient "mutuality of obligations" between the parties for the work agreement to amount to a full contract of employment.

A mutuality of obligations concerns the extent to which an employer has an obligation to provide work (with pay) and the obligation a worker may have to accept the work and supply that work on a personal basis. As a reminder here, think of our lorry drivers in the above case who could supply alternative drivers if it suited them.

A good essay or exam question here would be how might the court have used the concept of mutuality of obligations in the Ready Mixed Concrete case had the concept existed at the time of the case?

As the agreement with your employer forms a contract, there will be a number of terms in the contract which are not express but will be implied within the contract. These have, over a number of years, been implied into such contracts by common (case) law. Terms can also be implied into such contracts which come from other sources. Two of these other sources are terms implied by statute (for example the Working Time Regulations 1998) and terms which are occasionally implied into employment contracts by trade usage and custom.

It might be a good idea here to take a quick look back at Chapter 2 on implied terms in contracts just to refresh your memory. It's worthwhile taking a look at these implied terms in employment contracts as these can be the subject of essay or written exam questions or they can be easily used in MCQs; e.g. "which of the following 4 are an example of an implied term in a contract of employment…?"

I'll give you some of these examples of implied terms but not all of them. The reason for this is that, if you chase it far enough, there are dozens. A lot of these implied terms, luckily, are far too obscure to interest most first-year business studies law students. These are more suitable for someone taking a straight law degree. So, I'll give you the more well-known and, in my view, the more important ones.

Some common law duties (implied by case law) employers have to employees

A duty to provide work?

A very interesting question this. It appears that in most cases an employer doesn't really have a duty to provide you with work. Do you think this seems a bit counter-intuitive? I do. A quote which exemplifies this comes from *Collier v Sunday Referee Publishing Ltd (1940) 2 KB 647*. The quote which I'm about to give you was by Asquith and gives you an idea of the sort of social background and class which important judges tend to come from. He said, "Provided I pay my cook her wages regularly she cannot complain if I choose to take any or all of my meals out". I hope you remember to pay your cook regularly? I must admit, I personally often forget to do this.

From this case and others, we can take it that although your employer may not be under a duty to provide work for you, they're actually under a duty to pay you under your contract of employment, as long as you continue to offer your work to them. This sounds good to me. It means that you may be able at times to be paid for doing nothing. What more can any of us ask?

There are a few exceptions to this work/pay situation. Let's say you're a person where your particular work skill is something which needs constant practice, then the situation may be different. These are the sort of situations where you can make a good case to say that if you've got no chance to keep up your practice then you'll lose your skills. These could be where you may be a professional ballroom dancer or professional actor.

You may then be able to complain that you must be provided with work as you may well start to lose your acting skills or status as a well-known film or TV actor through long periods of not being offered work. The ability of an employee to demand that work is provided is also seen where an employee is working on commission. This can occur in various sales jobs where your main income very substantially depends upon the amount of sales that you are able to generate. You often rely on your employer to supply your sales 'leads'.

A duty of confidentiality?

This duty goes far back in history to the beginning of the old master/servant relationship. It is seen nowadays in an employer being under a duty not to pass on information about you to anyone else – for example your name and address or any other personal information about you. If you've done something naughty which your employer is aware of, they must disclose this to the police but the police will need a court order in order to view this information.

A duty to provide a safe place of work

Most of us are aware these days of the existence of the duty that the employer owes to their workers. If an employee is injured at work because an employer hasn't ensured a safe working environment, then the employer can potentially be liable in tort and/or contract law. The employer can also potentially be liable in criminal law. The numerous Health and Safety regulations are relevant here.

The duty to provide and to have in place systems to deal with employee grievances

This is relatively new duty for employers. Nowadays they are expected to have procedures in place to deal with any allegations of injustices coming from employees. The lack of such a system can allow a worker to complain to an industrial tribunal.

Some duties the employee has to the employer

Confidentiality

This duty as discussed above works both ways. An employee is under a duty, for example, not to reveal information about any research and development the employer may be undertaking. Similarly, an employee must not reveal any confidential information or trade secrets or contacts the employer may have entered into to a third party.

To take reasonable care and skill in his/her work

Obviously, there may well be many types of person employed in any business each with their own particular levels of knowledge and skill. Levels of skill will then vary quite a lot. The level of care and skill required from a worker will depend on the level of care and skill expected from the reasonable worker at that level (back to the objective test again). For example, a worker who is working as a professionally qualified accountant will be expected to use the level of care and skill which is to be reasonably expected from qualified accountants.

A duty of fidelity?

Fidelity means faithfulness. So, you must at all times be faithful to your employer. This implied duty, if no other implied term, goes right to the heart of the master/servant relationship. You mustn't at any time let your employer down by, for example, setting up in competition with them. You must at all times have their best interests in mind. This duty, apart from sounding quite religious, sounds very old fashioned. Believe me it still exists and covers such a wide range of possible actions that an employer might well be able to bring an action against you for almost anything. Remember, keep the faith!

What do you need to know?

The extent to which you may be expected to know the above duties and in how much depth you will be expected to know them, will as always depend upon the design and preferences of the lecturers who have written your course specification. If you read your course specification you should be able quite quickly to work out what areas you need to know. If you become aware that employer/employee duties are likely to be examined in some detail, you need to add at least one case to each of the above duties (and learn more of these duties and cases if you really want to do well). There are plenty of cases to choose from under each heading. Remember also that there are far more of these duties than I've been able to give here.

A good tip for most students is to wait and see what revision areas are going to be covered by your tutor. Unfortunately, for many students, taking this approach may come a bit too late as they want to start revising well before any revision sessions are put into place. If this is the case a great fall-back approach is to simply ask the relevant lecturer. They of course won't be able to tell you specifically what's included in your exam question by question. But also, they won't tell you to revise an area which isn't going to be of any use to you at all.

Vicarious liability in workplace situations

It's about time to look at vicarious liability in tort and how this could affect you as a business owner and your employees. Remember that the concept of vicarious liability means that in some instances the careless acts of one person can lead to another person becoming liable for these acts. At first sight this looks very unfair. After all, I hear you saying, why should you be blamed because some other person has acted in a stupid way and caused some damage? I hear you say this because I've mentioned it before!

The concept of vicarious liability isn't restricted to the workplace only but this is where we see its operation most commonly. If you remember when we looked at partnerships in the chapter on business organisations, we saw that one partner in a partnership can be liable for the torts of another partner (jointly and several liability).

To establish vicarious liability there must exist some kind of special relationship between the parties involved. A partnership is one example of this special relationship. We also see it in the employer/employee relationship for two main reasons.

To explain this, it's best to use an example. Imagine a building company which is engaged in building houses and flats in some particular area. Scaffolding is in place and several staff members are working high up on the scaffolding. One of these workers is not taking his work very seriously and manages to drop a scaffolding pole off the roof. This pole drops to the street below and falls on top of the head of a person passing by. This person suffers serious injuries and ends up in hospital for several weeks.

Normally, the injured person is likely to sue the person who caused the injury in the tort of negligence, expecting compensation (damages). Under the principle of vicarious liability, it's more likely that the owner of the construction company will be sued for damages. Of course, the reckless employee could be sued for damages in this example but he, (a scaffolder is quite likely to be a he), probably won't be sued for a couple of reasons.

The employer generally is thought of as being the person who is likely to be in a better financial position to be able to pay the damages claimed and it is far more likely that the employer will be covered by insurance for such acts. What's more, the law likes to drive home to employers that they should have the correct systems of safety in place to stop such occurrences from happening in the first place.

I don't know what you think, but to me what seems *prima facie* to be an unfair situation, suddenly starts to makes a bit of sense. I must emphasise the point here that in these sorts of situations, the injured person is quite within their rights to sue both the worker and the employer. We mentioned a similar example of this elsewhere, using an illustration a person falling over in a supermarket owing to the negligence of a worker. You are unlikely to sue the employee and far more likely to take action against the store itself for the negligence of its worker. But you could, if you want, sue them both.

I reckon that if you think that you're likely to have to have to cover vicarious liability in your exams, you're going to need to know a minimum of four cases at least on this.

Generally, an employer will be liable for the torts performed by an employee during "the course of their employment". This makes sense as you can hardly blame a worker for some negligent act when they're at home and not on company time. What might seem strange (or indeed unfair) is that the law in this area has decided that an employer can be liable in vicarious liability for acts done during the course of an employee's employment, even if the worker has been told very strongly that they are not to do what they then go ahead and do.

This is shown in the case of *Limpus v London General Omnibus (1862)*. This case always raises a giggle or two in class which is why I make sure to use it as often as I can.

Limpus v London General Omnibus (1862)

Here we have two bus companies which were in competition with each other. The first bus to get to a bus stop got the passengers. The driver of the bus belonging to the London General Omnibus Co. had been expressly told that under no circumstances was he allowed to race his bus to get passengers first. Of course, he did just this. The driver cut across the path of the other bus which was overturned. Not unexpectedly perhaps, the crash caused injury to the driver of the overturned bus, Mr Limpus. Unfortunately for the company, they were found liable for the actions of their own driver. The image of two buses racing each other along busy London streets, you have to admit, is pretty funny. At least it is, if seen from the distance of 60 years or so.

It's worth noting that it was stated in the case that the injury resulted from, "an act done by the driver in the course of his service and for his master's purposes". Does that ring any bells in relation to what we've said above?

Off on a 'frolic'

The origins of the expression, "off on a frolic of their own" can be traced back at least a couple of hundred years in English law. Judges have used this expression to mean where a person has been acting entirely for themselves and not under the instructions of their master.

'Frolic' is a word which doesn't seem to be used much these days in ordinary English usage. It simply means that a person is on some adventure or exploit of their own which is unconnected to the work they were supposed to be doing for their employer.

A case which explains this well is *Hilton v Thomas Burton (1961)*.

Hilton v Thomas Burton (1961)

Here some workers who were involved in demolition work, took a van belonging to their employer to a café for lunch. Owing to negligent driving on the way back to work, the van crashed and Mr Hilton was killed. Mrs Hilton sued the company under the principle of vicarious liability. The court found that although the worker was allowed to drive the van under his employment contract, he was not allowed to drive the van to go to lunch. As a result, the employer wasn't liable.

The same result would come about for example if a lorry driver 'borrowed' his employer's lorry on a Sunday when he wouldn't normally be working, to help his friend to move house. If this lorry driver crashed the lorry injuring someone, his employer wouldn't be liable for this. Effectively the 'helpful' lorry driver would be acting outside of the scope of his employment. As he would be acting not in the course of his employment, he would be off on frolic of his own so his employer wouldn't be liable for his tortious acts.

The way to answer any question on this is pretty much the same as any other legal question. You simply put both sides of the equation by stating that given the facts of the question, an employer will be liable if the court finds that the employee is not off a frolic of his own: the employer will not be liable if the court finds that he is off on a frolic of his own. Mention a few relevant cases and draw a conclusion along the lines of, "it is not always easy to predict which way the court will decide in these cases as sometimes cases which seem to have similar facts are decided differently. Given the present facts, probably the better view is that the court will follow the reasoning in (state your chosen case, one which seems closest to the facts of the question) and decide in favour of the employer or employee depending on which seems to be the most likely outcome".

By doing the above you've done all you've been asked to do. You've stated the legal position, given your legal authority (relevant cases), and concluded one way or the other. Mostly there is no real answer. What the examiners are looking for is that you know, and can apply, the relevant case law. By doing the above you'll be very likely to get very close to the top marks. If you've researched the case law in this area and can supply substantially more relevant case law, then you'll get a first for your answer. The definition of a first, is to show that substantial extra independent research has been done outside of lecturer/student contact hours. This is the position in any legal answer to any legal question. Also, what you're doing by answering questions this way is to exactly replicate how an actual court would deal with any such problem. Who can ask more than this?

Negligence and vicarious liability

I'll use this next case to highlight issues of vicarious liability but it can also be used to help you answer questions regarding the law of tort (negligence) as well as issues of occupier's liability. Quite a versatile case.

Woodward v Mayor of Hastings (1945)

In Woodward, we have the situation of a school being relocated during the 2nd World War. This was quite a common occurrence during this time as schools were often temporarily relocated in an effort to avoid areas which were being heavily bombed.

During a very cold time of year, a cleaner was asked to clear ice on steps leading into and out of the school. She cleared away the ice as best as she could but, crucially as it turned out, did nothing to prevent the overall slipperiness of the steps. She probably should have scattered ashes from a coal fire over the steps, which was a common thing to do at the time,

Anyway, she didn't do this and a young pupil of the school fell down the steps and injured himself quite badly. His mum didn't like this very much and attempted to sue the school in her son's name for negligence.

The court considered issues of duty of care of the school to its pupils and whether there had been a breach of any duty owed.

The court held that the actions (or lack of action) by the cleaner meant that the school was liable for damages under the heading of vicarious liability.

Please make a mental note here back to our discussion on the basics of the law of the tort in negligence where we said that a person can equally become liable where there is established that a duty of care exists and they do some injurious act or they don't do some act which leads to injury.

If you want to use this case when asked to consider occupiers' liability, you would simply say that the occupiers (in this case the school governors) were liable as they had the opportunity to check the steps but just didn't do so.

Independent contractors

The position with an independent contractor is that the person or company using such a contractor will not normally be liable for torts committed by them. This brings to the surface another important reason why it's so important to be able to distinguish as to whether a person or business might be employed by another person or company or whether they are acting independently. Remember the difficulty we talked about above? Was our plumber actually working for the person whose cold-water system sprang a leak or were they independent contractors? We said above that normally plumbers will be working for themselves but they don't have to be. What we're talking about here is that any legal liability for work done will be different depending whether a person is actually in our employment or working independently. So, to be clear, if we've employed someone then we may well be vicariously liable for their torts. If they're independent, then normally we won't be liable.

There are a number of situations when we as employers can still be vicariously liable for the torts committed by, shall we say, a self-employed person you've decided to use for some particular job. These are unusual types of cases but to give you an example it can occur if the work may involve a special risk of damage occurring to neighbouring properties.

A recent case concerning vicarious liability

This case is the very recent case (2020) heard by the Supreme Court – *Barclays Bank v Various Claimants*. The case is so new there isn't as yet much comment on it coming from the normal sources. The importance of this case to us is that it appears to reinforce the concept that vicarious does not apply liability to independent contractors.

Barclays Bank v Various Claimants (2020)

The case concerned Dr Gordon Bates (no relation as far as I know), who had been asked by Barclays Bank to perform medical examinations, mainly on prospective employees in the bank's recruitment drive. 126 people alleged that Dr Bates had sexually abused them in the course of their examinations. The issue to be decided was whether Barclays Bank could be held liable for the alleged sexual abuses by the doctor. The Court of Appeal had initially decided that the bank was liable. The case was looked at again on appeal to the Supreme Court which decided that Barclays Bank couldn't be held to be vicariously liable. The issue hinged upon whether the doctor actually worked for the bank or was an independent contractor.

As we know, if the doctor could satisfy the conditions necessary to be an independent contractor, then the bank would not be vicariously liable. After a thorough review of past cases, the Supreme Court decided that Dr Bates was acting as a "classic independent contractor".

If you get the time it's really worth chasing the case through from the High Court where it was first heard, up to the Court of Appeal and then up to The Supreme Court. The reason for taking the time to do this is twofold. First, it's fascinating to follow the different reasoning of the courts. Second, if you think that you might get a question on this area, it's going to be worth extra marks.

Section 2: The main rights of an employee

This is area where MCQs are likely to be used in employment law exams.

As we've seen above, the traditional view of the employer/employee relationship was that of master and servant. We made the point that under English law this relationship still is the basis for virtually all employment law. This continued to be the case, at least until European law began to be incorporated into English law. Perhaps unfortunately the older relationship has tended, for many years, to give the employer the 'upper hand' in work situations.

This imbalance of power (remember that ultimately the employer/employee relationship is primarily contractual), gave rise to a 'hire and fire' culture. Hire and fire here means that employers could take on workers whenever they were wanted and could get rid of someone they didn't want at the employers' own free will. Some commentators suggest that the ability of employers to manage their workforce on this basis is great for business. Looking at the situation purely from an employer's point of view, it probably is great for businesses. It's not quite so great though for workers. Under this system a worker would have no security of employment and in some cases could be dismissed at the fancy of the employer, with no explanation given at all. Importantly the sacked worker had very little comeback if they suddenly found that they'd lost their job.

Without wanting to get too much into politics, it's been suggested that the growth of the gig economy and 'alternative' working practices today, is an attempt by employers to get themselves back into the free and easy employment situation they used to be in. It's said that this will give us a much more flexible and efficient workforce. Well, employers would say this wouldn't they?

The 'gig economy' is just a way of describing the situation where there is much more use of part time work, temporary workers, job share and short-term contract work. In short, it's supposed to produce a more flexible workforce.

This tends to be a messy area of law, in that some aspects are governed by statute and some by common law and still others can be governed by statute and/or case law. As indicated above this seemingly muddled field of law makes it look more complicated than it really is. This is the reason why in a first-year business law course, it's generally only the main elements which you'll be expected to have a working knowledge of.

Remember that the most important act which operates in this area is the Employment Rights Act 1996. You will be expected to aware of this act and its main provisions. It's very doubtful (unless you have particularly sadistic law lecturers) to be expected to know the act, section by section.

Termination of employment

Termination can be, and often is, governed by your contract of employment. As an employee you will be expected to be aware of the terms of notice contained within your contract even if you haven't read it. It might be a good idea, if you're currently working, to take a look at it now. Periods needed for employment termination is governed by your particular contract of employment and by statute.

Termination governed by statute (above) include statutory notice of termination. Situations may include:

☐ Summary dismissal for *gross misconduct*.

☐ Constructive dismissal – where there has been a very serious breach of the employment contract by the *employer*.

If notice has been given to the employee, then the minimum statutory period of notice which must be given if you're employed for at least one month is one week. If a greater period than that above is given in your contract of employment, then this statutory period can be extended accordingly.

Termination upon notice

Statutory notice to be given by employer to employee

Time in Employment	Statutory Minimum Notice (in weeks)
Less than 1 month	None
1 month – 2 years	1
2 years	2
3 years	3
4 years	4
And so on until 12 years	Max 12

If your employer really wants to get rid of you quickly, then payments can be offered to you in lieu (meaning instead) of working out your notice. By this time, you might well be happy to take anything you can get.

Statutory notice required by the employee to the employer

Time Worked	Minimum Notice
1 month to 2 years	1 week
2 years or more	1 week for each full year worked continuously

The minimum statutory notice which must be given by you as an employee if you've been working at least one week is one week only. It's possible that your contract of employment may state that you must give a longer period of notice than this. If so, you must stick to the contract. In reality of course in these situations, many workers simply "go sick".

Dismissal – types of claim

Unfair dismissal

This type of dismissal is governed by the Employment Rights Act, but to claim that your dismissal was unfair, you have to have had a period of continuous employment of at least two years.

The act gives five reasons which will justify a dismissal. These are:

- ☐ capability (i.e. you have shown yourself incapable of doing the job for which you were employed);
- ☐ conduct (bad enough for you to be fairly sacked);
- ☐ redundancy (see below);
- ☐ illegality (oh dear what've you been up to?); and
- ☐ some other 'substantial' reason.

Your employer has to show that your dismissal was "fair and reasonable" under the above conditions. If your employer can't show this then you can claim compensation.

Wrongful dismissal

This is a common law contractual matter meaning that here you won't have the protection of the Employment Rights Act – this is one reason why I said earlier that your knowledge of contract law and the various types of breach which can occur would be useful. Any alleged breach of your employment contract by your employer can cause a situation of wrongful dismissal. The most common reason by far, is alleged failure by your employer to give you the appropriate period of notice as required under your contract of employment.

Redundancy

There are three main reasons why your employer may make you redundant.

- First, where the employer's business is closing;
- Second, where the workplace is closing. This just means the office or factory where you actually are working is to be closed.
- Third, where there is a diminishing need for you to do the particular work you were doing.

To be eligible for a redundancy pay-out you must be categorised as an actual 'employee'. Note how this now ties in with all the above work we did on what constitutes an employee? This is one reason why the courts need to know whether you're an employee or not. If it turns out that you're not an employee, then you can say goodbye to that nice little redundancy payment you were going to use to buy that gleaming little Porche 911.

The redundancy procedure needs full consultation which must be 'fair'. The amount of redundancy payment you will get depends on how long you've been working for your employer (you must have been working continuously for 2 years as a minimum), your average weekly pay and your age.

There have been many times during my employment career when I've wished someone would make me redundant – sadly this has never happened.

Note that all the figures given above can and do change over time. Make sure that if you're facing an upcoming MCQ which is likely to involve employment law, then get up to speed with the current statutory time periods involved. Lecturers can be sneaky and if one or other of the above time periods has recently changed, the chances are that there will be a question or two on this.

Summary

We pointed out firstly that a good way of thinking of employment law is to imagine it as being split into two sections. We made the following two points:

1. The fact that the agreement between you and your employer is a contractual one, so a lot of your knowledge of contract law, including implied terms, will be of use to you here. This is the most likely area where longer exam questions may appear and case law will need to be used in any answer to such questions.

2. The second area is governed more by statute law (the Employment Rights Act 1996) and concerns such elements as wrongful or unfair dismissal, and makes use of the Employment Tribunals rather than the standard civil law court system. Generally, this is the area which is more likely to be examined using MCQs.

The definition of who actually constitutes an 'employee' was examined by use of the main cases in this area of law. We pointed out that it is crucial for you to know if you are actually an employee or not. This is because, if legally you are not an employee, then you may not be eligible for many benefits such as sick pay, holiday pay or redundancy payments.

We looked at the main common law (case law) duties which the courts have developed concerning the duties an employer has to the employee and the duties owed by employee to the employer.

We then looked at the concept of vicarious liability where your actions as an employee can lead to your employer becoming liable for your actions in tort. We said that workers who may be classified as 'independent contractors' generally do not render the person for whom they are working liable for actions in tort.

We then considered some issues about the termination of employment and the notice of termination which should be given by the employer and the employee.

This was followed by an outline of the situation where dismissal may be deemed to be wrongful or unfair. Finally, we looked at the main elements surrounding redundancy and payments for redundancy.

Revision questions

1. Why might it be so crucial for a worker to be sure that they are legally classified as an 'employee'?
2. Who might be an independent contractor to a business? State some possible examples of which type of person or business which might be classified as independent contractors.
3. Explain the concept of vicarious liability and how it operates within contract law.
4. Using instances of case law, provide some examples of the duties an employer may owe to their workers.
5. Using common laws cases, give some examples where an employee may owe duties to their employees.

Corporate governance

Some large corporations (particularly PLCs) get up to some very naughty things at times. Why they do this of course we'll never fully know because we're only aware of the ones that get caught. However, it's easy to speculate about what the main reasons are likely to be…

We looked earlier at the most common forms of business organisations and noted that PLCs have shareholders who they have to keep happy. We noted that, in the words of many writers and business leaders themselves, shareholders in general tend to take a much more short-term view about dividend pay-outs than probably the board of directors might like. Directors would often like to retain earnings within the company for reinvestment purposes, but they feel obliged to pay out dividends so as not to annoy existing shareholders and to hopefully attract potential new investors. The decision as to how much to retain as a proportion of earnings of course affects the funds available to allocate to shareholders' dividends. The greater the amount of retained earnings, the less is available for the shareholders.

Things are generally not too bad when times are good for a company, but decisions about how much earnings to retain become more difficult when times get hard. Whatever the trading climate, it's often been said, large companies are pretty much profit-driven. The ever-increasing demand by shareholders for increased dividends, means that ultimately, PLCs are really shareholder driven. Or driven by "shareholder greed" – not my words.

To an extent then, PLCs are in competition with each other, even if they're not in the same industry. Why should this be? Well, shareholders holding shares in a company that isn't for any reason paying out (or increasing) dividends, always have the option of selling their shares and switching to shares in a company which is paying higher dividends. Now, shareholders normally don't want to do this because the act of selling and buying shares isn't free. The costs of trading in shares is normally called 'transactions costs' or trading costs. These fees hit shareholders right in the pocket and they don't like it one little bit. So, shareholders naturally are quite reluctant to sell their shares unless they feel they have to. Companies know this and to an extent rely upon it. Transactions costs vary as a percentage of the number of shares that you want to trade. As is normal in life, the greater the amount of money you have in shares, the less you'll have to pay in trading costs as a percentage of your shareholding.

Having said that, although shareholders normally are reluctant sell their shares in a particular company, they certainly will do it when they see their dividends falling behind the dividend pay-outs of other companies for too long. So, a PLC isn't just in competition with other companies in the same industry, but is also in a sort of 'dividend war' with other PLCs in virtually every other industry. If you remember what we said in Chapter 6, *Types of business*, we mentioned that being a director of a PLC is not quite as entertaining as us ordinary folk seem to think.

What seems to be an eternal race for profit by large companies can have a very beneficial effect. In theory at least, it should give these firms great encouragement to improve their efficiency in production (a good thing) but it may unfortunately also encourage them to engage in certain other activities designed to increase profit, which may be not quite so moral. I once had a perceptive student who wrote me an essay regarding corporate governance and she said something along the lines of being a bit hesitant to use the words 'moral' and 'large corporations' in the same sentence. She'd obviously grasped the subject area well.

The concept of corporate governance is, to put it crudely, an attempt to encourage corporations to behave themselves. Some systems of corporate governance try to use force to 'tame' such companies, while other systems use a more gentlemanly (courteous and polite) approach. For those students who prefer a more formal definition of corporate governance, the Chartered Governance Institute website (www.cgi.org.uk) says, "Corporate governance is the system of rules, practices and processes by which a company is directed and controlled".

It does sometimes seem that the field of corporate governance is a new one, but it isn't. The concept of corporate accountability dates at least as far back as the emergence of large corporations such as the East India Company in the 1600s. The real position is that corporate governance has become more noticed in recent years because of a whole series of scandals which really shook the financial world. The term 'corporate governance' began to be a trendy term in the 1970s and hasn't as yet gone away.

We have to bear in mind that all incorporated companies under English law are ultimately governed by the 2006 Companies Act. Under this act, directors are given certain rules which they are expected to rigidly stick to. The main rules the act stipulates – from section 170 onwards – are:

- to promote the success of the company;
- to exercise independent judgment;
- to exercise reasonable care, skill and diligence;
- to avoid conflicts of interest; and
- not to accept benefits (which really means bribes) from third parties.

Company law in America has similar provisions as do all legal jurisdictions throughout the world. Whether directors always work within these provisions is what is in question regarding the question of corporate governance.

Failures of corporate governance

The whole concept is best explained by examples. We'll start with an example of corporate malpractice (misconduct) well known to many students of business studies and/or economics the world over. As many readers will know this was the shocking conduct of an American corporation known as Enron.

The Enron scandal

Enron was a giant corporation, one of the largest businesses in the United States. It was involved in a variety of business activities including energy and commodity trading, together with some service interests. It was founded in 1985 and bankrupted (or more correctly went into liquidation) in 2001. For years the company had produced reports and accounts which stated that it was in an excellent financial position. Its trading position and profits could hardly have been better, according to the company. At this time the shareholders were blissfully happy.

It was apparently one of the finest companies in the American tradition of hard work and reward. Of course, in reality it was nothing like this at all, otherwise we wouldn't be talking about it. Years of losing vast sums of dollars were hidden by some of the top company directors and accountants. Together these individuals engaged in what must be one of the finest examples of 'creative accounting' the world has ever seen. What we would now call 'toxic' debt of the company's many subsidiary companies were being cleverly hidden.

The methods used in hiding these gigantic losses almost became an art form of its own.

The company shareholders at the time had no idea about what was really happening behind the scenes, so it came as a huge shock when the company finally 'went bust'. Company investors lost over $74 billion when the company folded. Some of the directors involved, along with their accountants, when eventually discovered, were given criminal sentences of 5+ years in prison. The former CEO, Jeffrey Skilling, received an initial 24 years in a penitentiary. This was later reduced to 10 years. The overall charges the offenders faced, and were found guilty of, included wilful fraud, conspiracy and corruption.

Now this is bad enough I think we'll all agree but the shock the collapse caused to the US financial community and the average American investor is difficult to describe. This sort of thing just didn't happen in the United States. Just maybe this could happen in some unstable South American country but not to 'Uncle Sam', and in the so-called Land of Liberty. The 'American Dream' suddenly turned into an 'American Nightmare'.

The 'successful fraudster'

Just to show you that misconduct is not just an American phenomenon, let's take a couple of other examples which took place in the UK. The first of these involves a person called Asil Nadir who became known at least to the British press as the successful fraudster as mentioned in the title above. Nadir came to this country together with his family in the 1950s from Northern Cyprus. The family were Turkish Cypriots and he was then just a young boy. But by all accounts, he had so much ambition that it must've been coming out of his ears. First, he acquired a small company called Polly Peck, which produced clothing and textiles of various types.

By a process of takeovers of other companies, he managed to grow this company vastly, and by 1989 he obtained a listing for Polly Peck on the London Stock Exchange. By this time the company was involved in a wide variety of businesses, such as fruit packing, consumer electronics and fashion products. The growth of the company became exponential and it even managed to buy the giant US canned fruit company Del Monte (you may have seen this name on tins in your local supermarket). This was the time when prime minister Margaret Thatcher was encouraging anyone who was listening to buy shares in PLCs – and at the same time selling off public utility companies. This was the so called 'yuppy' era when entrepreneurship was cheered on by all.

If you were a city trader at this time, you measured your success by being able to buy enough differently coloured Porches to see you through the week – one for each day. It certainly seemed that financial success was the only true measure of your achievements. Money seemed to be the new religion.

Well, at first Asil Nadir and his Polly Peck company seemed to fit in very well with this money-based culture. Then things started to go wrong for Nadir. Serious doubts and certain rumours about the company began to appear. Various questioning articles appeared in the financial press and journals. Amongst many other rumours there were questions being asked about Polly Peck's less than transparent accounting methods. Allegations began to be made about alleged share price manipulations (insider trading). Eventually the Serious Fraud Office decided to take a close look at the company. What the Fraud Office found resulted in Polly Peck being forced to go into liquidation in 1990 and Nadir being charged with a total of 66 criminal offences, including a charge of stealing £29 million from the company and systematically falsifying the company accounts. Company debts were reported as being in the region of £1.3 billion. Not surprisingly, company shareholders didn't like this very much.

Here's where I became interested in Asil Nadir, because before he stood trial for these alleged offences, he literally took flight from the UK. I say literally, because he took his private plane one night, and having persuaded a pilot to fly the plane, landed back in Northern Cyprus where he came from in the first place. Nadir had taken refuge in Norther Cyprus as there was no extradition treaty between that area of Cyprus and the UK. He remained there for 17 years. Now I had been studying the affairs of Polly Peck as a student at university around this time and one evening, which must have been in 2010, I was watching the evening BBC TV news and there on the screen appeared the face of Asil Nadir. In this country! What on earth was he doing back here I asked myself? Apparently, everyone else was asking the same question. Nadir's story was that he believed so strongly in British justice that he had faith that a trial here would find him innocent of any wrongdoing. I thought at the time that it seemed a bit odd that it took him 17 years to reach this conclusion. He seemed to blame everyone apart for himself. It was, according to him, all the fault of his accountants and financial advisors.

His trial took place at the Old Bailey in London (London's central criminal court). The jury, who presumably did have faith in the British system of justice, found him guilty and he was awarded a 10-year prison sentence. He allegedly stole in total just short of £150 million.

To be fair, he reportedly repaid around £7 million of his debts including some of his legal aid costs. I expect he thought "ah that'll do". After spending four years or so in a British prison, he was transferred to a Turkish prison under a government prisoner relocation scheme. The Turkish authorities let him out of the prison just the next day. He was treated as a bit of a celebrity figure for quite a while (at least in Turkey).

Currently he seems to be doing quite well for himself in Northern Cyprus (aren't we all pleased for him). He is, by all accounts, chairman of a company called Kibris Media which seems to be involved in substantial investment in an airport the name of which I can't pronounce.

I hope they don't let him anywhere near the cash register...

'The Bouncing Czech'

This nickname was given to Czechoslovakian businessman Robert Maxwell by *Private Eye* magazine. It's a pity that I can't tell you that I came up with this wisecrack, but I didn't. *Private Eye* came up with this near genius pun. You may have seen this magazine on the newspaper shelves in your local shops. It is known as being a little, shall we say, satirical – it's a jolly good read and I recommend it to everyone. It's worth it if only for the cartoons. The magazine has often been sued for defamation (printing insulting and untrue statements, for which they can be sued) about politicians, business leaders and other well-known public figures. What they printed about our new friend Robert Maxwell cost them damages of around £250,000. Basically, the magazine alleged that Maxwell was not only a crook but had tried to buy himself into a peerage. This means that the magazine suggested that Maxwell wanted to be able to call himself "Sir Maxwell" or "Lord Maxwell" and to achieve this he would allegedly pay whatever it took. The result of Maxwell bringing a successful libel action nearly sent the magazine into liquidation.

Anyway, time has shown that *Private Eye* really did get it spot on as he was proven in many later cases of being a crook. It turned out that he was indeed a comprehensive liar, a thief and an embezzler.

He certainly was a larger than life character both physically and in his business dealings. He stood at over 6 foot 4 inches and weighed well over 20 stones. He also certainly knew how to throw his weight around in his corporate activities as we shall see.

Robert Maxwell came to Britain in 1940 and enlisted in the army. It wasn't long before he was promoted and went on to fight with great distinction in Nazi Germany. He was certainly no coward and was awarded the Military Cross during the second world war. After the war he became involved with publishing and started the Pergamon Press business. Incidentally this company is still in existence but now trades under a different name. In 1984 he acquired the Mirror Group of newspapers which published the *Daily Mirror* and several other daily national newspapers. His other media enterprises included cable television and the purchase of the Macmillan publishing company. In addition, he bought the Oxford United football club. A very busy man indeed. On paper he was a fantastically rich man and was well known for acquiring large houses and expensive cars. Unfortunately for those around him, he could be a very dangerous and intimidating person. This was the case at least as far as his business empire was concerned but his behaviour extended to potential competitors. It's been said that this could also extend to his private life.

Maxwell had certain connections with Israel in arranging the supply of aircraft components to this country during the 1947 to 1948 Palestine War of Independence. He had acquaintances and 'friends' stretching pretty much over most of the world. In 1991 while he was holidaying on his £15 million luxury yacht (*The Lady Chislaine*) near the Canary Islands, he died from drowning after falling off the side of the boat. Accountants trying to sort out Maxwell's business affairs soon after his death, were shocked to discover that at least £300 million was missing from the accounts. Some reports put the figure at closer to £460 million. Maxwell, it was said, illegally spirited away huge sums to prop up his "failing and debt ridden" empire. Thousands of Maxwell's pension fund holders lost out because of his actions. I told you at the start of this chapter that PLCs can get up to some very naughty things. Well this is another real-life example of this sort of thing happening.

As soon as his death was announced, the rumours started. All the national newspapers jumped onto the story with their own speculations Did Maxwell jump off his yacht on purpose? After all he must have known that he couldn't hide a £300 plus million discrepancy in the accounts for long.

One report mentioned that Maxwell was due to have a meeting with his accountants shortly after coming back from holiday. Other speculations were that MOSAD might well have had some insight into his death given his Israeli, connections. The recovered body had no real physical damage evident apart for a small graze on one shoulder. So, did he fall or was he pushed? I expect we'll never really know the true answer.

Conspiracy theories of course spring up very quickly in these sorts of situations – a friend of mine swears blind he saw him a couple of weeks ago serving full English breakfasts in his local Wetherspoons in Leamington Spa.

Some commentators suggested the Maxwell didn't have the sort of personality which would allow him to face financial ruin and a long prison sentence, which he must've know was soon be likely to be coming his way. This supports the falling off the boat hypothesis. Roy Greenslade, a one-time editor of the *Daily Mirror*, was quoted as saying, "That was the nature of the beast. What you have here is a kind of sociopathic possibly borderline psychopathic character". Would this type of person commit suicide I wonder?

As a postscript to the whole affair, Maxwell's accountancy firm, PwC (called Price Waterhouse Coopers at that time, and then and now one of largest of accountancy firms in the world), were fined nearly £3.5 million for failing to notice fraudulent activities and financial irregularities in the Maxwell empire. Just who can we trust if we can't trust our accountants…

So, that's just three of the major corporate scandals we've taken a look at. There are plenty more I can assure you. I'll mention a few more in passing later on, but for now let's take a look at how first the U.S. authorities reacted to the Enron scandal (as it was so unexpected and unprecedented). Then we'll take a look at the reaction of the UK authorities to similar financial scandals. The reactions of the two countries were similar in style but contained at least one fundamental difference. The one major difference in the U.S. system is that it's now compulsory for a corporate firm to run new governance schemes but in the UK it's not essential for a PLC to 'join' our similar system.

The SOX Act

If you remember that Enron collapsed in 2001, you'll possibly be not too surprised that the U.S. government was so shocked by this that they reacted by passing a new piece of legislation in 2002. This legislation was thought up by two Senators, Senator Sarbanes and Senator Oxley. Again, hardly surprisingly, this has become known as the SOX act.

This act seems to be either loved or hated depending upon who you are – a corporation or an investor (mainly shareholders in a corporation). From the corporate point of view, it introduced a wide range of new financial rules and regulations which had, and still have, teeth with a real bite to them. These teeth can bite you very badly. Believe me, as a corporate executive you don't want to fall foul of the SOX regulations. If you do then you'll be likely to face enormous fines and the sort of jail sentence which'll guarantee that you won't see your children again until they've got children of their own.

Just to give you an idea some of the changes the act made to US corporate financial reporting, let's just look at a few of them.

- ☐ Loans by the company to company executives are banned;
- ☐ Auditing of company accounts now have to be made by an independent body and not by the company itself;
- ☐ SOX compliance audits are to be made available to any stakeholder;
- ☐ 'Whistle-blowers' to be given protection (these are individuals who know something about the company that the company want to keep quiet); and
- ☐ The big one, this is the dreaded Rule 404, CEOs are to personally guarantee that the financial figures for the end of the trading year are correct in all respects. Phew, get this wrong and you're going away for up to 20+ years.

Unfortunately, it's very difficult to get up to date and exact prosecution numbers under SOX regulations, as U.S. law has other approaches to fraud law which are easier to use to get a successful prosecution. This is a bit of a pity as I think we'd all like to know the real numbers involved. There is evidence, however, which does suggest that SOX regulations have increased investor confidence very considerably. That's really the whole object of the new regulations in the first place. Result!

From the point of view of large corporations though, SOX really hasn't made them very happy. It wasn't designed to do this of course. The main complaint is simply about the greatly increased costs involved in making sure that a corporation is fully compliant with the regulations.

In some instances, companies complain that a whole new compliance department need to be developed within a company simply to ensure that SOX is adhered to. A related argument is that these increased costs affect profit margins. Also, some large corporations are in direct competition with foreign companies, where the regulations are much easier to deal with and in some cases non-existent. So, it's argued the overall effects of SOX is to make US companies less competitive.

The UK response to corporate misgovernance

Having dealt with the U.S. response to corporate financial scandals, it's time to look at how the UK attempted to deal with these. The story is a similar one in that it was obvious that some extra regulatory control was needed given Polly Peck, Robert Maxwell and other scandals. The Enron scandal frightened the UK, as did scandals such as WorldCom in 2002, Tyco also in the same year, and HealthSouth and Freddie Mac, both in 2003. There are plenty more of these scandals which I could mention and they're worldwide. A half hour trawl on the net just looking for "financial scandals" and I'll bet you'll find several hundred or more examples. They are more common in certain countries than others, but very few countries seem immune to them.

One of the first examples of the new interest in corporate governance in the UK was shown by the setting up of the Corporate Governance Committee in 1991 by the Financial Reporting Council (FRC) and the London Stock Exchange. The report came about partly as a result of the Maxwell scandal. It was published in 1992 and became known as the Cadbury Report as it was chaired by Lord Adrian Cadbury of the chocolate maker family. (Incidentally, the Cadbury chocolate business was sold to the giant U.S. Kraft Corporation in a hostile takeover in 2010 for £11.9 billion. As part of the deal Kraft promised to keep the Cadbury manufacturing factory in Somerset open. One week later they closed it.)

I won't bore you with the details but there were various reports into UK corporate governance over the following years. We had the *Corporate Governance Combined Code* published, just known the '*Code*'. This was updated every year or so until 2018 when the FRC published a '*New Style Code*'. Around this time and in the following year the UK faced the collapse of Carillion (a major construction company), BHS or British Home Stores (a department store chain) and Thomas Cook (which I think I hardly need to say was a travel agency and airline). About this time, it became a bit frightening just venturing out onto the high street in most towns for fear of finding out whether any of your favourite shops would still be there. I remember thinking it would be a good story line for some kind of science fiction disintegration film. Maybe I'll send the idea to Disney? I've come up with a good title for my film which I feel that I really should share with you. It's going to be called, '*Gone with the Wind*'. I have been told that this may've been covered before, so I'll promote it as a sort of futuristic remake.

Back to corporate governance. After about 2018 in the UK things became a bit hazy. We'd had the 2018 'New Style Code', but other things were being speculated by the FRC and the press. The government has recently said that it has plans to replace the old regulatory body, the FRC, with a new regulatory body to be called the Audit, Reporting and Governance Authority (ARGA) as soon as time becomes available in Parliament. Although this new body sounds like a posh type of cooker, it is by all accounts to have greater powers than ever before. Unfortunately, parliamentary time, at the time of writing, is in very short supply. Again, we'll just have to wait and see. A firm recommendation of the original Cadbury report was that more use should be made of non-executive directors in company boards of directors. A non-executive director in a person who is a specialist in certain areas of business and who sist on a part time basis, as and when required by the board. They are there in an advisory capacity only and have nothing to do with the day to day running of the company. The Cadbury report said non-executive directors (usually shortened to non-execs), should, "bring an independent judgement to bear on issues of strategy, performance and resources, including key appointments and standards of conduct." It's often been said that non-execs are there to police the board of directors to make sure that they don't do anything too silly. Nowadays the use of non-execs has become widespread thankfully. In fact, the job at least from the outside, seems to be an ideal one to have. It's well paid and if you're lucky and/or well known, you can pick up a string of non-exec jobs each with its own salary. If you're really well known or happen to have the title 'Sir' or 'Lord' in your name, then companies love to employ you. It looks great on the company letterhead to have someone with a title. Very impressive. The downside is the difficulty in getting awarded the title in the first place.

If you're lucky enough to become a CEO or a director of a major PLC, then you probably got where you are as a result of a couple of character traits. First, it's very likely that you have great ambition and an enormous desire to succeed. Second, the chances are that you possess great entrepreneurial skills. All this is well and good. Trouble can come in that some top flight entrepreneurs sometimes have wild ideas. These ideas may look great on paper but turn out to be not quite so brilliant in practice.

Now, if entrepreneurs start to spend their own money on these sorts of ideas and make a success and become fabulously rich as a result, none of us are in a position to complain. If these ideas are put into practice and result in a spectacular financial loss, well also it's not our business to become involved.

The trouble is that such high-ranking members of boards of directors are not using their own money on wild speculative ideas. They're using money which doesn't belong to them – i.e. shareholders' money. This is why I mentioned above that one of the major roles of the non-execs is to ensure that such directors have an eye kept on them to try to ensure that they don't go off spending shareholders' money on schemes which are doomed to failure.

The UK approach to corporate regulation is fundamentally different from that taken by the U.S. Remember that in the U.S. a corporate institution after SOX, had no choice whatever but to adopt their form of corporate governance practices. If you didn't adopt these to the letter, then you faced fines and ultimately your company could be de-listed. (That is, your company could lose its stock exchange listing altogether and you had a company no longer). This was a bit frightening, as it was meant to be.

The situation in the UK was that a large corporation was expected to adopt a corporate governance system within their operation but (at first at least) weren't forced into doing this. The system became known as 'comply or explain'. So, a company running a corporate governance scheme, had to comply with the necessary requirements of the code in successive years as codes were updated. The company had to comply with the code, but if it for some reason couldn't do so, they had to explain why this should be so. All this information had to be explained in each company's annual financial reports. The idea, as ever, behind all types of corporate governance systems is to make the activities of each company far more transparent to the shareholders and other potential investors. The UK Stock Exchange have now introduced listing rules which have a stipulation that to retain corporate status, comply or explain is compulsory. Remember that the word 'listing' is just another name for taking a company on to the Stock Exchange.

The UK adoption of the 'comply or explain' system is based on the idea that a 'one size fits all' approach would not be suitable for companies which are involved in a hugely diverse range of activities. This point may be a valid one. We mentioned elsewhere that a PLC could be involved in anything from uranium/oil/coal prospecting extraction, to pet insurance, to IT and AI. The list of possible business activities is simply vast.

The approach taken by the U.S. authorities is said to be a rule-based approach. That is, rules are set by a regulatory body, and must be followed under threat of punishment. The UK approach is said to be a principles-based approach working on the idea that you, as a company, will adopt the principles set out in the codes as doing the 'right thing'. The UK approach has been said to be a more 'gentlemanly' approach – but not by me. Don't forget that in the UK, corporations still have regulators watching over what they're doing – whether they decide to comply or take the explain why they haven't route.

Which system works best in practice is a question which the academics are still arguing about. I don't want to get into this too deeply here because if I do, I know I'm going to annoy an awful lot of people. Again.

The great financial crash of 2007/8 is often blamed on the fact that at the time PLCs in most countries didn't have adequate financial regulation. Undoubtedly the crash originated in the US, but English bankers were very keen to 'jump on the bandwagon' by buying cheap US securities, thereby helping to spread the financial breakdown to this country. Who was to blame? Well, everyone blamed everyone else. Politicians blamed the banks and financial regulators; the regulators blamed the politicians and banks. The media blamed the whole lot put together.

The crash came unexpectedly according to most commentators. A handful of American economists, to be fair, had given a few warnings that trouble might be ahead, but no single person seemed to be able to foresee the whole thing that was about to happen. Whether the radical changes in US and UK corporate governance which occurred since (and because of the big crash), will serve to warn us that something similar is approaching again, only time will tell. I sincerely hope so.

Corporate governance, banking and financial regulation

The relation between the banking and financial corporations and the system of regulation meant to keep an eye on what they're actually doing, is a complicated one. The relation is usually a bit of a catch-up game. It's quite similar to the relationship between criminals and the police. Unfortunately, criminals will always be one step ahead, leaving the police in a position of trying to anticipate what they might get up to next.

Obviously, we need some system of banking and regulation of banks and other financial institutions but the main problem is how heavily should we regulate the sector as a whole? If a system of regulation is too 'light' then it's suggested that banks in particular will just run rings around the regulators. If we introduce a system of very heavy regulation, then the banks will simply introduce new financial products and services which are not yet regulated. When these new products and services become regulated, the financial service sector will just move on again to newer less regulated products. This actually does happen more often than most people realise.

You can say what you like about banks but they are certainly very clever.

With all our talk about corporate wrongdoings and the various worldwide legal attempts to eradicate it, you might be tempted to think that things are improving. Well, you'd be wrong. In fact, it's really easy to make the case that actually things are getting worse in recent years.

A quick Google will confirm this. Type in something like "corporate scandals" or similar and your eyes will drop out of your head! I've just done this and picked out just three of the many results which I've listed below.

Wirecard – "the Enron of Germany"

This corporation was founded in Germany and its company activities involved the provision of certain financial services and processing electronic payments around the world. There had been various investigations into the company and in particular its finances. Suspicions had been roused about its accounting practices and difficult questions were beginning to be asked.

In 2020 the company announced that somehow around $2.3 billion had "gone missing" from company funds. Later investigations by the German financial authorities revealed a succession of accounting shortfalls.

The company CEO, one Markus Braun, was arrested and put in jail. He is still in jail and engaging in a great deal of expensive litigation. This is an on-going story so keep an eye on the press, particularly the financial sections, to see how the story develops.

Wells Fargo

If you've ever watched an old cowboy film you'll have come across the name Wells Fargo before.

Wells Fargo is a US bank originating from around the 1850s. It is a high street bank known all over the United States and was very well trusted and respected by all its customers.

The trouble was that the internal culture of the bank encouraged bank employees to do just about anything they could to make money from their customers. I hear you say, "well isn't that what all banks do?" It is, but not all banks had the US Treasury reporting that Wells Fargo's high-pressure sales culture "fostered an atmosphere that perpetrated improper and illegal conduct". This report was published in 2020.

In short, and in non-legal terminology, bank employees were encouraged to 'rip off' bank customers wherever they could.

As a result, the bank got fined $25 million and over 5000 employees were sacked for creating false accounts. The CEO was personally fined $17.5 million and was banned for life from ever again operating in the banking industry.

Luckin Coffee

Luckin Coffee is a Chinese based coffee chain company. It was originally intended to become a major competitor of Starbucks and consequently one of its chains of coffee shops operated in the US. All did not go well to say the least.

An accountancy scandal was revealed in 2020 and the company filed for bankruptcy protection. It was alleged that management had 'inflated' the company sales figures by $300 million.

At the end of 2020 the company was fined $180 million for misstatement of its "revenues, expenses and losses". The company was also delisted from NASDAQ. (The full title of NASDAQ is the National Association of Securities Dealers Automated Quotations.) Phew – losing membership of NASDAQ is not to be recommended. This was soon reflected in Luckin Coffee's market status – and share price.

A note on possible exam questions

Most exam questions in the area of corporate governance are of a comparative type. They involve you demonstrating that you are aware of the need for effective corporate governance, and often ask for a comparison of the UK and US systems and the crucial difference between the mandatory system in the US and the "comply or explain" system in the UK.

Summary

In this chapter we took a look at how the incentive some for large companies to get up to dishonest behaviour is great. This if fuelled by two main pressures. First, the pressure coming from the fiercely competitive environment in which they exist and second by shareholder short-termism, and consequent demands for ever greater dividend pay-outs.

It was suggested that there is a need for systems to be introduced to curb some of the more extravagant activities of some large corporations. These controlling systems should work in addition to the normal company law of each of the counties the corporations operate in.

Examples were given of some of the more infamous financial scandals which resulted in huge losses to company investors (mainly shareholders).

Two separate systems of corporate governance were looked in the US and the UK. Each of these, we pointed out, are different in their methods of implementation in both countries.

Finally we looked at the last great financial crash which occurred in 2007/8 and asked the question of whether the corporate governance systems introduced mainly as a result of the crash will be helpful in avoiding any similar financial breakdown.

Revision questions

1. How would you define 'corporate governance'?
2. Why do you think that there has been increased interest in the field of corporate governance in recent years?
3. What do you think should be the key features of an effective system of corporate governance which a company should make clear to its shareholders?
4. Do you think that the increased use of non-executive directors by companies may affect an investor's decision to buy shares in a company?
5. Which company would you be more interested in buying shares in? A company that has a policy of reporting to shareholders exactly how its corporate governance system operates or another company which states that it's far too expensive to operate a corporate governance system and will therefore be able to pay far above average dividend pay-outs.

10 Cases and Acts

List of cases used

Adams v Lindsell (1818) 1 B & Ald 681

Balfour v Balfour (1919) 2 KB 571

Barclays Bank v Various Claimants UK SC 13

Barnett v Chelsea & Kennington Hospital (1969) 1 QB 428

Bettini v Gye (1876) QBD 183

British Railways Board v Herrington (1972) AC 877

Caparo Industries v Dickman (1990) 2 AC 605

Carlill v Carbolic Smoke Ball Co (1893) 1 QB 256

Carmichael v Natural Power PLC (1999) 1 WLR 2042

Chapple v Nestlé (1959) AC 87

Chaudry v Prabhakar (1988) 1 WLR 29

Collier v Sunday Referee Publishing Ltd (1940) 2 KB 647

Collins v Godefroy (1831) 1 B & Ad 950

Cassidy v Ministry of Health (1951) 2 KB 343

D & C Builders v Rees (1966) 2 QB 617

Daniel v Drew (2005) EWCA Civ 507

Derry v Peek (1889) LR 14 AC 337

Donoghue v Stephenson (1932) AC 562, ER Rep 1

Earl (The) of Oxford's case (1616) 1 CH REP

Fisher v Bell (1961) 1 QB 394, 1960 ER 731

Grant v Australian Knitting Mills (1936) AC 85

Guilford Motor Homes v Horne (1933) 1 CH 935

Hedley Byrne v Heller & Partners (1964) AC 465

Hilton v Thomas Burton (1961) 1 WLR 705

Holwell Securities v Hughes (1974) 1 WLR 155

Hong Kong Fir Shipping v Kawasaki (1962) 2 QB 26 (CA)

Hutton v Warren (1836) 1 M & W 460

Hyde v Wrench (1840) 49 ER 132

Lampleigh v Braithwaite (1615) HOB 105, 80 ER 255

Lievre v Gould (1893) 1 QB 491

Limpus v London General Omnibus (1862) 2 QB 530

McArdle, Re (1951) CH 669, All ER 905

Moorcock, The, (1889) 14 PD 64, All ER 530

Paradine v Jane (1647) EWHC KB J5

Poussard v Spiers (1876) 1 QBD 410

Ready Mixed Concrete v Ministry of Pensions and National Insurance (1968) 2 WLR 775

Royal Bank of Scotland v Etridge (2002) 2 AC 773

Salomon v Salomon (1897) AC 22

Sayers v Harlow Urban District Council (1958) AALL ER 342

Shirlaw v Southern Foundries (1939) 2 KB 206, AC 701

Stevenson, Jordan & Harrison v MacDonald & Evans (1952) 1 TLR 101

Taylor v Caldwell (1863) EWHC QB J1

Tweddle v Atkinson (1861) 121 ER 762

Weller v Foot and Mouth Research Institute (1966) 1 QB 569

Wheat v Lacon (1966) AC 552

White v Bluet (1853) 23 LJ Ex 36

Woodward v Mayor of Hastings (1945)   1945.KB 174.

Yewen v Noakes (1880) 6 QBD 530

List of Acts of Parliament and Regulations

1873 to 1875 Judicature Acts

1890 Partnership Act

1893 Sale of Goods Act

1903 Motor Car Act

1907 Limited Partnership Act

1930 Road Traffic Act

1943 Law Reform (Frustrated Contract) Act

1945 Law Reform (Contributory Negligence) Act

1957 Occupiers' Liability Act

1966 Employment Rights Act

1967 Misrepresentation Act

1968 Theft Act

1977 Unfair Contract Terms Act

1978 Theft Act

1979 Sale of Goods Act

1982 Supply of Goods and Services Act

1984 Occupiers' Liability Act

1998 European Convention on Human Rights

1999 Contracts (Rights of Third Parties) Act

2000 Limited Lability Partnership Act

2002 Regulatory Reform

2002 Sarbanes-Oxley Act (The SOX Act) – An American case

2006 Companies Act

2007 Tribunals, Courts and Enforcement Act

2015 Consumer Rights Act

2018 Road Traffic (Amendment) Act

Index

abuse of trust, undue influence 91
acceptance, of contract 51
Acts
   Companies Act (2006) 21
   Consumer Rights Act (2015) 19, 75
   Employment Act (1966) 167
   Employment Rights Act (1966) 169
   Human Rights Act (1998) 39
   Judicature Acts of 1873 to 1875. 37
   Law Reform (Frustrated Contract) Act (1943) 96
   Limited Lability Partnership Act (2000) 150
   Limited Partnership Act (1907) 151
   Motor Car Act (1893) 17
   Occupier's Liability Act (1957) 120
   Occupier's Liability Act (1984) 120, 124
   Partnership Act (1890) 148
   Road Traffic Act (1930) 17
   Sale of Goods Act (1979) 18
   SOX Act (2002) 198–199
   Supply of Goods and Services Act (1982) 18
   Theft Act 16
   Tribunals, Courts and Enforcement Act (2007) 169
Acts of Parliament 14–21
   from bill to law 14
agency problem, public limited company 145
All England Law Reports 31

balance of probabilities 9
bilateral contracts 67
Blackstone Ratio 10
Bouncing Czech. *See* Robert Maxwell
breach
   of condition 94
   of contract 84–86
   of contract 94
   of warranty 94
British law 1
business, types of 130–153
business efficacy 76
by-laws 22

Caparo Test
   duty of care 109
case citations 32
case law 7, 23–29
   leading cases 27
cases
   Adams v Lindsell (1818) 54
   Barclays Bank v Various Claimants (2020) 184
   Barnett v Chelsea & Kennington Hospital (1969) 112
   Bettini v Gye (1876) 82
   Caparo Industries V Dickman (1990) 109
   Carlill v Carbolic Smoke Ball Co (1893) 26, 63–66
   Carmichael v Natural Power PLC (1999) 175
   Cassidy v Ministry of Health (1951) 172

Chaudry v Prabhakar (1988) 119
Collins v Godefroy (1831) 59
Daniel v Drew (2005) 89
D & C Builders v Rees (1966) 88
Donoghue v Stephenson (1932) 104–105
Earl of Oxford (1616) 37
Fisher v Bell (1960) 49
Grant v Australian Knitting Mills (1933) 108
Guilford Motor Homes v Horne (1933) 141
Hedley Byrne v Heller & Partners (1964) 117
Hilton v Thomas Burton (1961) 182
Holwell Securities v Hughes (1974) 54
Hong Kong Fir Shipping v Kawasaki 83
Hutton v Warren (1836) 79
Hyde v Wrench (1840) 51
Lampleigh v Braithwaite (1615) 58
Lampleigh v Braithwaite 1615 25
Lievre v Gould (1893) 111
Limpus v London General Omnibus (1862) 181
Paradine v Jane (1647) 95
Poussard v Spiers (1876) 81
Ready Mixed Concrete v Ministry of Pensions & National Insurance (1968) 173
Re McArdle (1951) 58
Royal Bank of Scotland v Etridge (2002) 91
Salomon v Salomon (1897) 134
Sayers V Harlow Urban District Council (1958) 127
Shirlaw v Southern Foundries (1939) 77–78
Stevenson, Jordan & Harrison v MacDonald & Evans (1952) 172
Taylor v Caldwell (1863) 96
The Moorcock (1889) 76
Tweddle v Atkinson (1861) 92
Weller v Foot and Mouth Research Institute (1966) 114
Wheat v Lacon (1966) 123
White v Bluet (1853) 60
Woodward v Mayor of Hastings (1945) 183
Yewen v Noakes (1880) 172
case stated, appeal 28
Chancery Division, High Court of Justice 158
civil and criminal courts 154
civil and criminal systems, differences 162
civil law and criminal law 7, 23
claimant 6
common law, definitions 35
common law duties of employers 177
companies
    allowable names 137
    fraudulent activities 140
    governance 191–206
    'off the shelf' 138
Companies Act 21
Companies House 136
company prospectus 137
conditions 80–81
consensus ad idem 68
consideration 55–60
    before agreement 58
    defined 56
    other rules 60–61
    requirements for validity 59
    value of 57
consumer law 18–20
contract law, basis of trust 45
contracts
    acceptance 51
    bilateral and unilateral 67–68
    breach 94
    breach of 84–86
    counter offer 50
    express and implied terms 74

legally binding 62
of employment 167–179
offer 47
privity 91–93
simple verbal 44
speciality 44
transparency of terms 61
contracts ending 93–96
by performance 94
frustration 95
impossibility of performance 95
part performance 94
quantum meruit 94
contractual discharge 94–95
contractual 'ingredients' 44–73
defined 46
contractual relationship
and negligent advice 117
contractual terms 79–86
contributory negligence 126
control test of employment 171
corporate governance 191–206
Corporate Governance Combined Code 200
failures of 193–199
corporate malpractice
Asil Nadir 194–196
Enron scandal 193–194
Luckin Coffee 204
Robert Maxwell 196–198
UK response 199–202
Wells Fargo 204
Wirecard 204
counsel 7
counter offer 50
County Court 158
Court of Appeal 157
courts, superior and inferior 161–162
criminal law and civil law 6

damages 24
defamation 101
defendant 6
delegated legislation 21–23
dismissal 186
types of claim 187–188
unfair 187
wrongful 188
dividend war 192
duress 86–88
contract 87
duty of care 107
and negligent advice 118
Caparo Test 109
tests for 108

economic duress 87
economic loss 114–116
economic reality test of employment 173
efficacy 76
electronic commerce and law of contract 96–97
Electronic Commerce Directive (2002) 97
employed or self employed? 170–176
employee
duties to employer 178–179
or contractor? 170–171
rights 185–188
employee rights 169
employers, common law duties 177–178
employment
dismissal 186
termination 186, *See also* dismissal
termination, redundancy 188
tests of 171
type 169
employment contracts 168–179
employment law 167–190
employment law tribunals 169
English law 1
Enron scandal 193–194

European Convention on Human Rights 39
European Law 39
executive 8

Family Division, High Court of Justice 158
fiduciary duty 149
financial regulation 203
fraud 194, 197
frustration, contractual 95–96

gig economy 168, 185–188

hierarchy of the courts 27
High Court of Justice 158
higher courts 27
HM Revenue and Customs (HRMC) 130
House of Commons 14, 15
House of Lords 14, 15, 106, 156, 176
Human Rights Act 1998 39

implied terms 74–79
incorporation 134–146
independent contractor 184
indictable offences 159
injunction 38
innominate terms 83–84
integration test of employment 172
intra vires 5
invitation to treat 47

jargon. *See* terminology
John Doe 34
judge made law. *See* case law
judiciary 8
jurisprudence 6

Keeper of the King's Conscience 37
King's Counsel (K.C.) 11

Latin, reasons for using 4–5
law of contract 44–73, 74–99

law of equity 36–37
law of tort 100–129
Law Reports 31–33
leading cases 27
leave to appeal 155
legal entity 134
legal fiction 10
legal intent 62
legally binding 51
legislation 14–21
legislature 8
liability or guilt, tests of 9
lifting the corporate veil 139
limited company 135
    setting up 136
limited liability 134
limited liability company 136–145
limited liability partnerships 150. *See also* partnerships
limited partnerships 151
litigation 9
LLP. *See* limited liability partnerships
London Stock Exchange 138
Lord Chancellor, Keeper of the King's Conscience 37
lower courts 27

Magistrates' Courts 159–160
Man on the Clapham Omnibus 34
'master and servant' relationship 171
Maxwell, Robert 196–198
misrepresentation 68–71
    three types 71
Montesquieu 8

Nadir, Asil, fraudster 194–196
NASDAQ 205
negligence 103–113
    and vicarious liability 183
    contributory 126
    Lord Atkin's argument 106

professional advice 116–117
   tests for liability 110
negligent
   advice 116–117
   physical acts (or omissions) 104–113
   statements or misstatements 116–120
neighbour, legal definition 106
nuisance 101

obiter dicta 29
objective person 35
objective test 35
occupier, defined 123
occupier's liability 120–127
   avoiding 125–127
offences, summary and indictable 159
offer 47
   when ended? 61
offeree 59
offeror 59
'officious bystander' test 78
'off on a frolic' 181
Orders in Council 22

Parent Act (Enabling Act) 22
Parliament, law making 14
partnerships 147–151
   limited 151
   limited liability 150–151
   number of partners 149
   ordinary or general 148–150
performance
   impossibility of 95
   of contracts 94
plaintiff 6
PLC. *See* public limited company
points of law 28
Poll tax 21
postal rule of acceptance 52–53
precedent 7, 24–27
prima facie 28

private limited company 136–137
privity 91–93
promisee 59
promisor 59
public limited company 135, 137–139
   advantages and disadvantages 141–145
   agency problem 145
   divorce of ownership from control 144
   shares and shareholders 142–143
'pure' economic loss 114

QBD - Queen's Bench Division 32, 158
quantum meruit 94
Queen's Counsel (Q.C.) 11

ratio decidendi 25, 29
reasonable doubt 10
reasonable man test 107
rebuttable presumption 52
rectification 38
redundancy 188
rescission 39
rules for success as a student 1

self-employment 130–133. *See also* sole trader
separation of the powers 8
share capital 137
shareholder greed 191
shareholder 'problem'
   public limited company 145
shares and shareholders
   public limited company 142
'social and domestic' arrangements 52
sole trader 130–133
   advantages/disadvantages 131
   legal requirements 132–133
sources of law 13–43
special relationship
   and vicarious liability 180
   undue influence 89

specific performance 38
stare decisis 28
Star Wars 103
statute law 14–21
statutory instruments 22
successful fraudster 194–196
summary offences 159
superior and inferior courts 161–162
Supreme Court 156
Sweeny Todd 23
system of courts 154–166

termination of employment
    statutory notice 186–187
terminology 3–11
terms of contracts
    express and implied 74
    implied by case law 75–77
    implied by custom or practice 78–79
    types in contracts 79–86
tests of liability or guilt 9
torts 100–129
    main types 101
    of negligence 103–113
trespass to land 102
tribunal system 163–164

UK law 1
ultra vires 5
undue influence 88–91
    abuse of trust 91
    actual 89
    presumed 89–90
    special relationship 89
unilateral contract 67
US legislation, SOX Act 198–199

VAT (Value Added Tax) 130
veil (lifting of corporate veil) 139
vicarious liability 11
    and negligence 183
    independent contractors 184
    in workplace situations 179–185
    special relationship 180
visitor, lawful, defined 121
volenti non fit injuria 126

warranty 82

Printed by Printforce, United Kingdom